ALBERT SCHWEITZER

AN ANTHOLOGY

ALBERT SCHWEITZER

An Anthology

Edited by

CHARLES R. JOY

HARPER & BROTHERS · NEW YORK, LONDON
THE BEACON PRESS · BOSTON

PRINTED IN THE UNITED STATES OF AMERICA

PREFACE

Albert Schweitzer is considered by hundreds of thousands of people in many countries to be one of the foremost spiritual and ethical figures of our time. Indeed, there are many for whom there is no other of equal eminence. As one who has given to his simple creed supreme expression in his deed, he is more and more commanding the thought and arousing the interest of mankind.

It is a pity, therefore, that the books and articles which he has found time in the midst of the exhausting burdens of his life to write, covering now more than a half century of fruitful thinking and courageous living, should be so hard to find. Many of his books are no longer in print, some have never been translated from the French and the German which he uses with equal facility. They cover a wide range of subjects: philosophical, theological, ethical, biographical, autobiographical, musical, medical. Whatever the subject, they are all alike interpenetrated by the beauty of years well-spent, a mind well-stored, a spirit enriched and beautified by renunciation, dedication, and a boundless loyalty to life.

This anthology represents an effort to make available much that is now scattered and hidden, to gather together those passages from published books and ephemeral writings which have meaning and inspiration for us today, to introduce to a world careless of human, ethical, and spiritual values a man for whom only these values exist. His message of mystical, reverent, life-affirmation is a tonic word for this age, so recklessly eager to squander its heritage.

In most cases the passages brought together here appear as they have been translated in editions approved by Dr. Schweitzer. In those cases, however, where his writings have not yet appeared in English, there are a number of passages translated directly from the French or the German.

Grateful acknowledgment is made to the following publishers for permission to print copyrighted material from the books and periodicals used.

A. & C. Black, London, England, for excerpts from *The Quest of the Historical Jesus, Paul and His Interpreters, The Decay and Restoration of Civilization* (Part I of *The Philosophy of Civilization*), and *Civilization and Ethics* (Part II of *The Philosophy of Civilization*)

The Macmillan Company, New York, N. Y., for excerpts from *Memoirs of Childhood and Youth*, and *On the Edge of the Primeval Forest*

Henry Holt and Company, Inc., New York, N. Y., for excerpts from *The Forest Hospital at Lambaréné, African Notebook, Out of My Life and Thought, The Mysticism of Paul the Apostle*, and *Indian Thought and Its Development*

George Allen & Unwin, Ltd., London, England, for excerpts from *Christianity and the Religions of the World*

Dodd, Mead & Company, Inc., New York, N. Y., for excerpts from *The Mystery of the Kingdom of God*

The Contemporary Review, London, England, for excerpts from "The Relations of the White and Colored Races" (Vol. 133, No. 745)

The Christian Century, Chicago, Illinois, for excerpts from "Busy Days in Lambaréné" (Vol. 51, No. 11), and "Religion and Modern Civilization" (Vol. 51, Nos. 47 and 48)

Christendom, New York, N. Y., for excerpts from "The Ethics of Reverence for Life" (Vol. 1, No. 2)

This anthology is not intended to replace the books that Dr. Schweitzer has written. If the selections from his writings which are gathered here do not lead many a reader to seek the books themselves the purpose of this volume will be defeated. Here are literally the *hors d'oeuvres* which precede the meal and whet the appetite for the rich repast that is to follow. The editor's ardent desire is that no one should leave the table after the olives, radishes and celery, the tomatoes and anchovies have been eaten.

C. R. J.

BIBLIOGRAPHY OF BOOKS BY
DR. SCHWEITZER

I. AUTOBIOGRAPHICAL

Memoirs of Childhood and Youth. Translated by C. T. Campion. New York: The Macmillan Company. 1931.

On the Edge of the Primeval Forest. Translated by C. T. Campion. New York: The Macmillan Company. 1931.

The Forest Hospital at Lambaréné. Translated by C. T. Campion. New York: Henry Holt and Company, Inc. 1931.

African Notebook. Translated by Mrs. C. E. B. Russell. New York: Henry Holt and Company, Inc. 1939.

Mitteilungen aus Lambaréné. Three booklets. 1 and 2, 1924–25: 3, 1925–27. Bern: P. Haupt. München: Beck.

Selbstdarstellung. In Volume 7 of *Die Philosophie der Gegenwart in Selbstdarstellungen*. Edited by Dr. Raymund Schmidt. Leipzig: Felix Meiner, 1929.

Out of My Life and Thought. Translated by C. T. Campion. New York: Henry Holt and Company, Inc. 1933.

II. BIOGRAPHICAL

Eugène Munch. Mulhouse, Alsace: Brinkmann. 1898.

Goethe. (An address delivered by Dr. Schweitzer at the Goethe-Haus, Frankfort-am-Main, on receiving the Goethe Prize from the City of Frankfort, August 28, 1928.) Translated by C. T. Campion. New York: Henry Holt and Company, Inc. 1928.

Goethe Gedenkrede. (An address delivered on the one hundredth anniversary of Goethe's death, in his native city, Frankfort-am-Main, March 22, 1932.) Munich: Beck. 1932.

III. PSYCHIATRY

Die Psychiatrische Beurteilung Jesu. Darstellung und Kritik. Tübingen: Mohr. 1913.

IV. RELIGION AND THEOLOGY

The Quest of the Historical Jesus. A Critical Study of Its Progress from Reimarus to Wrede. Translated by W. Montgomery. New York: The Macmillan Company. 1926.

The Mysticism of Paul the Apostle. Translated by W. Montgomery. New York: Henry Holt and Company, Inc. 1931.

Paul and His Interpreters. Translated by W. Montgomery. New York: The Macmillan Company. 1912.

The Mystery of the Kingdom of God. Translated by Walter Lowrie. New York: Dodd, Mead and Company. 1914.

Christianity and the Religions of the World. Translated by Johanna Powers. New York: Henry Holt and Company, Inc. 1939.

V. PHILOSOPHY AND ETHICS

Die Religionsphilosophie Kants. Freiburg i/B.: J. C. C. Mohr (Paul Siebeck). 1899.

The Decay and Restoration of Civilization. Being Part I of *The Philosophy of Civilization.* Translated by C. T. Campion. New York: The Macmillan Company. 1932.

Civilization and Ethics. Being Part II of *The Philosophy of Civilization.* Translated by C. T. Campion. New York: The Macmillan Company. 1929.

Indian Thought and Its Development. Translated by Mrs. C. E. B. Russell. New York: Henry Holt and Company, Inc. 1936.

VI. MUSIC

Johann Sebastian Bach. Translated by Ernest Newman. 2 volumes. New York: The Macmillan Company. 1938.

Deutsche und französische Orgelbaukunst und Orgel-
kunst. Leipzig: Breitkopf und Härtel. 1927.

VII. ARTICLES BY ALBERT SCHWEITZER

"The Relations of the White and Colored Races." *The*
Contemporary Review. Vol. 133, No. 745, January
1928, pp. 65–70.

"Sunday at Lambaréné." *The Christian Century.* Vol. 48,
March 18, 1931, pp. 540–541.

"Le Secours Médical aux Colonies." *Revue des Deux*
Mondes. Series 8, vol. 5, September 15, 1931, pp.
390–404.

"Der runde Violinbogen." *Schweizerische Musikzeitung.*
No. 6. 1933.

"Busy Days in Lambaréné." *The Christian Century.* Vol.
51, March 14, 1934, pp. 355–357.

"Sermon on Forgiveness." *The Christian World.* Nov. 1,
1934, p. 11.

"Religion and Modern Civilization." *The Christian Cen-*
tury. Vol. 51, No. 47, November 21, 1934, pp. 1483–
1484. No. 48, November 28, 1934, pp. 1519–1521.

"The Ethics of Reverence for Life." *Christendom.* Vol. 1,
No. 2, Winter, 1936, pp. 225–239.

"Letter from Lambaréné." *The Living Age.* Vol. 355, September 1938, pp. 70 ff.

Note: Many of Dr. Schweitzer's books have been published
in a number of different languages, in addition to the original
French or German in which they were written. The same book
has occasionally been published in England and America under
different English titles. Sometimes the English translation is
abridged from the original. No effort has been made to make
the above bibliography complete for all languages and all editions. It lists books and articles in languages other than English,
only when no English translation has been made, and lists in
English only the one American edition which seems to the
editor most convenient. Only the most important magazine
articles have been added.

LIST OF ABBREVIATIONS

Bach	*J. S. Bach*, A. & C. Black, London
Busy Days	"Busy Days in Lambaréné," *The Christian Century*, Chicago
Childhood	*Memoirs of Childhood and Youth*, The Macmillan Company, New York
Christianity	*Christianity and the Religions of the World*, George Allen & Unwin, Ltd., London
Decay	*The Decay and Restoration of Civilization*, Part I in *The Philosophy of Civilization*, A. & C. Black, London
Edge	*On the Edge of the Primeval Forest*, The Macmillan Company, New York
Ethics	*Civilization and Ethics*, Part II in *The Philosophy of Civilization*, A. & C. Black, London
Gedenkrede	*Goethe Gedenkrede*, C. H. Beck'sche Verlagsbuchhandlung, Munich, Germany
Goethe	*Goethe*, Henry Holt and Company, Inc., New York
Hospital	*The Forest Hospital at Lambaréné*, Henry Holt and Company, Inc., New York
Indian	*Indian Thought and Its Development*, Henry Holt and Company, Inc., New York
Letter	"Letter from Lambaréné," *The Living Age*, New York
Life	*Out of My Life and Thought*, Henry Holt and Company, Inc., New York
Mystery	*The Mystery of the Kingdom of God*, Dodd, Mead and Company, Inc., New York

Mysticism   *The Mysticism of Paul the Apostle*, Henry Holt
                and Company, Inc., New York

Notebook   *African Notebook*, Henry Holt and Company,
                Inc., New York

Paul   *Paul and His Interpreters*, A. & C. Black, Lon-
                don

Quest   *The Quest of the Historical Jesus*, A. & C.
                Black, London.

Races   "The Relations of the White and Colored
                Races," *The Contemporary Review*, London

Religion   "Religion and Modern Civilization," *The Chris-
                tian Century*, Chicago

Reverence   "The Ethics of Reverence for Life," *Christen-
                dom*, New York

Secours   "Le Secours Médical aux Colonies," *Revue des
                Deux Mondes*, Paris

CONTENTS

INTRODUCTION

A Modern Man's Quest for the Holy Grail

The poetry of Africa!

Before the window against a bright blue sky a palm tree rises. A light breeze blowing from the river rustles the fronds of it and brings a little soothing refreshment. Goats graze in the newly mown meadow, each of them with a white heron close beside it. It is a peaceful, silent Sunday afternoon. The weaver birds are quiet in the trees overhead, the monkeys have ceased to chatter.

The river below is a mirror. So unruffled is it that one can see in its placid glass not only the white birds and the blue birds that skim over the surface of the water, but also the ospreys that circle high in the air. Each bird is companioned by its bright image in the turbid stream. The huge mass of tree roots, which alone shows where the water meets the land, is covered with a tangle of vines gay with flowers. On the other side the forest rises, the primeval forest, deep, luxuriant, impenetrable, the great living trees mingling with the dead giants of the past. Far in the distance a low line of blue hills rises.

By the window a man sits writing letters to his friends. The small, neat handwriting, like copperplate in its delicacy, contrasts strangely with the size of the man himself. He is a big man, six feet tall; obviously a strong man also. He has a shock of brown hair, turning gray, and a bushy moustache. His deep-set eyes are blue and kindly. They twinkle with humor. A little fawn nudges him, asking to be petted, and the big hand drops its pen and gently strokes the animal.

He resumes his writing. He is describing with simple and touching sincerity a grace that has been given to him—strength to work. He pours out his heart in gratitude to the many friends in many lands who made it possible.

It all makes an idyllic picture—river and forest, birds and flowers and domestic animals, human strength and devotion and tenderness. Here is the poetry of Africa!

The prose of Africa!

Papyrus swamps, decaying villages round about, ragged Negroes inhabiting them, the unhealthiest climate on the face of the earth, tsetse flies bearing the germs of sleeping sickness, mosquitoes malignant with malaria, termites that destroy the work of man as quickly as the work is done, traveler ants leaving utter desolation in the wake of their marching columns, jiggers that burrow into the soles of unprotected feet, venomous snakes in the tall grass, deluded leopard-men, who wear leopards' claws on their hands and feet, or iron imitations of them, lurking in the forests to pounce on their human victims and sever the arteries of their throats. Disease, pain, distress everywhere!

The untiring activity, of which the big man with the graying hair is writing, has to do with very unpleasant things, for he is a doctor. He writes of patients stricken with dysentery, who dirty everything they sit or lie on, who have to be cared for by the white doctors and nurses, since the blacks will not do such disgusting work. He writes of men whose skin gradually changes from black to brown, whose fingers wear away, whose toes disappear. They are lepers. He describes his efforts to save a man who has been bored through by the tusks of an elephant, and another whose hand has been torn by the frightful teeth of a gorilla. He tells of the many thousands who die of sleeping sickness, which the natives call the "killing disease." He writes of the phagedenic ulcers which form on the lower legs of men, and he writes feelingly for he himself has suffered from them. He tells of the hideous pain caused by strangulated hernia, and the miraculous relief which an operation brings. He writes of the huge tumors of elephantiasis, of tuberculosis, the white man's scourge, which has now reached the black man, of little children lying in a state of malarial coma. With all these tragic ills he is concerned, he and a pitifully few companions in the only hospital for a radius of five hundred miles. This, to him, is the glorious activity of which he writes to his distant friends and supporters. This, to us, is the prose of Africa which underlies all the rhythm of its poetry.

Albert Schweitzer is seventy-two years old now. On the edge of this primeval forest, far from the hills and valleys of the Vosges, where a sheltered childhood was spent, far from the cultured circles of Europe where he moved about so easily during his early manhood, he has wrought a work of mercy, the meaning of which far surpasses the number of black lives he has saved, and the measure of devastating pain which he has assuaged. If, as his friends first thought, he has buried himself in the depths of the dark continent, then his is a living grave, lifted up, drawing all men unto it, seen by all the world.

On the banks of the Ogowe River, which flows into the Atlantic just north of the Congo, Dr. Schweitzer established his home. It stood on a small hill above Lambaréné, named Adende. A few kilometers away in the middle of the seventies of the nineteenth century, forty years before the appearance of Dr. Schweitzer, the young Trader Horn built his post at a place called Adolinanongo, to which the Schweitzer hospital was moved in 1925. If Trader Horn could return today he would find that the outward aspect of things had changed very little. "Crocodiles still sometimes sleep with wide-open jaws on sandbanks or on deadwood on the banks. Hippos still frequent the waters of Adolinanongo in the dry season. Pelicans still circle in the air. The islands and shores are still covered with bright green, impenetrable bush mirrored in the brown flood." [1]

From the veranda of the little bungalow the doctor looked out innumerable times over the river with its branches, its green islands, its native villages, over the dense forest to the dim blue hills. But from that same veranda the doctor likewise looked out on more distant scenes. He looked out over the black peoples of Africa. He looked out over the peoples of every race and color. He looked out over life in its farthest reaches, over the universe itself. The spiritual life of mankind became richer because this man sacrificed the rich cultural inheritance which was his, and defying all the conventions of his group he decided to minister to the neediest of earth's children in earth's most neglected and forgotten region. Now from Adolinanongo Albert Schweitzer still looks out over the people, for that is what this native place name means. And all over the world the people look up to him as a glowing exemplar of what religion can be in the life of man.

This selfless spirit has been able to work its miracle of healing on the bodies and the souls of men because the prose of the outer world was suffused with the essence of its poetry. Like Goethe, who has been for him one of life's most enduring influences, Schweitzer has lived in the closest communion with nature and with reality. But never has he been supremely contented in this contact. Even in the lovely Alsatian countryside, where he was born on January 14, 1875, he seldom knew a perfectly happy moment. He was troubled by the cruelty he saw, the sickness and pain he observed. He could not join the village boys in their bird hunts or their fishing expeditions. When the evening prayers were said, and his mother had kissed him good night, he

[1] *My African Notebook*, p. 39.

added his own little prayer of childish faith: "Protect and bless all things that have breath: guard them from all evil, and let them sleep in peace." So began in tender, plastic years his concern for the humblest of all living things, a concern which has developed into the crowning principle of all his ethics—reverence, not simply for human life, but for all that lives everywhere, the gnat that flies into his reading lamp, the toad that falls into the posthole he is digging, the wayside primrose so thoughtlessly struck down, the worm dying on the hard pavement. Who but Albert Schweitzer would have thought with searing anguish of all the living creatures whose lives were being forfeited, when the natives kindled fires in the forest to make clearings for their pathetic little banana plantations? Who but Albert Schweitzer would have prayed that the crazed hippopotamus, raging before his hospital, upsetting canoes in blind fury and killing the occupants in the water, might be led by some animal premonition to escape before he was shot? Yet this abiding conviction of the sacredness of all life everywhere, maintained in the face of ridicule, is a bit of the poetry of his soul lighting with its gentle, luminous radiance the dark recesses of man's inhumanity and nature's tragic cruelty.

In the midst of life's dull prose his mind went in search of beauty. The dark caverns of superstition and error and ignorance needed the light, and truth was the torch he bore. Even as a boy he had a daring mind, questioning like Jesus in the temple the hoary errors of the past. "Why," he asked, "did the wise men never return in later years to Jesus?" "Why were the shepherds of Bethlehem not among his disciples?" "If the wise men brought such rich and precious gifts to the manger of the child Jesus, why were his parents always so poor?" The crawling things that live beneath the stone of institutionalized falsehood hated the light of reason, and Albert Schweitzer's torch of truth was not a welcome one. When he dared to disagree with his distinguished theological teachers, and proved that Jesus had been mistaken in his eschatological expectations which he shared with the Jews of his age, there were many who were convinced that he was overturning the temple of religion and bringing it down to the dust. Jesus could not be wrong at any point, and remain the Jesus of their worship, they thought. They could not see that in making Jesus and Paul men of their own age, and not men of our age, Schweitzer had lifted them above the passing generations, and endowed their genuinely spiritual insight with enduring significance. For there was, as Schweitzer convincingly showed, a transient and a permanent element in the teaching of both. The transient was tied to their time, the permanent was freed for all time. Truth was poetry to Schweitzer, and the prose of organized Christianity needed the warm magic of its transforming and vitalizing touch. No one who seeks sincerely for truth needed to fear the outcome. That was his abiding faith.

Schweitzer speaks of the parable of Dives and Lazarus to explain the mission which so startled his friends. "We are Dives," he says, "for, through the advances of medical science, we now know a great deal about disease and pain, and have innumerable means of fighting them. . . . Out there in the colonies, however, sits wretched Lazarus, the colored folk, who suffers from illness and pain just as much as we do, nay, much more, and has absolutely no means of fighting them." [2]

Here, again, we have the great gulf yawning between poetry and prose, which Schweitzer has given his life to bridge. He could not endure the thought of suffering. He could not accept privileges for himself denied to others. The steaming broth on the parsonage table of his childhood became nauseous to him because the other village

---

[2] *On the Edge of the Primeval Forest*, pp. 1 f.

boys did not enjoy such nourishing food. Since the boys had no overcoat he would not wear one. He refused to wear leather shoes on weekdays, because all the others wore clogs. His mittens had no fingers because theirs had none. There in Günsbach, his boyhood home, the dominant motif of his life was clearly set down.

He could go on, it is true, to a distinguished career as a theologian, a philosopher, a musician, a teacher, but it was inevitable that in the end this must be given up, for there were always those who had no broth, no overcoat, no shoes. Out there beyond the horizon of his early vision was the beggar Lazarus, full of sores, lying at the gate, waiting for the crumbs to fall. Schweitzer could not long continue to be the rich man, clothed in purple and fine linen, faring sumptuously every day, even though the callous world tried to blind his eyes of pity by calling Dives the daring and brilliant critic of Kant, the pioneering New Testament scholar, the distinguished teacher and director of a theological faculty, the widely acclaimed organist and expert on organ construction, the sympathetic interpreter of the music of Bach. His cultured friends might call him all of these names, but his conscience used another term. He was still Dives, the rich man, clothed in purple and fine linen, dining sumptuously day by day! And out there was Lazarus!

Suddenly, the academic degrees earned with such exhausting intellectual toil, doctor of philosophy, doctor of theology, doctor of music, became vain baubles to him, and he knew that he must win another doctorate, that of medicine. The title meant nothing to him, but the title would take him out to Lazarus in Africa. So he became "the old doctor" to his black brothers, a man whose friends in Europe thought mad, whose friends in Africa thought a fool on earth, but not a fool in heaven.

To the prose of African degradation and deprivation

Schweitzer brought the poetry of his gifted life, and in the blending of this prose and poetry found his happiness. When in 1927 he returned to Europe for a time, he had a feeling of pain that he had to tear himself loose from what had become to him a second home. "It seems to me incomprehensible," he wrote, "that I am leaving the natives for months. How fond of them one becomes, in spite of all the trouble they give one! How many beautiful traits of character we can discover in them, if we refuse to let the many and varied follies of the child of nature prevent us from looking for the man in him! How they disclose to us their real selves, if we have love and patience enough to understand them!" [3]

Music was one of the earliest passions of Schweitzer's life. Here was poetry in a new, enchanting form. There was a long line of organists in his family, so that the appearance of a talent for music was not surprising. He himself tells us that when he first heard the duet sung "In the mill by the stream" he had to hold on to the wall to keep himself from falling. "The charm of the two-part harmony of the song thrilled me all over, to my very marrow, and similarly the first time I heard brass instruments playing together I almost fainted from excess of pleasure." [4]

At five the boy was playing on the old square piano, and even before his legs were long enough to reach the pedals, he was at the organ. At nine he had already taken the place of the regular organist at a Günsbach service. The gifted young musician of Saint Stephen's in Mülhausen, Eugène Munch, introduced him to Bach, and the distinguished Parisian organist, Charles Marie Widor, took him as a private pupil. But the pupil quickly became himself a teacher, a master of the organ, a recitalist in universal de-

---

[3] *The Forest Hospital at Lambaréné*, p. 186.
[4] *Memoirs of Childhood and Youth*, p. 24.

mand, a writer in two languages on the life and work of
Johann Sebastian Bach.

The poetry of his life flowered again in music, but this,
too, had to be offered up on the altar of renunciation. It is
true that he took with him to Africa a zinc lined piano,
the gift of the Bach Society of Paris, but he fully expected
to sacrifice his music in the medical service of Lazarus.
Once more, however, he found that the poetry and prose
of life made a new synthesis. In the quiet of the late tropical
evenings he kept up with his musical technique; in the long
months of his internment during the First World War he
was able to practise assiduously on a table and the floor.
The full measure of the final sacrifice was not exacted.
Music and medicine harmonized in the equatorial forest.
The prose of his life was interfused with the poetry of it.

In Albert Schweitzer's writings about religion, civilization, ethics, and philosophy, certain *word-pairs* appear again
and again. They are key words to the understanding of
his thought. Among them are *rationalism* and *mysticism*,
pessimism and *optimism*, *decay* and *restoration*, *world*-
and *life-negation* and *world*- and *life-affirmation*. The exact
meaning of these words will appear in the selections that
follow. It is enough to point out now that in them we
hear again the treble and bass of his life, undertones of sadness and pain, overtones of confidence and joy, dissonance
and consonance, out of which he is trying to build a divine
symphony of sound and love.

Here, then, is Albert Schweitzer, the teacher, the thinker,
the healer, the singer, the seeker. The world is becoming
aware that his life and thought are destined to influence profoundly the spirit of our time. At once a Savonarola preaching doom and a St. Francis teaching and showing mercy,
he can help this new world of ours, which stumbles blindly
into the atomic age, to stop and ponder before it is too late.
Over us hangs a fate that may turn our cities and our civiliza-

tion into ashes. Schweitzer with his mystic reverence for
love and light and life can save us from that fate. He can
help us to spread balm on the wounds of the nations. He can
give us beauty for ashes.

—CHARLES R. JOY

Newton Highlands
Massachusetts
1947

ALBERT SCHWEITZER

AN ANTHOLOGY

THE SANCTUARY OF THOUGHT

The Deepest Thinking Is Humble

The deepest thinking is humble. It is only concerned that the flame of truth which it keeps alive should burn with the strongest and purest heat; it does not trouble about the distance to which its brightness penetrates.   [Indian, p. 257]

Thought Demands Acquiescence

Only when thinking becomes quite humble can it set its feet upon the way that leads to knowledge. The more profound a religion is, the more it realizes this fact—that what it knows through belief is little compared with what it does not know. The first active deed of thinking is resignation—acquiescence in what happens. Becoming free, inwardly, from what happens, we pass through the gate of resignation on the way to ethics.   [Religion, p. 1520]

Dissonance and Harmony

The spirit of the age dislikes what is simple. It no longer believes the simple can be profound. It loves the complicated, and regards it as profound. It loves the violent. That is why the spirit of the age can love Karl Barth and Nietzsche at the same time. The spirit of the age loves dissonance, in tones, in lines and in thought. That shows how far from thinking it is, for thinking is a harmony within us.   [Religion, p. 1484]

Elemental Thinking

Elemental thinking is that which starts from the fundamental questions about the relations of man to the universe, about the meaning of life, and about the nature of goodness. It stands in the most immediate connection with the thinking which impulse stirs in everyone. It enters into that thinking, widening and deepening it.   [Life, p. 260]

Fearless Thought

If thought is to set out on its journey unhampered, it must be prepared for anything, even for arrival at intellectual agnosticism. But even if our will-to-action is destined to wrestle endlessly and unavailingly with an agnostic view of the universe and of life, still this painful disenchantment is better for it than persistent refusal to think out its position at all. For this disenchantment does, at any rate, mean that we are clear as to what we are doing.   [Decay, p. 104]

Realistic Thinking

Thinking which keeps contact with reality must look up to the heavens, it must look over the earth, and dare to direct its gaze to the barred windows of a lunatic asylum. Look to the stars and understand how small our earth is in the universe. Look upon earth and know how minute man is upon it. The earth existed long before man came upon it. In the history of the universe, man is on earth for but a second. Who knows but that the earth will circle round the sun once more without man upon it? Therefore we must not place man in the center of the universe. And our gaze must be fixed on the barred windows of a lunatic asylum, in order that we may remember the terrible fact

that the mental and spiritual are also liable to destruction.
[Religion, p. 1520]

The Riddle of the Universe

All thinking must renounce the attempt to explain the universe. We cannot understand what happens in the universe.
What is glorious in it is united with what is full of horror.
What is full of meaning is united to what is senseless. The
spirit of the universe is at once creative and destructive—
it creates while it destroys and destroys while it creates,
and therefore it remains to us a riddle. And we must inevitably resign ourselves to this.   [Religion, p. 1520]

Thought and Freedom

A man's ability to be a pioneer of progress, that is, to
understand what civilization is and to work for it, depends
on his being a thinker and on his being free. He must be
the former if he is to be capable of comprehending his
ideals and putting them into shape. He must be free in order
to be in a position to launch his ideals out into the general
life. The more completely his activities are taken up in any
way by the struggle for existence, the more strongly will
the impulse to improve his own condition find expression
in the ideals of his thought. Ideals of self-interest then get
mixed up with and spoil his ideals of civilization.

Material and spiritual freedom are closely bound up with
one another. Civilization presupposes free men, for only by
free men can it be thought out and brought to realization.
[Decay, p. 16]

A Plea for Thought

It is with complete confidence that I step forward to press
the claims of unprejudiced rational thought. I know well

that our times have no affinity whatever for anything that is branded as rationalistic, and would like to dismiss everything of the sort as an eighteenth-century aberration. But it will soon become evident that we shall be obliged to take up the same position which the eighteenth century defended so stoutly. The period which lies between those times and the present is an intermezzo of thought, an intermezzo which had extraordinarily rich and interesting motifs, but yet was all the same a fatal intermezzo. Its inevitable end was that we should founder absolutely in a total lack of any world-view or civilization at all, and it is the latter state which is responsible for all the spiritual and material misery amid which we languish at present. [Ethics, p. xvii]

The Riches of Rationalism

Nowadays it belongs to the complete duty of the well-trained theologian to renounce the rationalists and all their works; and yet how poor our time is in comparison with theirs—how poor in strong men capable of loyalty to an ideal, how poor, so far as theology is concerned, in simple commonplace sincerity!   [Quest, p. 57]

A Deeper Rationalism

All the movements that have claimed to take the place of rationalism stand far below it in the matter of achievement. From speculative thought, from history, from feeling, from aesthetics, from science, they tried to obtain something like a world-view, grubbing at haphazard in the world around them instead of excavating scientifically. Rationalism alone chose the right place for its digging, and dug systematically, according to plan. If it found only metal of small value, that was because, with the means at its disposal, it could not go deep enough. Impoverished and ruined as we are because we sought as mere adventurers, we must make up our minds to sink another shaft in the ground where rationalism worked, and to go down through all the strata to see whether we cannot find the gold which must certainly be there.   [Decay, p. 89]

"O World Unknowable"

The rationalist thought of former times aimed at intellectual comprehension of the world, and thought that by means of such knowledge it would be able to interpret the highest impulses of our will-to-live as possessing meaning in connection with the world totality and the world process. But these hopes were doomed to failure. We are not destined to attain to such an understanding of the objective world and ourselves as forming a mutual harmony. In a cruder fashion we ventured the supposition that a view of life must be sought for in a world-view, in which, we imagined, it must necessarily be contained. Facts do not justify this supposition. Thus we come to see that our thought arrives at a dualism, from which there is no escape. It is the dualism of world-view and life-view, of knowledge and volition.   [Ethics, pp. xiii f.]

A Necessary Rationalism

Rationalism is more than a movement of thought which realized itself at the end of the eighteenth and the beginning of the nineteenth centuries. It is a necessary phenomenon in all normal spiritual life. All real progress in the world is in the last analysis produced by rationalism. [Decay, pp. 88 f.]

Rationalism and Orthodoxy

That thoroughgoing theological rationalism which accepts only so much of religion as can justify itself at the bar of reason, and which conceives and represents the origin of religion in accordance with this principle, was preceded by a rationalism less complete, as yet not wholly dissociated from a simple-minded supernaturalism. Its point of view is one at which it is almost impossible for the modern man to place himself. Here, in a single consciousness, orthodoxy and rationalism lie stratified in successive layers. Here, to change the metaphor, rationalism surrounds religion without touching it, and, like a lake surrounding some ancient castle, mirrors its image with curious refractions.

This half-developed rationalism was conscious of an impulse—it is the first time in the history of theology that this impulse manifests itself—to write the Life of Jesus; at first without any suspicion whither this undertaking would lead it. No rude hands were to be laid upon the doctrinal conception of Jesus; at least these writers had no intention of laying hands upon it. Their purpose was simply to gain a clearer view of the course of our Lord's earthly and human life. The theologians who undertook this task thought of themselves as merely writing an historical supplement to the life of the God-Man Jesus.   [Quest, pp. 27 f.]

A Theory of the Universe

The reconstruction of our age can begin only with a reconstruction of its theory of the universe. There is hardly anything more urgent in its claim on us than this which seems to be so far off and abstract. Only when we have made ourselves at home again in the solid thought-building of a theory which can support a civilization, and when we take from it, all of us in cooperation, ideas which can stim-

ulate our life and work, only then can there again arise a
society which can possess ideals with magnificent aims and
be able to bring these into effective agreement with reality.
It is from new ideas that we must build history anew.
[Decay, pp. 85 f.]

The Direction Is Clear

The ways along which we have to struggle toward the goal
may be veiled in darkness, yet the direction in which we
must travel is clear. We must reflect together about the
meaning of life; we must strive together to attain to a theory
of the universe affirmative of the world and of life, in which
the impulse to action which we experience as a necessary
and valuable element of our being may find justification,
orientation, clarity and depth, may receive a fresh access
of moral strength, and be retempered, and thus become
capable of formulating, and of acting on, definite ideals of
civilization, inspired by the spirit of true humanitarianism.
[Decay, p. 105]

What Do I Think?

Descartes built an artificial structure by presuming that
man knows nothing, and doubts all, whether outside himself or within. And in order to end doubt he fell back on
the fact of consciousness: *I think.* Surely, however, that is
the stupidest primary assumption in all philosophy! Who
can establish the fact that he thinks, except in relation to
thinking *something?* And what that something is, is the
important matter. When I seek the first fact of consciousness, it is not to know if I think, but to get hold of myself.
Descartes would have a man think once, just long enough
to establish the certainty of being, and then give over any
further need of meditation. Yet meditation is the very thing
I must not cease. I *must* ascertain whether my thoughts
are in harmony with my will-to-live.   [Reverence, p. 228]

A Return to Reflection

It seems, indeed, little better than mockery that we should urge men to anything so remote as a return to reflection about the meaning of life at a time when the passions and the follies of the nations have become so intense and so extended, when unemployment and poverty and starvation are rife, when power is being used on the powerless in the most shameless and senseless way, and when organized human life is dislocated in every direction. But only when the general population begins to reflect in this way will forces come into being which will be able to effect something to counterbalance all this chaos and misery. Whatever other measures it is attempted to carry out will have doubtful and altogether inadequate results.

When in the spring the withered gray of the pastures gives place to green, this is due to the millions of young shoots which sprout up freshly from the old roots. In like manner the revival of thought which is essential for our time can only come through a transformation of the opinions and ideals of the many brought about by individual and universal reflection about the meaning of life and of the world.   [Decay, pp. 100 f.]

Through Knowledge to Religion

Every conviction which possesses real value is nonrational and enthusiastic in character, since it cannot be the product of knowledge about the universe, but arises from the reflective experience of the will-to-live, in virtue of which we leave behind all mere intellectual knowledge of the world. This is what rational thought, when continued to its final conclusion grasps and understands as the real truth, in the strength of which we have to live. The way to true mysticism leads us through and beyond rational reflection to profound experience of the world and of our will-to-live. We must all venture once more to become "thinkers," in order to attain to that mysticism which is the only immediate and the only profound world-view. We must all make pilgrimage through the realm of knowledge until we reach the point where it passes into actual experience of the world's essential being. We must all become religious as the result of reflection.   [Ethics, p. xviii]

History and Modern Thought

We have not yet arrived at any reconciliation between history and modern thought—only between halfway history and halfway thought. What the ultimate goal towards which we are moving will be, what this something is which shall bring new life and new regulative principles to coming centuries, we do not know. We can only dimly divine that it will be the mighty deed of some mighty original genius, whose truth and rightness will be proved by the fact that we, working at our poor half thing, will oppose him might and main—we who imagine we long for nothing more eagerly than a genius powerful enough to open up with authority a new path for the world, seeing that we cannot succeed in moving it forward along the track which we have so laboriously prepared.   [Quest, p. 2]

Historical Instinct

There are some who are historians by the grace of God, who from their mother's womb have an instinctive feeling for the real. They follow through all the intricacy and confusion of reported fact the pathway of reality, like a stream which, despite the rocks that encumber its course and the windings of its valley, finds it way inevitably to the sea. No erudition can supply the place of this historical instinct, but erudition sometimes serves a useful purpose, inasmuch as it produces in its possessors the pleasing belief that they are historians, and thus secures their services for the cause of history. In truth they are at best merely doing the preliminary spadework of history, collecting for a future historian the dry bones of fact, from which, with the aid of his natural gift, he can recall the past to life.   [Quest, p. 25]

Skepticism

The city of truth cannot be built on the swampy ground of skepticism. Our spiritual life is rotten throughout because it is permeated through and through with skepticism, and we live in consequence in a world which in every respect is full of falsehood. We are not far from shipwreck on the rock of wanting to have even truth organized.

Truth taken over by a skepticism which has become believing has not the spiritual qualities of that which originated in thinking. It has been externalized and rendered torpid. It does obtain influence over a man, but it is not capable of uniting itself with him to the very marrow of his being. Living truth is that alone which has its origin in thinking.

Just as a tree bears year after year the same fruit and yet fruit which is each year new, so must all permanently valuable ideas be continually born again in thought. But our age is bent on trying to make the barren tree of skepticism fruitful by tying fruits of truth on its branches. [Life, p. 259]

Life Without Thought

No one who opens the sluices to let a flood of skepticism pour itself over the land must expect to be able to bring it back within its proper bounds. Of those who let themselves get too disheartened to try any longer to discover truth by their own thinking, only a few find a substitute for it in truth taken from others. The mass of people remain skeptical. They lose all feeling for truth, and all sense of need for it as well, finding themselves quite comfortable in a life without thought, driven now here, now there, from one opinion to another. [Life, p. 258]

The Religion of the Age

If one reviews the development of religion since the middle of the nineteenth century, one understands the tragic fact that although really living religion is to be found among us, it is not the leaven that leavens the thinking of our age. [Religion, p. 1484]

The Man of Today

The man of today is exposed to influences which are bent on robbing him of all confidence in his own thinking. The spirit of spiritual dependence to which he is called on to surrender is in everything that he hears or reads; it is in the people whom he meets every day; it is in the parties and associations which have claimed him as their own; it pervades all the circumstances of his life.

From every side and in the most varied ways it is dinned into him that the truths and convictions which he needs for life must be taken by him from the associations which have rights over him. The spirit of the age never lets him come to himself. Over and over again convictions are forced upon him in the same way as, by means of the electric advertisements which flare in the streets of every large town, any company which has sufficient capital to get itself securely established, exercises pressure on him at every step he takes to induce him to buy their boot polish or their soup tablets.

By the spirit of the age, then, the man of today is forced into skepticism about his own thinking, in order to make him receptive to truth which comes to him from authority. To all this constant influence he cannot make the resistance that is desirable because he is an overworked and distracted being without power to concentrate. Moreover, the manifold material trammels which are his lot work upon his mentality in such a way that he comes at last to believe himself unqualified even to make any claim to thoughts of his own.   [Life, pp. 255 f.]

The Loss of Self-confidence

The circumstances of the age do their best to deliver us up to the spirit of the age.

The seed of skepticism has germinated. In fact, the modern man has no longer any spiritual self-confidence at all. Behind a self-confident exterior he conceals a great inward lack of confidence. In spite of his great capacity in material matters he is an altogether stunted being, because he makes no use of his capacity for thinking. It will ever remain incomprehensible that our generation, which has shown itself so great by its achievements in discovery and invention, could fall so low spiritually as to give up thinking.   [Life, p. 257]

Contempt for Thinking

Karl Barth, who is the most modern theologian, because he lives most in the spirit of our age, more than any other has that contempt for thinking which is characteristic of our age. He dares to say that religion has nothing to do with thinking. He wants to give religion nothing to do with anything but God and man, the great antithesis. He says a religious person does not concern himself with what hap-

pens to the world. The idea of the Kingdom of God plays
no part with him. He mocks at what he calls "civilized
Protestantism." The church must leave the world to itself.
All that concerns the church is the preaching of revealed
truth. Religion is turned aside from the world.   [Religion,
p. 1484]

The Lack of Reason in Our Time

The history of our time is characterized by a lack of reason
which has no parallel in the past. Future historians will one
day analyze this history in detail, and test by means of it
their learning and their freedom from prejudice. But for all
future times there will be, as there is for today, only one
explanation, viz., that we sought to live and to carry on
with a civilization which had no ethical principle behind it.
[Decay, p. 61]

Modern Thinking Unequal to Its Task

The spirit of the age rejoices, instead of lamenting, that
thinking seems to be unequal to its task, and gives it no
credit for what, in spite of imperfections, it has already
accomplished. It refuses to admit, what is nevertheless the
fact, that all spiritual progress up to today has come about
through the achievements of thought, or to reflect that
thinking may still be able in the future to accomplish
what it has not succeeded in accomplishing as yet.   [Life,
p. 255]

The Ideals We Need

Humanity has always needed ethical ideals to enable it to
find the right path, that man may make the right use of the
power he possesses. Today his power is increased a thou-

sandfold. A thousandfold greater is now the need for man
to possess ethical ideals to point the way. Yet at the very
moment when this happens, thinking fails. In this period of
deepest need thinking is not giving to humanity the ideals
it needs so that it may not be overwhelmed. Is that our
destiny? I hope not. I believe not. I think that in our age
we are all carrying within us a new form of thought which
will give us ethical ideals.   [Religion, p. 1520]

Thinking Drops the Tiller

In modern thinking the same thing happens as in religion.
Thinking drops the tiller from its hand in the middle of
the storm. It renounces the idea of giving to human beings
ideals by the help of which they can get on with reality.
It leaves them to themselves, and that in a most terrible
moment. For the present moment *is* terrible. Man has won
power over the forces of nature and by that has become
superman—and at the same time most miserable man! For
this power over the forces of nature is not being used ben-
eficially, but destructively.   [Religion, p. 1520]

Modern Thought Has No Goal

With the spirit of the age I am in complete disagreement,
because it is filled with disdain for thinking. That such is
its attitude is to some extent explicable by the fact that
thought has never yet reached the goal which it must set
before itself. Time after time it was convinced that it had
clearly established a world-view which was in accordance
with knowledge and ethically satisfactory. But time after
time the truth came out that it had not succeeded.

Doubts, therefore, could well arise as to whether thinking would ever be capable of answering current questions
about the world and our relation to it in such a way that

we could give a meaning and a content to our lives.   [Life, p. 254]

Secondary Issues Prevail

Our philosophizing has become more and more involved in the discussion of secondary issues. It has lost touch with the elemental questions regarding life and the world which it is man's task to pose and to solve, and has found satisfaction more and more in discussing problems of a purely academic nature and in a mere virtuosity of philosophical technique. It has become increasingly absorbed in side issues. Instead of genuine classical music it has frequently produced only chamber music, often excellent in its way, but not the real thing. And so this philosophy, which was occupied only in elucidating itself, instead of struggling to achieve a world-view grounded in thought and essential for life, has led us into a position where we are devoid of any world-view at all, and, as an inevitable consequence of this, of any real civilization.   [Ethics, p. viii]

The Danger of Technical Language

Technical expressions are a danger for every system of philosophy, whether Indian or European. For they may become formulae which hinder the natural development of thought in the same way as ruts in a road hinder traffic. So to find out what are its real contents it is reasonable to test a system of thought by setting aside the expressions which it has coined for its own use and compelling it to speak in ordinary comprehensible language.   [Indian, p. ix]

The Divorce of Science and Reflection

Today thought gets no help from science, and the latter stands facing it independent and unconcerned. The newest

scientific knowledge may be allied with an entirely un-
reflecting view of the universe. It maintains that it is concerned only with the establishment of individual facts,
since it is only by means of these that scientific knowledge
can maintain its practical character; the coordination of the
different branches of knowledge and the utilization of the
results to form a theory of the universe are, it says, not its
business. Once every man of science was also a thinker who
counted for something in the general spiritual life of his
generation. Our age has discovered how to divorce knowledge from thought, with the result that we have, indeed,
a science which is free, but hardly any science left which
reflects.   [Decay, p. 72]

The Clogged Spirit

A fundamental impulse to reflect about the universe stirs
us during those years in which we begin to think independently. Later on we let it languish, even though feeling
clearly that we thereby impoverish ourselves and become
less capable of what is good. We are like springs of water
which no longer run because they have not been watched
and have gradually become choked with rubbish.

More than any other age has our own neglected to
watch the thousand springs of thought; hence the drought
in which we are pining. But if we only go on to remove
the rubbish which conceals the water, the sands will be irri-
gated again, and life will spring up where hitherto there
has been only a desert.   [Decay, pp. 92 f.]

The Tragedy of Western Thought

Western thought is not governed like mystical thought by
the idea that the one thing needful is the spiritual union of
man with infinite Being, and therefore (if it is obliged to

renounce the hope of attaining to a knowledge of the universe that corresponds to ethical world- and life-affirmation), it is in danger of saying it is satisfied not only with lowered ideals, but also with an inferior conception of world-view. That is the tragedy that is being enacted before our eyes.   [Indian, pp. 253 f.]

Spiritual Bankruptcy

Renunciation of thinking is a declaration of spiritual bankruptcy. Where there is no longer a conviction that men can get to know the truth by their own thinking, skepticism begins. Those who work to make our age skeptical in this way, do so in the expectation that, as a result of renouncing all hope of self-discovered truth, men will end by accepting as truth what is forced upon them with authority and by propaganda.   [Life, p. 258]

Obstructive Erudition

Obstructive erudition is the special prerogative of theology, in which, even at the present day, a truly marvelous scholarship often serves only to blind the eyes to elementary truths, and to cause the artificial to be preferred to the natural. And this happens not only with those who deliberately shut their minds against new impressions, but also with those whose purpose is to go forward, and to whom their contemporaries look up as leaders.   [Quest, p. 25]

Mistrust of Thought

Today in addition to that neglect of thought there is also prevalent a mistrust of it. The organized political, social, and religious associations of our time are at work to induce the individual man not to arrive at his convictions by his own thinking, but to make his own such convictions as they keep ready made for him. Any man who thinks for himself and at the same time is spiritually free, is to them something inconvenient and even uncanny. He does not offer sufficient guarantee that he will merge himself in their organization in the way they wish. All corporate bodies look today for their strength not so much to the spiritual worth of the ideas which they represent and to that of the people who belong to them, as to the attainment of the highest possible degree of unity and exclusiveness. It is in this that they expect to find their strongest power for offense and defense.   [Life, p. 255]

The Lost Feeling for Sincerity

Not less strong than the will to truth must be the will to sincerity. Only an age which can show the courage of sincerity can possess truth which works as a spiritual force within it.

Sincerity is the foundation of the spiritual life.

With its depreciation of thinking our generation has lost its feeling for sincerity and with it that for truth as well. It can therefore be helped only by its being brought once more onto the road of thinking.

Because I have this certainty I oppose the spirit of the age, and take upon myself with confidence the responsibility of taking my part in the rekindling of the fire of thought.   [Life, pp. 259 f.]

The Enigma of Creative Force

We shall not solve our problem by blotting out the dualism which exists in the world as we know it, but rather by taking it up into our lives as something which has no longer any sinister power over us. And we shall arrive at this point when we leave behind all the artificialities and fictions of thought and admit the simple fact that we cannot bring world-view and life-view into harmony with each other, and are therefore obliged to make up our minds to give preference to the latter. The volition given in our will-to-live transcends and is superior to our knowledge of the world. What is decisive for our view of life is not our knowledge of the world, but rather the positive nature of the volition which is given in our will-to-live. In nature we encounter the eternal spirit as an enigmatic creative force. In our will-to-live we experience it in ourselves as world- and life-affirmation and as ethical will.

Our real world-view is our relation to the world, as this is presented to us in the self-determination of our will-to-live when it attempts to comprehend itself in thought. World-view is derived from life-view and not vice versa. [Ethics, pp. xiv f.]

Logic and Ethics

Logical thought about the nature of the universe cannot reach an ethic. . . . The more it is logical and consistent, the less has it of an ethical content. Lao-tse and Chang Tso-lin are much greater thinkers than Kung-fu-tse (Confucius) and Meng-tse (Mencius), but their philosophy is accordingly less ethical.   [Christianity, p. 70]

Despair of Intellectual Knowledge

I think I am the first Western thinker who has dared to be absolutely skeptical with regard to our knowledge of the objective world, without at the same time renouncing world- and life-affirmation and ethics. Despair of any attempt to comprehend the world intellectually does not involve for me a hopeless lapse into a skepticism which would mean our drifting through life like rudderless wrecks. It seems to me to afford us the very truth which we must dare to grasp in order to find in it that world-view of which we dream, a world-view which will put us in touch with reality and inspire us to action. On the other hand every world-view not based on despair of intellectual knowledge is artificial and fictitious, for it rests on an unreliable interpretation of the world.   [Ethics, p. xiii]

Invisible Barriers

The more we try to see into the development of things, in any field whatever, the more we become conscious that to each epoch there are set certain limits of knowledge, before which it has to come to a halt, and always at the very moment when it was apparently bound to advance to a higher and definitive knowledge that seemed just within its grasp. The real history of progress in physics, philosophy, and religion, and more especially in psychology, is the history of incomprehensible cessations of conceptions that were unattainable by a given epoch, in spite of all that happened to lead it up to them—of the thoughts it did not think, not because it could not, but because there was some mysterious command upon it not to. In the same way, the true history of art is the history of invisible, insuperable barriers, which only fall when the due time comes, without anyone understanding why this happens exactly when it does, and not just as well earlier or later.   [Bach, I, p. 48]

Reason the Only Method

I was convinced—and I am so still—that the fundamental principles of Christianity have to be proved true by reasoning, and by no other method. Reason, I said to myself, is

given us that we may bring everything within the range
of its action, even the most exalted ideas of religion. And
this certainty filled me with joy.   [Childhood, p. 60]

Thought the Foundation of Faith

Christianity cannot take the place of thinking, but it must
be founded on it.

In and by itself it is not capable of mastering lack of
thought and skepticism. The only age which can be receptive for the imperishable elements in its own thoughts is
one animated by an elemental piety which springs from
thinking.

Just as a stream is preserved from gradually leaking
away, because it flows along above subsoil water, so does
Christianity need the subsoil water of elemental piety which
is the fruit of thinking. It can only attain to real spiritual
power when men find the road from thought to religion
no longer barred.

I know that I myself owe it to thinking that I was able
to retain my faith in religion, and Christianity.   [Life,
p. 276]

Christianity Needs Thought

Christianity has need of thought that it may come to the
consciousness of its real self. For centuries it treasured the
great commandment of love and mercy as traditional truth
without recognizing it as a reason for opposing slavery,
witch-burning, torture, and all the other ancient and medieval forms of inhumanity. It was only when it experienced
the influence of the thinking of the *Aufklärung* [Age of
Enlightenment] that it was stirred into entering the struggle
for humanity. The remembrance of this ought to preserve
it forever from assuming any air of superiority in comparison with Thought.   [Life, p. 275]

The Revolt against Thoughtlessness

If men can be found who revolt against the spirit of
thoughtlessness, and who are personalities sound enough
and profound enough to let the ideals of ethical progress
radiate from them as a force, there will start an activity of
the spirit which will be strong enough to evoke a new
mental and spiritual disposition in mankind.   [Life, p. 261]

A Cloistered Christianity

The situation today is that Christianity has completely
withdrawn into itself, and is concerned only with the prop-
agation of its own ideas, as such. It no longer sees any use
in proving them to be in agreement with thought, but
prefers that they be regarded as something altogether outside it, and occupying a superior position. It loses, however, thereby its connection with the spiritual life of the
time and the possibility of exercising any real influence
upon it.

The emergence of the world-view of Reverence for Life
now summons it to face once more the question whether
it will or will not join hands with Thought which is ethical
and religious in character.   [Life, pp. 274 f.]

Quench Not the Spirit

It has significance for all future times that the Symphony
of Christianity began with a tremendous dissonance between faith and thought, which later resolved itself into a
harmony. Christianity can only become the living truth for
successive generations if thinkers constantly arise within it
who, in the Spirit of Jesus, make belief in Him capable of
intellectual apprehension in the thought-forms of the world-
view proper to their time. When Christianity becomes a

traditional belief which claims to be simply taken over by the individual, it loses its relationship to the spiritual life of the time and the capacity of assuming a new form adapted to a new world-view. If the debate between tradition and thought falls silent, Christian truth suffers, and with it Christian intellectual integrity. This is why it is so deeply significant that Paul undertakes as an entirely obvious duty to think out Christianity in its whole scope and its whole depth by the use of the materials provided by the eschatological world-view of his time. The sayings "Quench not the Spirit" and "Where the Spirit of the Lord is, there is liberty," which owe their place in the records of the origin of Christianity to him, carry the significance that thinking Christianity is to have its rights within believing Christianity, and that the "little faiths" will never succeed in suppressing loyalty to truth. Never must Christianity lay aside the large simplicity with which Paul claims thought also as having its origin in God. Never must the spring-like freshness of Pauline Christianity die out from amid our own. [Mysticism, p. 377]

Thought Renews Faith

The result of the first appearance of thought in Christianity is calculated to justify, for all periods, the confidence that faith has nothing to fear from thinking, even when the latter disturbs its peace and raises a debate which appears to promise no good results for the religious life. How strongly the faith of the primitive Christian community resisted the thinking of Paul! And yet it was the raising, by the Apostle of the Gentiles, of the belief in Jesus Christ to a reasoned faith which provided a solution of the problem set to the Christianity of the next generation by the non-fulfilment of the eschatological hope. The idea which looked so dangerous to the leaders of the primitive Church enabled the

Gospel of Jesus after its rejection by Judaism to find entrance and understanding in the Greek world. It is the thoughts of the Apostle of the Gentiles, who was opposed by the faith of his own time, which have again and again acted as a power of renewal in the faith of subsequent periods. Thus it appears, from the course of this first conflict of Christian thought with Christian faith, that the thought proved an investment for the future which brought profit to the faith of later generations, as has proved to be the case again and again in the history of Christianity. [Mysticism, pp. 376 f.]

The Rights of Thought

Paul vindicated for all time the rights of thought in Christianity. Above belief which drew its authority from tradition, he set the knowledge which came from the Spirit of Christ. There lives in him an unbounded and undeviating reverence for truth. He will consent only to a limitation of liberty laid on him by the law of love, not to one imposed by doctrinal authority.   [Mysticism, p. 376]

The Patron Saint of Thought

Paul is the patron saint of thought in Christianity. And all those who think to serve the faith in Jesus by destroying freedom of thought would do well to keep out of his way. [Mysticism, p. 377]

Stoicism

Stoicism seemed to me great in that it goes straight for its goal; that it is universally intelligible, and is at the same time profound; that it makes the best of the truth which it recognizes as such, even if it is unsatisfying; that it puts life into such truth by the earnestness with which it devotes itself to it; that it possesses the spirit of sincerity; that it urges men to collect their thoughts, and to become more inward; and that it arouses in them the sense of responsibility. I felt, too, that the fundamental thought of Stoicism is true, namely that man must bring himself into a spiritual relation with the world, and become one with it. In its essence Stoicism is a nature-philosophy which ends in mysticism. [Life, p. 261]

Lao-tse

Just as I felt Stoic thinking to be elemental, so I felt that of Lao-tse to be the same, when I became acquainted with his Tao Te King. For him, too, the important thing is that man shall come, by simple thinking, into a spiritual relation to the world, and prove his unity with it by his life.

There is, therefore, an essential relationship between Greek Stoicism and Chinese. The only distinction between them is that the former had its origin in well-developed, logical thinking, the latter in intuitive thinking which was undeveloped and yet marvellously profound. [Life, p. 261]

Always Something New

In the far interior, where the cult of Islam is widespread, young men were making merry over an old one who was a zealous reader of the Koran. "You will soon know your Koran by heart," they said. "Don't you get sick of always reading the same thing?"

"For me," he replied, "it is by no means the same Koran. When I was a boy, I understood it as a boy. When I was a man in my prime, I understood it as a man, and now I am old I understand it as an old man. I read it again and

again because, for me, it always contains something new."
[Notebook, pp. 118 f.]

Negro Reflective Powers

I am astonished at the reflective powers which I so frequently meet with in Negroes. They are preoccupied with
the questions of existence in a direct and living fashion,
although they seldom say anything about such things to us.
But on the occasions when this does happen, it becomes
evident that they have an inner life which we should never
have suspected in them. I have had conversations with
Africans that affected me deeply. Doctors and nurses at my
hospital and Europeans of our acquaintance have had similar experiences.

Anyone who has once arrived at knowing the inner personality of the African knows that he has a fine nature in
spite of his curious weak points and faults. During the
many years in which I have had to do with Negroes,
although I have had so many occasions for anger, I have
learned to respect and value them, and I believe this will be
the experience of every European who associates with them
not alone as a superior but as a human being.   [Note-
book, pp. 135 f.]

Negroes Are Deeper than We

The child of nature thinks a great deal more than is generally supposed. Even though he can neither read nor write,
he has ideas on many more subjects than we imagine. Conversations I have had in the hospital with old natives about
the ultimate things of life have deeply impressed me. The
distinction between white and colored, educated and uneducated, disappears when one gets talking with the forest
dweller about our relations to each other, to mankind, to

the universe, and to the infinite. "The Negroes are deeper than we are," a white man once said to me, "because they don't read newspapers," and the paradox has some truth in it.   [Edge, pp. 153 f.]

The Two Problems of Thought

There are two great fundamental problems common to all thought: (1) the problem of world- and life-affirmation and world- and life-negation, and (2) the problem of ethics and the relations between ethics and these two forms of man's spiritual attitude to Being.   [Indian, p. vii]

Enthusiastic Thought

The enthusiasm which comes from thought has the same relation to that which is produced by mere random feeling as the wind which sweeps the heights has to that which eddies about between the hills. If we venture once more to seek help from the light of reason, we shall no longer keep ourselves down at the level of a generation which has ceased to be capable of enthusiasm, but shall rise to the deep and noble passion inspired by great and sublime ideals. These will so fill and expand our being that that by which we now live will seem to be merely a poor kind of excitement, and will disappear.   [Decay, p. 88]

THE STRUGGLE FOR TRUTH

Truth Has No Special Hour

Truth has no special time of its own. Its hour is now—always, and indeed then most truly when it seems most unsuitable to actual circumstances.   [Edge, p. 174]

Testing for Truth

The highest honor one can show to a system of thought is to test it ruthlessly with a view to discovering how much truth it contains, just as steel is assayed to try its strength. [Indian, p. viii]

The Power of Truth

Because I have confidence in the power of truth and of the spirit, I believe in the future of mankind. Ethical world- and life-affirmation contains within itself an optimistic willing and hoping which can never be lost. It is, therefore, never afraid to face the dismal reality, and to see it as it really is.   [Life, p. 281]

Faith in Truth

The beginning of all spiritual life of any real value is courageous faith in truth and open confession of the same. The most profound religious experience, too, is not alien to thought, but must be capable of derivation from this if it

is to be given a true and deep basis. Mere reflection about
the meaning of life has already value in itself. If such reflection should again come into being amongst us, the ideals,
born of vanity and of passion, which now flourish in rank
profusion like evil weeds among the convictions of the
generality of people, would infallibly wither away and die.
How much would already be accomplished towards the improvement of our present circumstances if only we would
all give up three minutes every evening to gazing up into
the infinite world of the starry heavens and meditating on
it, or if in taking part in a funeral procession we would reflect on the enigma of life and death, instead of engaging in
thoughtless conversation as we follow behind the coffin!
The ideals, born of folly and passion, of those who make
public opinion and direct public events, would have no
more power over men if they once began to reflect about
infinity and the finite, existence and dissolution, and thus
learned to distinguish between true and false standards, between those which possess real value and those which do
not. The old-time rabbis used to teach that the Kingdom of
God would come if only the whole of Israel would really
keep a single Sabbath simultaneously! How much more is
it true that the injustice and violence and untruth, which
are now bringing so much disaster on the human race,
would lose their power if only a single real trace of reflection about the meaning of the world and of life should
appear amongst us!   [Decay, pp. 102 f.]

Inherent Truth

From my youth I have held the conviction that all religious
truth must in the end be capable of being grasped as something that stands to reason. I, therefore, believe that Christianity, in the contest with philosophy and with other religions, should not ask for exceptional treatment, but should

be in the thick of the battle of ideas, relying solely on the power of its own inherent truth.   [Christianity, p. 3]

Piety and Truth

The deeper piety is, the humbler are its claims with regard to knowledge of the suprasensible. It is like a path which winds between the hills instead of going over them.   [Life, p. 277]

Truth Undismayed

It is the fate of the "little faiths" of truth that they, true followers of Peter, whether they be of the Roman or the Protestant observance, cry out and sink in the sea of ideas, where the followers of Paul, believing in the Spirit, walk secure and undismayed.   [Paul, p. 249]

Public Opinion

A new public opinion must be created privately and un-obtrusively. The existing one is maintained by the press, by propaganda, by organization, and by financial and other influences which are at its disposal. This unnatural way of spreading ideas must be opposed by the natural one, which goes from man to man and relies solely on the truth of the thoughts and the hearer's receptiveness for new truth. Unarmed and following the human spirit's primitive and natural fighting method, it must attack the other, which faces it, as Goliath faced David, in the mighty armor of the age.   [Decay, pp. 74 f.]

Truth Must Be Won

Since the essential nature of the spiritual is truth, every new truth means ultimately something won. Truth is under all circumstances more valuable than non-truth, and this must apply to truth in the realm of history as to other kinds of truth. Even if it comes in a guise which piety finds strange and at first makes difficulties for her, the final result can never mean injury; it can only mean greater depth. Religion has, therefore, no reason for trying to avoid coming to terms with historical truth.   [Life, p. 65]

In Returning Shall We Be Saved

What does Goethe say to our time?

He says to it, that the frightful drama that is being enacted in it, can come to an end only when it sets aside the economic and social magic, in which it has trusted, when it forgets the magic formulas with which it deludes itself, when it is resolved to return at any cost to a natural relationship with reality.   [Gedenkrede, p. 48]

The Painful Struggle for Truth

Those who tried to bring Jesus to life at the call of love found it a cruel task to be honest. The critical study of the life of Jesus has been for theology a school of honesty. The world had never seen before, and will never see again, a struggle for truth so full of pain and renunciation as that of which the lives of Jesus of the last hundred years contain the cryptic record. One must read the successive lives of Jesus with which Hase followed the course of the study from the 'twenties to the 'seventies of the nineteenth century [Karl August Hase, the Jena professor, whose first *Life of Jesus* was published in 1829] to get an inkling of what it must have cost the men who lived through that decisive period really to maintain that "courageous freedom of investigation" which the great Jena professor, in the preface to his first *Life of Jesus*, claims for his researches.

One sees in him the marks of the struggle with which he
gives up, bit by bit, things which, when he wrote that
preface, he never dreamed he would have to surrender. It
was fortunate for these men that their sympathies sometimes
obscured their critical vision, so that, without becoming
insincere, they were able to take white clouds for distant
mountains.   [Quest, pp. 5 f.]

The Pursuit of Truth

Paul is no mere revolutionary. He takes the faith of the
primitive Christian community as his starting point: only
he will not consent to halt where it comes to an end, but
claims the right to think out his thoughts about Christ to
their conclusion, without caring whether the truths which
he thereby reaches have ever come within the purview of
the faith held by the Christian community and been recognized by it.   [Mysticism, p. 376]

German Research

It is impossible to overestimate the value of what German
research upon the life of Jesus has accomplished. It is a
uniquely great expression of sincerity, one of the most
significant events in the whole mental and spiritual life of
humanity.   [Quest, p. 397]

The Philosophy of Values

The philosophy of values resorts to a type of thinking
which becomes dualistic. It asserts that there are spiritual
truths alongside theoretical truths, and that all valuable
conviction has truth in itself—a dangerous assertion. The
real father of this doctrine of double truth is Hume. To
escape skepticism, Hume says, we need convictions which

will help us to live, and in regard to which we ask, not, Are they true? but, Are they necessary for our life?   [Religion, pp. 1519 f.]

Pragmatism

What is pragmatism compared with this philosophy of values? [The philosophy of Hume.] It is a philosophy of values which has given up the criterion of ethics. Pragmatism says: Every idea that helps me to live is truth. Europeans got this pragmatism sent, all ready for use, from America, in William James. So modern thinking arrives at the doctrine of double truth. The theory of double truth is a spiritual danger. If there is a double truth, there is no truth. The sense of sincerity is blunted and the last thing that thinking can give humanity is a feeling for truth— for sincerity is fundamental in all spiritual life and when this fundamental is shaken, there is no spiritual life remaining. In pragmatism, not only sincerity and truth, but ethics is in danger. For ethics is no longer the criterion of what is valuable. Pragmatism is filled with the spirit of realism. It permits men to take their ideals from reality. [Religion, p. 1520]

Success and Truth

Many famous lives of Jesus, which have prolonged an honored existence through many successive editions, make but a poor figure, while others, which have received scant notice, appear great. Behind Success comes Truth, and her reward is with her.   [Quest, p. 12]

The Valley of Reality

The pathway from imperfect to perfect recognized truth leads through the valley of reality. European thought has

already descended into this valley. Indian thought is still
on the hill on this side of it. If it wishes to climb to the hill
beyond, it must first go down into the valley.   [Indian,
pp. 256 f.]

Revolutionary Ideas in Theology

The fact is that in theology the most revolutionary ideas
are swallowed quite readily so long as they smooth their
passage by a few small concessions. It is only when a
spicule of bone stands out obstinately and causes choking
that theology begins to take note of dangerous ideas.
[Quest, p. 37]

The Progress of Truth

The traveler on the plain sees from afar the distant range
of mountains. Then he loses sight of them again. His way
winds slowly upwards through the valleys, drawing ever
nearer to the peaks, until at last, at a turn of the path, they
stand before him, not in the shapes which they had seemed
to take from the distant plain, but in their actual forms.
[Quest, p. 23]

THE SEARCH FOR BEAUTY

The Artists in the Soul

We classify the arts according to the material they use in order to express the world around them. One who expresses himself in tones is called a musician; one who employs colors, a painter; one who uses words, a poet. This, however, is a purely external division. In reality, the material in which the artist expresses himself is a secondary matter. He is not only a painter, nor only a poet, nor only a musician, but all in one. Various artists have their habitation in his soul. His work is the product of their cooperation; all have a part in each one of his ideas. The distinction consists only in this, that one idea is dominated by one of these artists, another by another of them, and they always choose the language that suits them best.   [Bach, II, p. 8]

The Other Artist in Us

Let us ask the audience of a performance of a work by Palestrina to account for the solemn effect it has made on them. The majority would confess that they had felt themselves transported into the vast nave of a church, and saw the sunlight streaming through the windows of the choir into the twilight of the building. We all poetize more than we are apt to imagine. This can be shown by a simple experiment. Try to look but not hear, and to hear but not let any visual associations step over the threshold of con-

sciousness, and the other artist in us, whom we imagined
to be uninterested, will at once spring up and demand his
rights.   [Bach, II, p. 15]

Poet and Painter

Many other authors since Goethe's time have passed from
painting to verbal description and remained pictorial in
essence, though choosing the material in which they could
best depict the world as they saw it. Taine is certainly a
painter. We can only understand rightly the loose and yet
wonderfully clear structure of Gottfried Keller's stories
when we realize that it is not the poet but the dramatic
painter who guides the pen. In Michelangelo, again, who is
the greater—the poet or the painter? We call Heine our
greatest lyrist. Should we not call him from the standpoint
of "the universal art," the most inspired painter among the
lyric poets? Böcklin is a poet who has got among the
painters. It is the poetic imagination that has led him to the
fictions of his wonderful but, in the last resort, unreal landscapes. His visions master him to such an extent that im-
possibilities in the composition, even errors of drawing that
are at first sight disconcerting, are matters of indifference to
him. He had recourse to pencil and palette because he
thought he could thus reproduce most vividly his poems
of the elemental forces. His paintings are in the last resort
symbols of poems that were inexpressible in words. It is
thus quite natural that the reaction against him comes from
the French painters, who, with their objective realism,
have no sympathy with such a relation of poetry and painting, and combat an art showing tendencies of this kind from
the standpoint of absolute painting, just as the partisans of
absolute music make war on the music that bases itself
on poetry.   [Bach, II, pp. 10 f.]

German and French Painting

The essential distinction between German and French painting comes from their attitudes towards poetry. Anyone who comes in contact with artists of both countries, and analyzes the first impressions of German artists in Paris and the impressions of French artists at the sight of German works, and tries to see to the root of the unjust judgments on both sides, will soon observe that the difference in their views has its origin in the difference of their attitudes toward poetry. The German painter is more of a poet than the French. Therefore French painting reproaches German painting with a lack of real, objective feeling for nature. German painting, on the other hand, in spite of its admiration for the splendid technique of the French, feels somewhat chilled by a kind of deliberate poverty of imagination that it detects in it. In literature these contrasted ways of looking at nature have given Germany a splendid lyrical poetry that the French have never been able to achieve.   [Bach, II, p. 11]

Intercoloration

Painting is suffused with poetry, and poetry with painting. The quality of either of the arts at a given moment depends on the strength or the weakness of this intercoloration. As regards their means of expression each of them passes into the other by imperceptible gradations. [Bach, II, p. 11]

The Rivalry of the Arts

The close and tense relation in which the arts stand among each other gives each of them a desire for expansion that allows the art no peace until it has attained its utmost possible limit. Then it is further impelled to appropriate a

portion of the territory of another art. Not only does music
try to paint and narrate like the two other arts; they in their
turn do likewise. Poetry tries to paint pictures that really
need to be taken in by the eye, and painting tries to seize
not only the visible scene but the poetic feeling underlying
it. Music, however, working in a medium so little fitted to
depict concrete ideas, soon reaches its limits of clear representation of poetic and pictorial ideas. For this reason pictorial and poetic tendencies have in all epochs exercised a
pernicious influence upon music, and have given birth to
a false art, that imagined it could express objects and ideas
which it is far beyond the powers of music to render. This
false music lives by pretensions and self-deception. Its arrogant view of itself as the only perfect music has always
brought it into discredit.   [Bach, II, pp. 13 f.]

Art Is an Act of Creation

Every artistic idea is complex in quality until the moment
when it finds definite expression. Neither in painting, nor
in music, nor in poetry is there such a thing as an absolute
art that can be regarded as the norm, enabling us to brand
all others as false, for in every artist there dwells another,
who wishes to have his own say in the matter, the difference being that in one his activity is obtrusive, and in
another hardly noticeable. Herein resides the whole distinction. Art in itself is neither painting nor poetry nor
music, but an act of creation in which all three cooperate.
[Bach, II, p. 13]

Complex Emotions

Not only is the creative art complex; our reception of it
is not less so. In every true artistic perception there come
into action all the feelings and ideas of which a man is

capable. The process is multiform, though it is only in the
rarest cases that the subject has any inkling of what is going
on in his imagination, and what mental overtones compli-
cate the ground tone which, as it seems to him, exclusively
occupies his attention.

Many a man erroneously thinks he sees a picture whereas
he really hears it, his artistic emotions arising from the
music—perhaps silent—that he perceives in the scene represented on the canvas. Anyone who does not hear the bees
in Didier-Pouget's picture of the flowery heath does not
see it with the eye of the artist. Again, anyone who is not
fascinated by the most ordinary painting of a pine wood—
hearing the infinite distant symphonies of the wind sweep-
ing over the treetops—sees only as half a man, i.e., not as
an artist.

So again in music. Musical sensibility is to some extent
a capacity for tone-visions, of whatever kind it may be,
whether it deals with lines, ideas, forms, or events. Associations of ideas are always going on where we would not
suspect them.   [Bach, II, p. 14]

The Translation of Ideas

Art is the translation of aesthetic associations of ideas. The
more complexly and intensely the conscious and uncon-
scious concepts and ideas of the artist communicate themselves to us through his art work, the deeper is the impression. It is then that he succeeds in stimulating others to that
vivacity of imaginative feeling which we call art, in contra-
distinction to what we hear and see and experience in our
ordinary moments.   [Bach, II, p. 15]

The Accident of Speech

Every artistic feeling is really an act. Artistic creation is
only a special case of the artistic attitude towards the world.

Some men have the faculty of reproducing in speech, colors, tones, or words the artistic impression made on them and many others by what goes on in the world around them. It is not so much that these are more fundamentally artists than the others, but only that they can speak and the others are dumb. When we see the passionate effect made by art on men who are only "receptive," and how much their mute imagination can add to the works of others, it no longer seems a paradox that it is only by accident that some of the great ones have received the gift of speech.   [Bach, II, p. 15]

The Inexpressible Speaks

In poetry and painting . . . the language . . . is also the language of daily life. We need, however, only read a poem by Goethe, and test the words of which it consists by the wealth of suggestions that they arouse in us, to see at once that words in art become suggestive symbols, by means of which the imaginations of two artists hold converse together. "In truth," says Wagner, "the greatness of the poet can be best measured by what he refrains from saying, in order to let the inexpressible itself speak to us in secrecy."

In painting, the inadequacy of the thing said is still more striking. We cannot estimate how much the spectator must add of his own before a colored canvas can become a landscape. An etching, indeed, makes extraordinary demands on the imagination, for the representation in black and white is only a symbol of the landscape, and has no more reality than a symbol. And yet this symbolical delineation is, for anyone who can interpret it, perhaps the most potent means of conjuring up the faculty of complete vision.

In this way there comes into painting, in the place of the naïve "This is," the noteworthy "This signifies" of artistic speech. It will be learned and assimilated by familiarity. It even happens at times that the speech fails, the symbols not being clear to the spectator, and appear merely as agglomerations of lines and colors, either because the artist has put more into them than they can express, or because the spectator has not caught the secret of his speech. [Bach, II, p. 16]

The Signs and Symbols of Art

The part of a work of art that is perceptible by the senses is in reality only the intermediator between two active efforts of the imagination. All art speaks in signs and symbols. No one can explain how it happens that the artist can waken to life in us the existence that he has seen and lived through. No artistic speech is the adequate expression of what it represents; its vital force comes from what is unspoken in it. [Bach, II, p. 16]

The Mystery of Music

In music the expression is wholly symbolical. The translation of even the most general feelings and ideas into tone is a mystery. The latest researches into the physiology of musical sensation do not help us in the least; they merely conquer for musical aesthetics a wonderful colonial territory, which, however, to the end of time will yield it nothing. "The thing that is most important is, and will remain, unexplained," says Hanslick,—"the nervous process by which the sensation of tone becomes converted into feeling, a mental mood." [Bach, II, pp. 16 f.]

The Tragedy of Music

The tragedy of music is that it can only express with limited intelligibility the concrete image from which it has sprung. From the indefiniteness of the tone picture itself, however, we must not conclude a corresponding indefiniteness of the fancy that prompted it, and claim that music of this kind is the absolute music. We have a warning example in Weber's *konzertstück*. In 1821, on the morning of the day of the first performance of *Der Freischütz*, Weber brought his wife the *konzertstück* which he had just completed, and played it to her and his favorite pupil, Benedict, telling them at the same time what the music was meant to represent:

"*Larghetto*. On the terrace of the castle stands the châtelaine, looking sadly into the distance. Her husband is with the Crusaders in the Holy Land. She has no news of him. Is he dead? Will she see him again?

"*Allegro appassionato*. Horror! She sees him lying on the battlefield, abandoned, wounded. The blood flows from his wounds . . . and she cannot hasten to his side!

"*Adagio e tempo di marcia*. Tumult and glittering of weapons in the distance, coming from the wood. They draw nearer. They are knights carrying the cross. The banners wave, the people break out into cries of joy, and . . . he is there!

"*Più mosso, presto assai*. She runs to meet him. He embraces her. Wood and field add their jubilant cries to the hymn of faithful love."

The pupil immediately wrote out the "explanation," but Weber would not allow it to be published with the music. Had it not been preserved by accident, no one would have imagined the events depicted in the *konzertstück*, and it would naturally be regarded as a piece of pure music.   [Bach, II, pp. 18 f.]

Pure and Representative Music

Just as there are painters and musicians among the poets, so there are poets and painters among the musicians. They become clearly distinguished from each other in proportion as the "other artist" is able to assert himself in their conceptions. Poetic music deals more with ideas, pictorial music with pictures; the one appeals more to the feeling, the other to our faculty of representation. The incoherency of the discussion upon tone-painting, program music and representative music has been due in great part to the fact that no account has been taken of the two main currents in music that now flow parallel to each other, now cross each other—it being assumed that every sin against pure music was of the same order.

Beethoven and Wagner belong more to the poets, Bach, Schubert and Berlioz more to the painters. [Bach, II, p. 21]

Descriptive Music

Beethoven's works were also written under the impression of definite scenes, in spite of the fact that they are claimed to be pure music. When asked for an explanation of the D minor sonata, he replied, "Read Shakespeare's *Tempest*." In the adagio of the F major quartet (*op*. 18, No. 1) he had in his mind the grave scene from *Romeo and Juliet*. The E major sonata (*op*. 81) even bears an authentic inscription; it depicts a farewell, a separation and a return. More particularly in his latest chamber music we have a strong feeling that the musical sequence of ideas is determined by a poetic mood of some kind; we have, however, no hints by which we can definitely reconstruct from the music the situation the composer had in his mind. [Bach, II, p. 19]

Beethoven, the Poet

Beethoven is often called a poet by Wagner, who thinks that the awakening of "the other artist" in him was the crucial point of his career. The first period of free and careless musical invention was followed by another, in which Beethoven speaks a language that often seems arbitrary and capricious, the ideas being held together only by a poetic purpose, which, however, could not be expressed with poetic clearness in music. Then comes the period in which the deeply sensitive man suffered acutely, when he could no longer make himself intelligible to his hearers, who regarded him simply as a mad genius. The successive symphonies relate the longing of music to transcend its own element and become universal art, until at last, in the ninth symphony, it seized upon speech, worked out its own salvation, and united the several arts in one.   [Bach, II, pp. 21 f.]

Goethe, the Painter

It may happen that the "other artist" and the possibilities of the "other language" assume so prominent a place in the consciousness of artists that they are at variance with themselves, not knowing which art they really ought to cultivate. It was so with Goethe, who on his return from Wetzlar, did not know whether he should devote himself to painting or to poetry. . . .

For all that he remained a painter. His designs indeed are amateurish, and his understanding of the masterpieces of painting is not so complete as he himself thought it was. But he sees and depicts everything like a painter. He is always congratulating himself on the gift of seeing the world with the eye of a painter, whose pictures were always before him. Venice appeared to him as a succession of pictures by the Venetian school. The unfathomable mystery of his style is the way in which a couple of sentences, without any real attempt at description on his part, will bring the whole scene as it appeared to him before the eye of the reader, suggesting to him all kinds of things he neither sees nor hears, but which he can no more forget than if they had been actually part of his own experience. In *Faust* we have a succession not so much of scenes as of vivid pictures. Goethe paints his own portrait at different periods of his life, against an idyllic, naïve, tragic, burlesque, fantastic or allegorical background. His landscapes are not merely built up out of words; like the painter, he has really seen them all, and he employs words like resonant spots of color, in such a way that they conjure up the living scene before the reader's eye. [Bach, II, pp. 8 ff.]

Bach, the Painter

Beethoven and Wagner poetize in music; Bach paints. And Bach is a dramatist, but just in the sense that the painter is. He does not paint successive events, but seizes upon the pregnant moment that contains the whole event for him, and depicts this in music. [Bach, II, p. 41]

The New and the Old

The German Reformation had this advantage over the French, that it found a spiritual song already existing in the popular tongue, and therefore a ground upon which it could build; but its great good fortune was that it possessed, in Luther, a man who would not permit the old wood to be cut down, recognizing with sure prescience that the new song must grow up in the shade of the old. On the other hand the sacred folk song withered away in the Romanesque countries, because it had no root in the Middle Ages, and had to exist as best it could upon the Psalter, as it does to the present day. [Bach, I, p. 7]

Out of the Bitter, Sweet

The really creative period of the hymn begins at the end
of the sixteenth century. The whole of German poetry is
impelled upon the religious path. While France, under a
monarchy conscious of its own goal, is developing into a
strong national state, in which there springs up a brilliant
literature, fostered by an art-loving court, Germany is on
the way to complete ruin. The nation as such disappears,
and with it that national feeling without which no true
literature is possible. When the country relapsed into barbarism during the Thirty Years' War, the only thing of
the soul that survived was religion. In its bosom poetry
took refuge. Thus Germany, in its bitterest need, created a
religious poetry to which nothing in the world can compare, and before which even the splendor of the Psalter
pales.   [Bach, I, pp. 10 f.]

One Will Live

These hymn writers [of the period beginning at the end of
the sixteenth century] are by no means talents of the first
order. Nevertheless the sincerity of devout feeling and the
grave beauty of a diction formed by a constant reading of
the Bible keep the average of the songs fairly high. Perhaps
all these poets wrote too much. It happens, too, with the
sacred poem as with the lyric: in one inspired song the poet,
become for the moment a genius, will express magically
what in other songs he could only stammer out. And this
one song will live.   [Bach, I, p. 11]

The Idea Always Conquers

An idea is, in the end, always stronger than circumstances.
Organ music did not come to perfection in Paris or in

Venice, where everything seemed to be in its favor, but
among the poor cantors and schoolmasters of an impoverished country, as the Germany of the two generations
after the Thirty Years' War was. How small Frescobaldi,
the organist of St. Peter's in Rome, whose fame among his
contemporaries was so great, seems beside a Samuel Scheidt,
whose name was unknown on the other side of the Alps!
[Bach, I, pp. 36 f.]

Only the Perfect Endures

In no other art does the perfect consign the imperfect to
oblivion so thoroughly as it does in music. Early painting
retains its own artistic charm for all time. It deals with
nature, with reality, and renders it, no matter how awk-
wardly, with a primitive truth that makes so direct an
appeal to the spectator of all epochs that he himself looks
at the scene with the childlike eyes of those early artists.
Music, however, does not depict the external universe, but
is the image of an invisible world, which can only be expressed in eternal tones by those who see it in its whole
perfection and can reproduce it as they have seen it. Anything less than this pales and fades in the course of time,
even to unrecognizability. It may indeed be of historical
interest, as the record of an aspiration towards a goal; but
it has lost the power of giving direct artistic satisfaction.
[Bach, I, p. 49]

All Unfolding Is a Kind of Withering

As we find it hard to part from the first spring days and
pass into the season of full unfolding and ripening, so we
tear ourselves almost regretfully away from primitive art,
with its buds full of coming wealth of ideas and forms, in

order to see what ultimately became of it. In art, as in everything else, is not all unfolding and ripening a kind of withering, since in the full bloom we no longer have truth and reality appealing to us with that mysterious directness that is more magically eloquent than even perfection itself? For primitive art of this kind, the later product, perfect though it be, is not a heightening of something less perfect, but merely the revelation of all that was latent in the primitive organism.   [Bach, I, p. 67]

Subjective and Objective Art

Some artists are subjective, some objective. The art of the former has its source in their personality; their work is almost independent of the epoch in which they live. A law unto themselves, they place themselves in opposition to their epoch and originate new forms for the expression of their ideas. Of this type was Richard Wagner.

Bach belongs to the order of objective artists. These are wholly of their own time, and work only with the forms and the ideas that their time proffers them. They exercise no criticism upon the media of artistic expression that they find lying ready to their hand, and feel no inner compulsion to open out new paths. Their art not coming solely from the stimulus of their outer experience, we need not seek the roots of their work in the fortunes of its creator. In them the artistic personality exists independently of the human, the latter remaining in the background as if it were something almost accidental. Bach's works would have been the same even if his existence had run quite another course. Did we know more of his life than is now the case, and were we in possession of all the letters he had ever written, we should still be no better informed as to the inward sources of his works than we are now.   [Bach, I, p. 1]

Superpersonal Art

The art of the objective artist is not impersonal, but super-personal. It is as if he felt only one impulse—to express again what he already finds in existence, but to express it definitively, in unique perfection. It is not he who lives— it is the spirit of the time that lives in him. All the artistic endeavors, desires, creations, aspirations and errors of his own and of previous generations are concentrated and worked out to their conclusion in him.   [Bach, I, p. 1]

Bach, a Universal Personality

Bach is clearly not a single but a universal personality. He profited by the musical development of three or four generations. When we pursue the history of this family, which occupies so unique a position in the art life of Germany, we have the feeling that everything that is happening there must culminate in something consummate. We feel it to be a matter of course that some day a Bach shall come in whom all those other Bachs shall find a posthumous existence, one in whom the fragment of German music that has been embodied in this family shall find its completion. Johann Sebastian Bach—to speak the language of Kant—is a historical postulate.

Whatever path we traverse through the poetry and the music of the Middle Ages, we are always led to him. [Bach, I, p. 2]

A Collective Soul

Bach is a terminal point. Nothing comes from him; everything merely leads up to him. To give his true biography is to exhibit the nature and the unfolding of German art that comes to completion in him and is exhausted in him— to comprehend it in all its strivings and its failures. This genius was not an individual, but a collective soul. Centuries and generations have labored at this work, before the grandeur of which we halt in veneration. To anyone who has gone through the history of this epoch and knows what the end of it was, it is the history of that culminating spirit, as it was before it objectivated itself in a single personality. [Bach, I, pp. 3 f.]

Lonely Greatness

Bach lived in the decadent epoch when music and poetry led each other astray, an epoch of excessive scribbling, of superficial art, . . . an epoch which seemed fated to be impotent to create anything of durable value. Whereas at other times and in other places the great artist has been only one star among others, whose light, if less brilliant than his, he nevertheless did not extinguish, Bach is surrounded by mere will-o'-the-wisps, which his epoch—and he with it —mistook for stars. Of the innumerable cantatas that were written and admired at that time, his alone have survived their own day, and even these exhibit, both in their form and in their texts, traces of the dead world from which they have come. There is no stronger testimony to the greatness of Bach than the fact that in an epoch of error, and sharing its errors, he nevertheless wrote imperishable works. We have finally, however, the sad consciousness that he was only great enough to save himself, but not his epoch as well —that he did not hurl himself against it and strive to lead it back from this stilted poetry and the empty forms of Italian recitative and the *da capo* aria, to the true, simple, and really dramatic church music.   [Bach, I, pp. 95 f.]

Bach, the End of an Epoch

Bach . . . was in fact not the beginning of a new epoch, but the end of an old one, in which the knowledge and the errors of successive centuries found expression for the last time, as if seeking salvation together by genius. Since Bach held his peace, and, though inwardly opposed to his epoch, nevertheless went its way with it, it was inevitable that his works should be thrown into the general grave with those of his contemporaries, there to await their resurrection.

If the talents succumb to the errors of their time, what matters? But when the men of genius are ensnared in them, centuries have to suffer for it. The very greatness of Aristotle held Greek natural philosophy back when it was already on the path that would have led it to the discoveries of Galileo and Copernicus. Bach, with an easy consciousness of his own strength, burdened himself with the Italian forms and formulas, and so retarded the progress of German religious music along the path that would have led it, even at that time, to an art such as Wagner was afterwards to realize in drama.   [Bach, I, p. 96]

Bach's Humility

Bach fought for his everyday life, but not for the recognition of his art and of his works. In this respect he is very different from Beethoven and Wagner, and in general from what we understand by an "artist."

The recognition that the world gave to the master of the organ and the clavier—really only the external and contemporary side of his artistic activity—he took as a matter of course. He did not ask the world for the recognition of that part of his work that was not of his own age, and in which his deepest emotions found expression. It did not even occur to him that he should or could expect this from his epoch. He did nothing to make his cantatas and Passions known, and nothing to preserve them. It is not his fault if they have survived to our day. . . .

The unique thing about him is precisely the fact that he

made no effort to win recognition for his greatest works,
and did not summon the world to make acquaintance with
them. Hence the kind of consecration that rests upon his
works. We feel an unaffected charm in his cantatas such as
we do not meet with in other art works. The gray volumes
of the old *Bachgesellschaft* [an organization founded in
1850 to publish a complete edition of Bach's works, the
final volume appearing in 1900] speak a moving language.
They discourse to us of something that will be imperishable
simply because it is big and true, something that was written
not in the hope of recognition but because it had to come
out of him. Bach's cantatas and Passions are not only children of the muse, but also children of leisure [the play
upon words in the German cannot be reproduced in English—"sind nicht nur Kinder der Muse, sondern auch
Kinder der Musse"], in the honorable and profound sense
that this word had in the old days, when it signified the
hours of a man's life that he employed for himself and
himself alone.   [Bach, I, pp. 165 f.]

Unconscious Greatness

Bach himself was not conscious of the extraordinary greatness of his work. He was aware only of his admitted mastery
of the organ and clavier and counterpoint. But he never
dreamed that his works alone, not those of the men all
round him, would remain visible to the coming generations. If it is one of the signs of the great creative artist,
born before his time, that he waits for "his day," and wears
himself out in the waiting, then was Bach neither great nor
born before his time. No one was less conscious than he
that his work was ahead of his epoch. In this respect he
stands, perhaps, highest among all creative artists; his immense strength functioned without self-consciousness, like

the forces of nature; and for this reason it is as cosmic and copious as these.   [Bach, I, p. 166]

Bach's World-View

The *Well-Tempered Clavichord* [two collections of preludes and fugues composed by Bach, and dating from 1722 and 1744] is one of those works by which we can measure the progress of artistic culture from one generation to another. . . . What so fascinates us in the work is not the form or the build of the piece, but the world-view that is mirrored in it. It is not so much that we enjoy the *Well-Tempered Clavichord* as that we are edified by it. Joy, sorrow, tears, lamentation, laughter—to all these it gives voice, but in such a way that we are transported from the world of unrest to a world of peace, and see reality in a new way, as if we were sitting by a mountain lake and contemplating hills and woods and clouds in the tranquil and fathomless water.   [Bach, I, pp. 338 f.]

Art Was Bach's Religion

Nowhere so well as in the *Well-Tempered Clavichord* are we made to realize that art was Bach's religion. He does not depict natural soul states, like Beethoven in his sonatas, no striving and struggling toward a goal, but the reality of life felt by a spirit always conscious of being superior to life, a spirit in which the most contradictory emotions, wildest grief and exuberant cheerfulness, are simply phases of a fundamental superiority of soul. It is this that gives the same transfigured air to the sorrow-laden E flat minor prelude of the First Part, and the carefree, volatile prelude in G major in the Second Part. Whoever has once felt this wonderful tranquility has comprehended the mysterious spirit that has here expressed all it knew and felt of life in this secret language of tone, and will render Bach the thanks we render only to the great souls to whom it is given to reconcile men with life and bring them peace.   [Bach, I, p. 339]

Music Is an Act of Worship

Music is an act of worship with Bach. His artistic activity and his personality are both based on his piety. If he is to be understood from any standpoint at all, it is from this. For him, art was religion, and so had no concern with the world or with worldly success. It was an end in itself. Bach includes religion in the definition of art in general. All great art, even secular, is in itself religious in his eyes; for him the tones do not perish, but ascend to God like praise too deep for utterance.

"Figured bass," he says in the rules and principles of accompaniment that he gave his pupils [which are preserved in a copy dating from 1738], "is the most perfect foundation of music. It is executed with both hands in such a manner that the left hand plays the notes that are written, while the right adds consonances and dissonances thereto, making an agreeable harmony for the glory of God and the justifiable gratification of the soul. Like all music, the figured bass should have no other end and aim than the glory of God and the recreation of the soul; where this is not kept in mind there is no true music, but only an infernal clamor and ranting."   [Bach, I, p. 167]

This Is Holy Ground

The great point is that Bach, like every lofty religious mind, belongs not to the church but to religious humanity, and that any room becomes a church in which his sacred works are performed and listened to with devotion. [Bach, I, p. 264]

Bach's Music Is Gothic

Bach's music is Gothic. Just as in Gothic architecture the great plan develops out of the simple motive, but enfolds itself in the richest detail instead of in rigid line, and only makes its effect when every detail is truly vital, so does the impression a Bach work makes on the hearer depend on the player communicating to him the massive outline and the details together, both equally clear and equally full of life.   [Bach, I, p. 363]

The Fundamental Mystery of Things

The Brandenburg concertos [six concertos written by Bach for Prince Christian Ludwig, Margrave of Brandenburg, and delivered to him in 1721], are the purest products of Bach's polyphonic style. . . . We really seem to see before us what the philosophy of all ages conceives as the fundamental mystery of things—that self-unfolding of the idea in which it creates its own opposite in order to overcome it, creates another, which again it overcomes, and so on and on until it finally returns to itself, having meanwhile traversed the whole of existence. We have the same impression of incomprehensible necessity and mysterious contentment when we pursue the theme of one of these concertos, from its entry in the *tutti*, through its enigmatic struggle with its opposite, to the moment when it enters into possession of itself again in the final *tutti*.   [Bach, I, pp. 406 f.]

Interpreting Bach's Spirit

Bach's music depends for its effect not upon the perfection but upon the spirit of the performance. Mendelssohn, Schelble and Mosewius, who were the first to waken the cantatas and Passions to new life, were able to do so because they were not only musicians but sincere and deep-feeling men. Only he who sinks himself in the emotional world of Bach, who lives and thinks with him, who is simple and modest as he, is in a position to perform him properly. If the director and the performer do not feel themselves in a consecrated mood, they cannot communicate such a mood to the hearer; something cold will settle upon the music and deprive it of its best strength. "One thing is needful," said Mosewius in 1845, when he was trying to interest the world in Bach's cantatas; and it is perhaps more needful now than ever it was. "An inner unity of soul," he says at the end of his essay, "is absolutely indispensable in performing Bach; and every individual chorister must not only have thoroughly mastered the work technically but must preserve his spiritual forces unbroken throughout."

May this perception penetrate everywhere; then will Bach help our age to attain the spiritual unity and fervor of which it so sorely stands in need.   [Bach, II, p. 468]

THE ALTARS OF THE WORLD

The Lines of Distinction in Religion

When examining the fundamental ideas of the higher religions, we notice three lines of distinction which are determinative for the character of each religion. The first is that between optimistic and pessimistic; the second that between monistic and dualistic; thirdly, there is the greater or lesser extent to which ethical motives are present.   [Christianity, p. 24]

Indian Answers to the Religious Problem

Religion is the search for a solution of the problem how man can be in God and in the world at one and the same time. The answer given by Brahmanism and Buddhism is this: "By dying to the world and to life, for God is mere spirituality." Hinduism says: "By performing every action as something decreed by God, for God is the power which works all in all." In thus making God and the world coincide, Hinduism blurs the difference between good and evil, which it otherwise feels with elemental vividness. Why? Because it desires to be a religion which explains everything, a consistent religion which issues from logical thinking on the world.   [Christianity, pp. 66 f.]

Intellectualism and Ethics

In the Indian mind intellectualism consumes the ethical element, just as sometimes a cloud which was to have given rain is consumed in a sultry atmosphere.   [Christianity, p. 40]

Inactive Sympathy

Indian religion likes to represent itself as the religion of universal sympathy. It talks a good deal about the compassion which we should feel for all creatures. At the same time, however, it preaches the ideal of being absolutely without interest and of ceasing from all activity and maintains that even the enthusiasm for doing good must be considered as a passion which in the end has to be overcome. From intellectual compassion the Brahmanist and the Buddhist do not advance to the compassion of deed. Why, indeed, should they render material assistance to a creature in distress? The only help which they can give, without being inconsistent, is to enable the individual to look behind the veil, and to tell him that he must die to life and world and thus rise to the passionless state.   [Christianity, pp. 39 f.]

Word and Deed

Brahmanism and Buddhism, really, attain to an ethic in words only, but not to an ethic of deed. These ultimate consequences to which Indian thinking leads must be exposed. We cannot allow this religion to represent itself as the higher form of the religion of love, basing its claim to such superiority on its origin in pure reasoning about the world. The battle between Brahmanism and Buddhism on the one side and Christianity on the other is a battle between the spiritual and the ethical. Again and again in discussions Indians will tell you this: "Spirituality is not morality—that is, to become spiritual by merging into the divine is something apart, something which ultimately, being supreme, is above all ethic." We Christians, on the other hand, say: "Spirituality and morality are one and the

same. It is through the most thoroughgoing morality that
the highest spirituality is attained, through the most
thoroughgoing morality that it is continually expressed."
[Christianity, pp. 38 f.]

Poverty-stricken Religions

Brahmanism and Buddhism make an impression because
they represent a type of religion that is unified in itself,
being the result of consistent reasoning on the world and
on life. They present a logical, monistic-pessimistic view of
the world and life. But it is a poverty-stricken religion. Its
God is mere empty spirituality. Its last word to man is absolute negation of life and of the world. Its ethical content
is meagre. It is a mysticism which makes man lose his individual existence in a god that is dead.

When discussing religious matters with us, the Indian
mind is to some extent conscious of this poverty. Again
and again it tries to have a warmer light play upon its cold
mysticism, so that it may shine in ethical coloring. But this
is a vain effort. Claiming, and rightly, to be the result of
logical reasoning, Indian religion may not assert anything
that would not be consistent with its own ideas. As far as
we have anything to do with it, we do not allow it to appear
to be something different from what it really is, namely, a
negation of life and of the world, purporting to be religion
and ethics.   [Christianity, pp. 43 f.]

Monastic Religions

One more point, which reveals a significant difference—
the Brahmans' and Buddha's doctrine of redemption is for
priests and monks only, for they alone are in a position to
live out this religion of withdrawing from the world. This
fact is usually passed over in silence by propagandists of

Indian religion. How often have I had to point out to thinking men that Brahmanism and Buddhism are not religions
for ordinary men, but solely for monks. At the conclusion
of Buddha's most profound discourses we generally find
some word which reminds us of the fact that here is not a
man speaking to men, but an Indian monk speaking to
Indian monks. And the charm is gone.   [Christianity,
pp. 40 f.]

Indian Religions and the Common Man

Brahmanism and Buddhism have nothing to offer to any
but those whose circumstances enable them to withdraw
from the world and to devote their lives to self-perfection
beyond the sphere of deeds. To the man who ploughs the
field or works in a factory, they can say nothing but that
he has not yet arrived at the true knowledge, otherwise he
would cease from an activity which binds him to the de-
ceitful and sorrowful world of sense. The only consolation
they can offer him is the prospect of his getting a chance,
in some future incarnation, to rise to the higher knowledge
and to seek the way which leads out of this world.
[Christianity, pp. 41 f.]

Jesus and the Indian Religions

The relation between Christianity and the Indian religions
resembles the relation which exists between Christianity
and the Greco-Oriental type of religion. Insofar as Christianity, too, is pessimistic, but only so far, a certain degree
of external relationship may be said to exist. In their inner
nature the two differ absolutely. The Brahmans and Buddha
say to man: "As one who has died, and to whom nothing
in the natural world is of interest any longer, you should
live in the world of pure spirituality." The gospel of Jesus

tells him: "You must become free from the world and from yourself, in order to work in the world as an instrument of God." [Christianity, p. 37]

The Divine in Jesus and the Indian Religions

The Indian idea of the divine is, that it is pure, spiritual essence. It is the ocean into which man, tired of swimming, wishes to sink. The God of the Gospel of Jesus is living, ethical Will, desiring to give to my will a new direction. He says to me: "Strike out courageously! Do not ask where your efforts will take you on the infinite ocean. It is my will that you should swim." [Christianity, p. 38]

The Distinctive Feature of Buddhism

The distinctive feature of the religion of the Buddha consists first of all in his rejection equally with the material enjoyment of life of the asceticism and self-torture practised by Brahmans and the adherents of the Samkhya doctrine and Jainism. Renunciation of the world, he preaches, consists above all in men attaining the inner state of deliverance from things, not so much in their achieving the uttermost renunciation outwardly. He whose spirit is really free from the world can concede his right to natural needs without becoming worldly. The Buddha was firm in this conviction because of his own experience that he did not attain enlightenment when he mortified and tormented his body, but when he took food again and ceased to be a "self-torturer." [Indian, pp. 91 f.]

Incomplete Compassion

Even if the commandment not to kill and not to hurt does not begin with the Buddha, he is nevertheless the originator of the ethic of compassion. For he it is who undertook to base on compassion this commandment which originally sprang from the idea of nonactivity and keeping unpolluted from the world.

In a discourse he describes in moving words how the thralls and hirelings receive from the king, who wants to organize a great sacrifice, an order to fetch the animals selected for slaughter, and how they set about carrying it out "from fear of punishment, cowed down by fear, their eyes filled with tears."

It is said that the representations of the silk weavers that in order to get silk they had to be guilty of the lives of so many little creatures was the reason why he forbade his monks the use of silk coverings.

But the Buddha's ethic of compassion is incomplete. It is limited by world- and life-negation. Nowhere does the Master demand that because all life is suffering man should strive, insofar as is possible, to bring help to every human being and to every living thing. He only commands the avoidance of pitiless actions. Of sympathetic helping he takes no account. It is excluded by the principle of non-activity which derives from world- and life-negation. [Indian, pp. 102 f.]

Buddha's Broad-mindedness

The Buddha . . . showed himself a freethinker in opening his monastic Order even to members of the despised Sudra castes. To whatever caste a man belongs, he says in one of his discourses, if he lives the true life of a monk, he can nevertheless reach perfection. Whether the fire be kindled with costly wood, or with wood from a dog trough, or from a pig trough, or a laundry trough, or from a castor oil tree: it has the same flame, the same brightness and the same power of illumination.   [Indian, pp. 93 f.]

THE ALTARS OF THE WORLD

The Ethics of Jesus and Buddha

The Buddha's ethics are different from the ethics of Jesus in that he did not demand real active love. Jesus and the Buddha have this in common, that their form of ethics, because it is under the influence of world- and life-negation, is not an ethic of action but an ethic of inner perfection. But in both the ethic of inner perfection is governed by the principle of love. It therefore carries within it the tendency to express itself in action and in this way has a certain affinity with world- and life-affirmation. With Jesus the ethic of the perfecting of the self commands active love: with the Buddha it does not get so far.

It must be noted that the world- and life-negation of Jesus is in origin and in essence quite different from that of the Buddha. It does not rest on the distinction between material and immaterial Being, but abandons the natural world as evil, in the expectation that it will be transformed into a world that is supernatural and good. The world- and life-negation of Jesus is conditioned by ethics.

Because of this fundamental difference in world- and life-negation the constantly renewed attempt to explain the teaching of Jesus as derived from Buddhist influence must be pronounced hopeless, even on the altogether improbable assumption that Jesus was acquainted with Indian thought.   [Indian, p. 113]

Buddha and Paul

The Buddha's broad-mindedness must not be understood in the sense of his having altogether declared himself for the abolition of caste distinctions. His opinion is that the monks alone, who are leaving behind them all earthly relationships, are no longer subject to them. They are still valid

for people who remain in the ordinary life of the world.
The thought of reforming society is as far from the Buddha
as from St. Paul. Both see their vocation only in leading
man out of the earthly and holding up before him the
perfection which he ought to reach. The terrestrial world
is for them something doomed to pass away. To trouble
about the improvement of worldly conditions seems to
them as little opportune as to undertake repairs in a house
that is about to be pulled down. That is why the Buddha
does not attack the validity of the caste distinctions in
ordinary life; and why Paul is not led by the principle of
Christian love to demand the abolition of slavery.   [Indian,
p. 94]

The Greatness of Buddha and Luther

In the world- and life-negation to which he was devoted,
the Buddha kept some measure of naturalness. This is what
was great in him. Whilst he mitigated the severity of world
renunciation, he made a fresh and great concession to
world- and life-affirmation.

In the same way, Luther, through his own innate naturalness, emancipated himself from the world- and life-
negation of medieval Christianity. Only he got further than
the Buddha did in world- and life-affirmation. He dared to
say that a man's calling and a man's work are sacred.
[Indian, p. 92]

Redemption in Buddha and Luther

The Buddha was a reformer and reminds us of Luther.

In the matter of religion there is a striking similarity
between them. Both of them began by struggling with the
problem of redemption. Luther was anxious about the question how forgiveness of sins may be attained, and the

Buddha about how liberation from the misery of constantly repeated rebirth can be possible.

In their struggle for redemption both were free spirits. They dared to sever connection with the principle of striving after works which dominated the piety of their age. Luther declared that medieval Christian justification by works and the monastic life were of no avail for redemption, while the Buddha rejected the asceticism and self-mortification of his time. Both sought to attain redemption by the path of works and both discovered by experience that it does not lead to the goal, and therefore turned their attention to a spiritualized form of religion. [Indian, p. 91]

Hinduism and Civilization

In Hinduism world- and life-affirmation has never succeeded in getting the mastery over world- and life-negation. In India there never came a break with the traditional pessimism, such as was brought about by powerful thinkers in the Christianity of the sixteenth, seventeenth, and eighteenth centuries. Hinduism, therefore, in spite of its ethical tendency, was never in a position to accomplish in the regions where it prevailed a work for civilization which was comparable to that of Christianity. [Life, p. 216]

Hinduism, a Religion of Compromise

Moved by ethical ideas Hinduism endeavors to become a religion of action. Not only does it preach, as do the Brahmans and Buddha, that man becomes perfect by withdrawing from the world, but it also tries to exhort him to the practice of love. As you know, Hinduism does no longer simply acquiesce, as did Brahmanism and Buddhism, in the great social evils in India, such as the unfortunate position of widows, but it is interested in actual life, and tries, though timidly, to bring about reforms.

What, then, is Hinduism, judged by the highest thoughts that stir within it? It is a reaction against the absolute, pessimistic negation of life and of the world, as found in the Brahmanist and Buddhist philosophy, and at the same time it is an attempt to rise from dead monism and pantheism to the conception of a personal, living, ethical God. But in order to become a living, ethical religion, Hinduism gives up the consistency and self-containedness of the older schools of Indian religious thought. It concatenates thoughts in order to obtain valuable results. In every respect it is a religion of compromise. Polytheism and monotheism, pantheism and theism, intellectual mysticism and personal piety of heart, spiritual religion and popular cults—all these it tries to unite, without acknowledging the evident impossibility of their being thus united. It lives on imperfect conceptions and on half-truths. Therein lies its strength—its weakness too.　[Christianity, pp. 63 f.]

Gandhi Mixes the Spiritual and the Worldly

Gandhi . . . is confident that by the nonworldly he can completely spiritualize and ennoble what is worldly, and he really seriously believes that he can practise passive resistance entirely in the spirit of freedom from hatred and of love. Again and again he points to his followers that the justification, the reason and the success of what they join him in undertaking for the good of the people is dependent on whether their minds are completely purified. And again and again he emphasizes his conviction that passive resistance, exercised in the spirit of Ahimsa, must not only be concerned with the achievement of this purpose or that, but that its real aim must be to bring about a mutual understanding founded on love. The nonviolent violence of passive resistance must merely form the river bed for the flood-waters of the spirit of love.

Thus, then, does Gandhi try to solve the problem whether, along with action by ethical and spiritual means, action by worldly means can also be justified. He sets up the first as a principle and at the same time retains a minimum of worldly procedure, the exercise, namely, of non-violent force; and this he places at the service of the ethical and the spiritual.

It must remain a question whether the restriction to nonviolent force and the combination of this (as being the procedure regarded as the least worldly) with the ethical and spiritual method is the right solution of the problem. All mixing up of what is different in essence is an unnatural and dangerous proceeding.   [Indian, pp. 232 f.]

The Origin of Passive Resistance

In a conversation with his friend, the Rev. J. J. Doke, a Baptist minister of Johannesburg, Gandhi said that he got the idea of passive resistance in the spirit of Ahimsa from the sayings of Jesus, "But I say unto you, that ye resist not evil," and "Love your enemies . . . pray for them which despitefully use you and persecute you, that ye may be the children of your father which is in heaven." And then his idea developed under the influence of the Bhagavad-Gita and Tolstoi's "The Kingdom of God Is Within You." [Indian, p. 234]

I Carry My Cave with Me

In spite of this strong world- and life-negation, Gandhi can no longer make his own the old ideal which is part and parcel of it—the ideal of a life withdrawn from the world. His friend the Brahman ascetic, who advised him to retire to a cave and live for meditation alone, received the reply, "I am striving to reach the Kingdom of Heaven which is called the liberation of the soul. In order to reach this I need not seek refuge in a cave. I carry my cave with me . . ."   [Indian, p. 237]

Vivekananda

Vivekananda dares not probe to its depths the question why Indian mentality is so poor in works. He puts the responsibility on the indifference of individuals. He will not admit to himself that the guilt lies with a mode of thinking which involves withdrawal from the world. He cannot concede indeed that Indian thought has undergone any development and that the idea of active love has only begun to play a part within it in recent times.   [Indian, p. 255]

Failure of Indian Mysticism

From time to time Vivekananda expresses himself quite despairingly to the effect that the West can point to such great social achievements, whilst in India, the home of the eternal verities, so little is done for the poor and the suffering. On one occasion he confesses, "No society puts its foot on the neck of the wretched so mercilessly as does that of India." In one of his letters to Indian friends one finds the sentence, "So far as the spiritual and mental qualities are concerned, the Americans are greatly our inferiors, but as a social community they are superior to us."   [Indian, p. 255]

India's Gift to the World

Vivekananda and the rest believe the world must accept mysticism from India. They do not take into consideration that in Western thought there is mysticism of a similar nature to and no less valuable than mysticism in Indian thought. They work with the fiction that Indian thought alone is capable of profundity and piety. They do not understand that mysticism only fails to make headway in European thought because it cannot comply with the demands of ethical world- and life-affirmation. [Indian, pp. 254 f.]

Is Indian Thought Superior?

Vivekananda and others are willing and glad to concede to European thought that it has the capacity for making scientific discoveries, for creating machines, for organizing the life of society in an expedient fashion, and in general for accomplishing the work of civilization. But in their utterances they take it as a matter of course that Indian thought is far superior in its achievements so far as thinking is concerned. Vivekananda wants "to revolutionize the world" with the eternal verities which are in the possession of India. According to a saying of Aurobindo Ghose, India holds in its hand the key to the progress of humanity. [Indian, p. 254]

Mysticism Is Timeless

We await the Indian thinker who will expound to us the mysticism of spiritual union with infinite Being as it is in itself, not as it is set down in the ancient texts or according to the meaning read into them by their interpreters.

It belongs to the nature of mysticism that it is timeless and appeals to no other authority than that of the truth which it carries within it. [Indian, p. 256]

Theosophy

Theosophy, which endeavors to create a unified religion, and therefore tries to bring Indian and Christian piety together, has a difficult task, because the two are so totally different from each other in character. Usually it sacrifices Christian thought to Indian thought. It only uses the former to give a stronger ethical coloring to the latter. [Christianity, p. 40]

The Religion of China

All the leading religious thinkers of China are at one in holding the conviction that the forces which are at work in the world are good. Therefore, in their opinion, true piety consists in understanding the meaning of the world and in acting in accordance with it. Being consistent monistic thinkers, they, like the Brahmans and Buddha, do not attain to the conception of a personal God; but whereas for the Indians God remains absolute, lifeless spirituality, he is to the Chinese the mere sum-total of the forces at work in the world. This Power, which they conceive as being above all things and in all things, they call "Heaven."   [Christianity, p. 46]

Christianity and the Religions of China

The religious mind of China has not attracted as much attention in the West as that of India. It is only recently that we have begun to know a little more about it. Let me tell you that to become acquainted with these thinkers was for me a vital experience; especially Lao-tse and Meng-tse fascinated me. They are much nearer to us than the Indian philosophers, for they do not move in an atmosphere of arrogant negation of life and world, but are battling with philosophy, therein to attain to really ethical piety. Chinese religion, unlike Brahmanism and Buddhism, bears not only an outward resemblance to the Gospel of Jesus, but, being moved by the great commandment of love, it has in many respects true spiritual affinity with the Gospel. [Christianity, pp. 52 f.]

Chinese Religion and the Knowledge of the World

As regards one thing, the religion of China is as far removed from us as that of India: it attempts to be unified, self-contained, logical knowledge of the world. Insofar as the Chinese philosophers are ethical, they idealize the natural forces at work in the world, and ascribe to them ethical character. Insofar as they dare to face reality, they must turn the wick of the lamp of ethics down, till in the end it is reduced to a dimly burning light. Slaves of their monism, they run after an illusion—as if religion could justify itself on the basis of "knowledge of the world." If they cannot comprehend the meaning of the world as the activity of the forces of love, they land in a cold religion, if not in skepticism. Thus, there are indeed some Chinese thinkers who say: "The meaning of the world is, that in the expectation of inevitable death we enjoy life." [Christianity, pp. 53 f.]

Pacifism in China

There were men in China who traveled all over the empire as preachers of love and peace. It is there that we find the first pacifists, probably in the fifth century B.C. In a record which has come down to our time with the writings of the philosopher, Chang Tso-lin, this is said about them: —

"They sought to unite men through an ardent love in universal brotherhood. To fight against lusts and evil desires

was their chief endeavor. When they were reviled, they did
not consider it a shame; they were intent on nothing but
the redemption of men from quarreling. They forbade
aggression, and preached disarmament in order to redeem
mankind from war. This teaching they carried throughout
the world. They admonished princes and instructed subjects. The world was not ready to accept their teaching,
but they held to it all the more firmly. It was said that high
and low tried to avoid meeting them, but that they forced
themselves upon people." [Christianity, p. 50]

God in Nature and in Ourselves

To the Brahmans and to Buddha we said: Religion is more
than a pessimism which denies life and world. To the religious minds of China we say: Religion is more than ethical
optimism. And to both types of thinkers, we say: Religion
is not a knowledge of the divine which springs from the
contemplation of the universe. God, we believe, is more
than merely the spiritual force underlying this world.
Monism and pantheism, however profound and spiritual,
do not lead into the ultimate problem of religion. That
problem is, that in ourselves we experience God as different
from the God we find in Nature: in Nature we recognize
Him only as impersonal creative Power, in ourselves we
recognize Him as ethical Personality. [Christianity, p. 55]

The Characteristics of Islam

There is no need for a comparison of spiritual values as
between Christianity and Islam. The latter arose in the
seventh century A.D., partly under the influence of Jewish
and Christian ideas. It lacks spiritual originality and is not
a religion with profound thoughts on God and the world.
Its power in the world is based on the fact that, while it

is a monotheistic and also to some extent an ethical religion, it has preserved all the instincts of the primitive religious mind and is thus able to offer itself to the uncivilized and the half civilized peoples of Asia and Africa as the form of monotheism most easily accessible to them. There are, it is true, some deeper, mystic elements in Islam fighting for existence, especially in the so-called Sufism, a movement which is dominated by Zoroastrian and Indian influences. Such movements are, however, being suppressed again and again.   [Christianity, pp. 22 f.]

Islam as a World Religion

Islam can be called a world religion only in virtue of its wide extension. Spiritually it could not develop to be such because it never produced any thinking about the world and mankind which penetrated to the depths. If ever any such thought stirred within it, it was suppressed in order to maintain the authority of traditional views.   [Life, p. 216]

THE TIMELESSNESS OF JESUS

There Came a Man

There came a Man to rule over the world; He ruled it for good and for ill, as history testifies; He destroyed the world into which He was born; the spiritual life of our own time seems like to perish at His hands, for He leads to battle against our thought a host of dead ideas, a ghostly army upon which death has no power, and Himself destroys again the truth and goodness which His Spirit creates in us, so that it cannot rule the world. That He continues, notwithstanding, to reign as the alone Great and alone True in a world of which He denied the continuance, is the prime example of that antithesis between spiritual and natural truth which underlies all life and all events, and in Him emerges into the field of history.   [Quest, p. 2]

Not Biographies, but Gospels

It is only at first sight that the absolute indifference of early Christianity towards the life of the historical Jesus is disconcerting. When Paul, representing those who recognize the signs of the times, did not desire to know Christ after the flesh, that was the first expression of the impulse of self-preservation by which Christianity continued to be guided for centuries. It felt that with the introduction of the historic Jesus into its faith, there would arise something new, something which had not been foreseen in the thoughts of the Master Himself, and that thereby a contradiction would be brought to light, the solution of which would constitute one of the great problems of the world.

Primitive Christianity was therefore right to live wholly in the future with the Christ who was to come, and to preserve of the historic Jesus only detached sayings, a few miracles, His death and resurrection. By abolishing both the world and the historical Jesus it escaped the inner division described above, and remained consistent in its point of view. We, on our part, have reason to be grateful to the early Christians that, in consequence of this attitude they have handed down to us, not biographies of Jesus but only Gospels, and that therefore we possess the Idea and the Person, with the minimum of historical and contemporary limitations.   [Quest, p. 3]

The Birth of the Historical Jesus

We can, at the present day, scarcely imagine the long agony in which the historical view of the life of Jesus came to birth. And even when He was once more recalled to life, He was still, like Lazarus of old, bound hand and foot with grave-clothes—the grave-clothes of dogma.   [Quest, p. 4]

Hate, the Biographer

It was not only each epoch that found its reflection in Jesus; each individual created Him in accordance with his own character. There is no historical task which so reveals a man's true self as the writing of a life of Jesus. No vital force comes into the figure unless a man breathes into it all the hate or all the love of which he is capable. The stronger the love, or the stronger the hate, the more lifelike is the figure which is produced. For hate as well as love can write a life of Jesus, and the greatest of them are written with hate. . . . It was not so much hate of the Person of Jesus as of the supernatural nimbus with which it was so easy to surround Him, and with which He had in fact been surrounded. They were eager to picture Him as truly and purely human, to strip from Him the robes of splendor with which He had been apparelled and clothe Him once more with the coarse garments in which He had walked in Galilee.

And their hate sharpened their historical insight. They advanced the study of the subject more than all the others put together.   [Quest, pp. 4 f.]

The Study of the Life of Jesus

The problem of the life of Jesus has no analogue in the field of history. No historical school has ever laid down canons for the investigation of this problem, no professional historian has ever lent his aid to theology in dealing with it. Every ordinary method of historical investigation proves inadequate to the complexity of the conditions. The standards of ordinary historical science are here inadequate, its methods not immediately applicable. The historical study of the life of Jesus has had to create its own methods for itself. In the constant succession of unsuccessful attempts, five or six problems have emerged side by side which together constitute the fundamental problem. There is, however, no direct method of solving the problem in its complexity; all that can be done is to experiment continuously, starting from definite assumptions; and in this experimentation the guiding principle must ultimately rest upon historical intuition.

The cause of this lies in the nature of the sources of the life of Jesus, and the character of our knowledge of the contemporary religious world of thought. It is not that the sources are in themselves bad. When we have once made up our minds that we have not the materials for a complete life of Jesus, but only for a picture of His public ministry, it must be admitted that there are few characters of antiquity about whom we possess so much indubitably historical information, of whom we have so many authentic discourses. The position is much more favorable, for instance, than in the case of Socrates; for he is pictured to us by literary men who exercised their creative ability upon the portrait. Jesus stands much more immediately before us, because He was depicted by simple Christians without literary gift. [Quest, p. 6]

Discoverers

The time is past for pronouncing judgment upon lives of Christ on the ground of the solutions which they offer. For us the great men are not those who solved the problems, but those who discovered them. [Quest, p. 159]

Its Jesus Is Not Alive

For the last ten years modern historical theology has more and more adapted itself to the needs of the man in the street. More and more, even in the best class of works, it makes use of attractive headlines as a means of presenting its results in a lively form to the masses. Intoxicated with its own ingenuity in inventing these, it becomes more and more confident in its cause, and has come to believe that the world's salvation depends in no small measure upon the spreading of its own "assured results" broadcast among the people. It is time that it should begin to doubt itself, to doubt its "historical" Jesus, to doubt the confidence with which it has looked to its own construction for the moral and religious regeneration of our time. Its Jesus is not alive. [Quest, p. 310]

Jesus Stays with His Time

Historical criticism became, in the hands of most of those who practised it, a secret struggle to reconcile the Germanic religious spirit with the Spirit of Jesus of Nazareth. It was concerned for the religious interests of the present. Therefore its error had a kind of greatness, it was in fact the greatest thing about it; and the severity with which the pure historian treats it is in proportion to his respect for its Spirit. For this German critical study of the life of Jesus is an essential part of German religion. As of old, Jacob wrestled with the angel, so German theology wrestles with Jesus of Nazareth and will not let Him go until He bless it—that is, until He will consent to serve it and will suffer Himself to be drawn by the Germanic spirit into the midst of our time and our civilization. But when the day breaks, the wrestler must let Him go. He will not cross the ford with us. Jesus of Nazareth will not suffer Himself to be modernized. As an historic figure He refuses to be detached from His own time. He has no answer for the question, "Tell us Thy name in our speech and for our day!" But He does bless those who have wrestled with Him, so that, though they cannot take Him with them, yet, like men who have seen God face to face and received strength in their souls, they go on their way with renewed courage, ready to do battle with the world and its powers. [Quest, pp. 310 f.]

The Nonexistent Jesus

The Jesus of Nazareth who came forward publicly as the Messiah, who preached the ethic of the Kingdom of God, who founded the Kingdom of Heaven upon earth, and died to give His work its final consecration, never had any existence. He is a figure designed by rationalism, endowed with life by liberalism, and clothed by modern theology in an historical garb.   [Quest, p. 396]

Jesus Passes Us By

The study of the Life of Jesus has had a curious history. It set out in quest of the historical Jesus, believing that when it had found Him it could bring Him straight into our time as a Teacher and Savior. It loosed the bands by which He had been riveted for centuries to the stony rocks of ecclesiastical doctrine, and rejoiced to see life and movement coming into the figure once more, and the historical Jesus advancing, as it seemed, to meet it. But He does not stay; He passes by our time and returns to His own. What surprised and dismayed the theology of the last forty years was that, despite all forced and arbitrary interpretations it could not keep Him in our time, but had to let Him go. He returned to His own time, not owing to the application of any historical ingenuity, but by the same inevitable necessity by which the liberated pendulum returns to its original position.   [Quest, p. 397]

Making Jesus Conform

There was a danger of our thrusting ourselves between men and the Gospels, and refusing to leave the individual man alone with the sayings of Jesus.

There was a danger that we should offer them a Jesus who was too small because we had forced Him into conformity with our human standards and human psychology. To see that, one need only read the lives of Jesus written since the 'sixties, and notice what they have made of the great imperious sayings of the Lord, how they have weakened down His imperative world-contemning demands upon individuals, that He might not come into conflict

with our ethical ideals, and might tune His denial of the
world to our acceptance of it. Many of the greatest sayings
are found lying in a corner like explosive shells from which
the charges have been removed. No small portion of elemental religious power needed to be drawn off from His
sayings to prevent them from conflicting with our system
of religious world-acceptance. We have made Jesus hold
another language with our time from that which He really
held.   [Quest, p. 398]

The Historical Jesus Is Not Important

We are experiencing what Paul experienced. In the very
moment when we were coming nearer to the historical
Jesus than men had ever come before, and were already
stretching out our hands to draw Him into our own time,
we have been obliged to give up the attempt and acknowledge our failure in that paradoxical saying: "If we have
known Christ after the flesh yet henceforth know we Him
no more." And further we must be prepared to find that
the historical knowledge of the personality and life of Jesus
will not be a help, but perhaps even an offense to religion.

But the truth is it is not Jesus as historically known, but
Jesus as spiritually arisen within men, who is significant for
our time and can help it. Not the historical Jesus, but the
spirit which goes forth from Him and in the spirits of
men strives for new influence and rule, is that which overcomes the world.   [Quest, p. 399]

The Eternal in Jesus

It is not given to history to disengage that which is abiding
and eternal in the being of Jesus from the historical forms
in which it worked itself out, and to introduce it into our
world as a living influence. It has toiled in vain at this un-

dertaking. As a water plant is beautiful so long as it is growing in the water, but once torn from its roots, withers and becomes unrecognizable, so it is with the historical Jesus when He is wrenched loose from the soil of eschatology, and the attempt is made to conceive Him "historically" as a Being not subject to temporal conditions. The abiding and eternal in Jesus is absolutely independent of historical knowledge and can only be understood by contact with His spirit which is still at work in the world. In proportion as we have the Spirit of Jesus we have the true knowledge of Jesus.   [Quest, p. 399]

The World-negating Spirit of Jesus

Because it is thus preoccupied with the general, the universal, modern theology is determined to find its world-accepting ethic in the teaching of Jesus. Therein lies its weakness. The world affirms itself automatically; the modern spirit cannot but affirm it. But why on that account abolish the conflict between modern life, with the world-affirming spirit which inspires it as a whole, and the world-negating spirit of Jesus? Why spare the spirit of the individual man its appointed task of fighting its way through the world-negation of Jesus, of contending with Him at every step over the value of material and intellectual goods—a conflict in which it may never rest? For the general, for the institutions of society, the rule is: affirmation of the world, in conscious opposition to the view of Jesus, on the ground that the world has affirmed itself! This general affirmation of the world, however, if it is to be Christian, must in the individual spirit be Christianized and transfigured by the personal rejection of the world which is preached in the sayings of Jesus. It is only by means of the tension thus set up that religious energy can be communicated to our time. There was a danger that modern theology, for the sake of peace, would deny the world-negation in the sayings of Jesus, with which Protestantism was out of sympathy, and thus unstring the bow and make Protestantism a mere sociological instead of a religious force. There was perhaps also a danger of inward insincerity, in the fact that it refused to admit to itself and others that it maintained its affirmation of the world in opposition to the sayings of Jesus, simply because it could not do otherwise.   [Quest, p. 401]

The Real Jesus Condemns the Modern Jesus

It is a good thing that the true historical Jesus should overthrow the modern Jesus, should rise up against the modern spirit and send upon earth, not peace, but a sword. He was not a teacher, not a casuist; He was an imperious ruler. It was because He was so in His inmost being that he could think of Himself as the Son of Man. That was the only temporarily conditioned expression of the fact that He was an authoritative ruler. The names in which men expressed their recognition of Him as such, Messiah, Son of Man, Son of God, have become for us historical parables. We can find no designation which expresses what He is for us. [Quest, p. 401]

Jesus Teaches Active Love

World- and life-negation is found in the thought of Jesus insofar as He did not assume that the Kingdom of God would be realized in this natural world. He expected that this natural world would very speedily come to an end and be superseded by a supernatural world in which all that is imperfect and evil would be overcome by the power of God.

But this form of world- and life-negation found in Jesus is different from that of India. Instead of denying the material world because its gaze is directed to pure Being, it only denies the evil, imperfect world in expectation of a good and perfect world which is to come.

It is characteristic of the unique type of the world- and life-negation of Jesus that His ethics are not confined within the bounds of that conception. He does not preach the inactive ethic of perfecting the self alone, but active, enthusiastic love of one's neighbor. It is because His ethic contains the principle of activity that it has affinity with world- and life-affirmation.   [Indian, pp. 4 f.]

Jesus Fights against the Modern Spirit

It is because Jesus does not think in a utilitarian way, but only according to the absolute ethic of "not being conformed to the world," that there is such a remarkable contrast between His thoughts and our modern views. Only when we experience this contrast, have we entered into relationship to the true Jesus. Therefore, we must not allow ourselves to be tempted into modernizing His views and inadvertently putting thoughts as we think them into His words. His significance for us is that He fights against the spirit of the modern world, forcing it to abandon the low level on which it moves even in its best thoughts and to rise to the height whence we judge things according to the superior will of God, which is active in us, and think no more in terms of human utilitarianism but solely in terms of having to do God's will—becoming forces of God's ethical personality.   [Christianity, pp. 19 f.]

The Imposing Personality of Jesus

The adherents of Jesus believed in the coming of the Kingdom because his imposing personality accredited the message. The Church after his death believed in his Messiahship and expected the coming of the Kingdom. We believe that in his ethical religious personality, as revealed in his ministry and suffering, the Messiah and the Kingdom are come.

The situation may be likened to the course of the sun. Its brightness breaks forth while it is still behind the mountains. The dark clouds take color from its rays, and the conflict of light and darkness produces a play of fantastic imagery. The sun itself is not yet visible: it is there only in the sense that the light issues from it. As the sun behind the morning glow, so appeared the personality of Jesus of Nazareth to his contemporaries in the pre-Messianic age.

At the moment when the heaven glows with intensest coloring, the sun itself rises above the horizon. But with this the wealth of color begins gradually to diminish. The fantastic images pale and vanish because the sun itself dissolves the clouds upon which they are formed. As the rising sun above the horizon, so appeared Jesus Christ to the primitive Church in its eschatological expectation.

As the sun at midday, so he appears to us. We know nothing of morning and evening glow; we see only the white brilliance which pervades all. But the fact that the sun now shines for us in such a light does not justify us in conceiving the sunrise also as if it were a brilliant disk of midday brightness emerging above the horizon. Our modern view of Jesus' death is true, true in its inmost nature, because it reflects his ethical religious personality in the thoughts of our time. But when we import this into the history of Jesus and of primitive Christianity we commit the same blunder as were we to paint the sunrise without the morning glow.   [Mystery, pp. 248 ff.]

The Piety of Jesus

Greco-Oriental piety, Plato, the mystery religions and the Gnostics, all alike say to man: "Free thyself from the

world!" Jesus says: "Get free from the world, in order to
work in this world in the spirit and in the love of God,
till God transplants you into another, more perfect world."
[Christianity, p. 15]

The Heroic in Jesus

The heroic recedes from our modern *Weltanschauung*, our
Christianity, and our conception of the person of Jesus.
Wherefore men have humanized and humbled Him. Renan
has stripped off His halo and reduced Him to a sentimental
figure, coward spirits like Schopenhauer have dared to
appeal to Him for their enervating philosophy, and our
generation has modernized Him, with the notion that it
could comprehend His character and development psycho-
logically.

We must go back to the point where we can feel again
the heroic in Jesus. Before that mysterious Person, who,
in the form of His time, knew that He was creating upon
the foundation of His life and death a moral world *which
bears his name*, we must be forced to lay our faces in the
dust, without daring even to wish to understand His nature.
Only then can the heroic in our Christianity and in our
Weltanschauung be again revived.   [Mystery, p. 274]

The Dignity of Jesus

As Jesus gave up the ghost, the Roman centurion said,
"Truly this man was the Son of God" (MARK, 15:39).
Thus at the moment of His death the lofty dignity of Jesus
was set free for expression in all tongues, among all nations,
and for all philosophies.   [Mystery, p. 252]

A Stranger to Our Time

Jesus as a concrete historical personality remains a stranger
to our time, but His spirit, which lies hidden in His words,

is known in simplicity, and its influence is direct. Every saying contains in its own way the whole Jesus. The very strangeness and unconditionedness in which He stands before us makes it easier for individuals to find their own personal standpoint in regard to Him.   [Quest, p. 399]

The Timeless Significance of Jesus

In reality that which is eternal in the words of Jesus is due to the very fact that they are based on an eschatological world-view, and contain the expression of a mind for which the contemporary world, with its historical and social circumstances, no longer had any existence. They are appropriate, therefore, to any world, for in every world they raise the man who dares to meet their challenge, and does not turn and twist them into meaninglessness, above his world and his time, making him inwardly free, so that he is fitted to be, in his own world and in his own time, a simple channel of the power of Jesus.   [Quest, p. 400]

As One Unknown He Comes

He comes to us as One unknown, without a name, as of old, by the lake side, He came to those men who knew Him not. He speaks to us the same word: "Follow thou me!" and sets us to the tasks which He has to fulfil for our time. He commands. And to those who obey Him, whether they be wise or simple, He will reveal Himself in the toils, the conflicts, the sufferings which they shall pass through in His fellowship, and, as an ineffable mystery, they shall learn in their own experience Who He is.   [Quest, p. 401]

THE HUMANITY OF PAUL

Bridging Two Worlds

By his doctrine of the Spirit, Paul has himself thrown a bridge from his world-view to ours. While the faith of his contemporaries was being dazzled by the outward phenomena of the possession of the Spirit, he grasped the concept of the Spirit as the manifestation of all the radiations which pass from the super-earthly into the earthly. Of these radiations he estimates the value not according to their degree of visibility, but according to the influence which they exert. Thus he values highest the unsensational ethical guidance of the Spirit, and recognizes love as the gift in which what in its essential nature is eternal becomes reality within the temporal. [Mysticism, p. 386]

Living Truth

It is not merely that Paul was the first to champion the rights of thought in Christianity; he has also shown it, for all time, the way it was to go. His great achievement was to grasp, as the thing essential to being a Christian, the experience of union with Christ. Out of the depths of the expectation of the Messiah and of the Messianic world this thought wells up to him, a thought to which expression had already been given by Jesus when He spoke of the mystery of the consecration of believers through fellowship with the unrecognized future Messiah who was dwelling among them. By penetrating to the depths of the temporarily conditioned, Paul wins his way to a spiritual result of permanent value. Strange as his thoughts are to us in the way they arise out of, and have their form moulded by, the eschatological world-view which for us is so completely obsolete, they nevertheless carry a directly convincing power in virtue of their spiritual truth which transcends all time and has value for all times. So we too should claim the right to conceive the idea of union with Jesus on the lines of our own world-view, making it our sole concern to reach the depth of the truly living and spiritual truth. [Mysticism, pp. 377 f.]

The Eschatological Expectation

In the effort to understand Paul some started out from his anthropology, others from his psychology, others from his manner of thought in his pre-Christian period (as though we knew anything about that!), others from his personal idiosyncrasy, others from his attitude to the Law, and others from the experience on the way to Damascus. In thus taking hold of any thread which came to hand they tangled the skein to start with, and condemned themselves to accept an inexplicable chaos of thought as Pauline teaching. The only practical procedure is to begin with the simple material which Paul shares completely with the Early Church, and then to see how his doctrine develops out of these. Until it is explained in this way it is not explained at all. This simple material is the eschatological expectation. In that conviction Paul was at one with all those who at that time were preaching the Gospel—the conviction that through the death and resurrection of Jesus the proximate coming of the Messianic Kingdom with Jesus as its ruler was assured. It was this elementary teaching which formed the burden of the discourse when he journeyed as a mis-

sionary from place to place. To it he constantly recurs in
his Letters. With this, therefore, the exposition of Paulinism
must logically begin.   [Mysticism, p. 40]

Paul, Not the Creator of a New Religion

One error of the students of Comparative Religion deserves
particular mention, for it is typical. In consequence of the
parallelism which they maintain between the mystery religions and Paulinism, they come to ascribe to the Apostle
the creation of a "religion." Nothing of the kind ever entered into his purpose. For him there was only one religion:
that of Judaism. It was concerned with God, faith, promise,
hope, and law. In consequence of the coming, the death,
and the resurrection of Jesus Christ, it became its duty to
adjust its teachings and demands to the new era thus introduced, and in the process many things were moved from
the shadow into the light, and others from the light into
the shadow. "Christianity" is for Paul no new religion, but
simply Judaism with the center of gravity shifted in consequence of the new era. His own system of thought is certainly for him no new religion. It is his belief, as fully
known and worked out in its implications, and it professes
to be nothing else than the true Jewish religion, in accord
both with the time and with the Scriptures.   [Paul, p. 227]

Paul and Hellenism

Understood on the basis of eschatology, Paul becomes a
thinker of elemental power who was alone in recognizing
the special character of the period which interposed itself
between the resurrection and return of Jesus, and the first
to seek a solution of the problem raised by the delay of this
return. Since all his conceptions and thoughts are rooted in
eschatology, those who labor to explain him on the basis

of Hellenism, are like a man who should bring water from a long distance in leaky watering-cans in order to water a garden lying beside a stream.

As the spider's net is an admirably simple construction so long as it remains stretched between the threads which hold it in position, but becomes a hopeless tangle as soon as it is loosed from them; so the Pauline mysticism is an admirably simple thing, so long as it is set in the framework of eschatology, but becomes a hopeless tangle as soon as it is cut loose from this.   [Mysticism, p. 140]

Unworldliness in the World

Side by side with Paul's achievement as a thinker must be set his achievement as a man. Having a personality at once simple and profound, he avoids an abstract and unnatural ideal of perfection, and makes perfection consist in the complete adjustment of spiritual with natural reality. So long as the earthly world with all its circumstances still subsists, what we have to do is so to live in it in the spirit of unworldliness that truth and peace already make their influence felt in it. That is the ideal of Paul's ethic, to live with the eyes fixed upon eternity, while standing firmly upon the solid ground of reality. He gives to the enthusiastic conception of the Good a practical direction, without thereby robbing it of its originality and power.

He proves the truth of his ethic by his way of living it. Alike in suffering and in action he shows himself a human being, who by the Spirit of Christ has been purified and led up to a higher humanity. Though his work lies in the world, he ventures to live the unworldly life, and to rely only on the power which is at his disposal, because of that which he, in the Spirit of Christ, has inwardly become. [Mysticism, p. 333]

Paul's Humanity

Paul is the only man of primitive Christian times whom we really know, and he is a man of a profound and admirable humanity.

Although he lives in the expectation of the imminent end of the world, an expectation in view of which all earthly things lose their significance and value, he does not in consequence become an ascetic zealot. For an external abandonment of the things of the world he substitutes an inner freedom from them. As though he had an intuition that it might be the fate of Christianity to have to make terms with the continuance of the natural world, he reaches by his spirituality that attitude towards earthly things by means of which Christianity must henceforth maintain its place in the world. Though living and thinking in his own day, he is at the same time preparing the future.   [Mysticism, p. 332]

The Power of Paul's Thought

Three things make up the power of Paul's thought. There belong to it a depth and reality, which lay their spell upon us; the ardor of the early days of the Christian faith kindles our own; a direct experience of Christ as the Lord of the Kingdom of God speaks from it, exciting us to follow the same path.

Paul leads us out upon that path of true redemption, and hands us over, prisoners, to Christ.   [Mysticism, p. 396]

THE STRENGTH OF CHRISTIANITY

The Solid Foundation of Christianity

Jesus means something to our world because a mighty spiritual force streams forth from Him and flows through our time also. This fact can neither be shaken nor confirmed by any historical discovery. It is the solid foundation of Christianity.   [Quest, p. 397]

The Essential Element in Christianity

The essential element in Christianity as it was preached by Jesus and as it is comprehended by thought, is this, that it is only through love that we can attain to communion with God. All living knowledge of God rests upon this foundation: that we experience Him in our lives as will-to-love.   [Life, p. 277]

The Mystery Religions

However much one may idealize the Greco-Oriental mystery religions—and some of the investigators have idealized them beyond measure—they are still poverty-stricken, compared with Christianity. If one forms an unbiased judgment, on the basis of the extant records concerning them, a great deal of the charm with which they are being surrounded today vanishes. They are concerned solely with the bestowal of immortality upon men through magic. The ethical element, which plays such a predominant part in Christianity, they contain in words, at best, but not in reality. The Mithras cult alone is really ethical. It derives its ethical energies from the religion of Zarathustra, of which it is a fragment that for some time whirled, like a flaming comet, in the Greco-Oriental and Greco-Roman world. But not even the wildest fanatic disputing the originality of Christianity can think of maintaining that it sprang from the cult of Mithras, for that cult appeared in the Greco-Oriental world only after Christianity had attained to full development. It was, however, the very vitality of its ethical ideas that made the Mithras religion, which Roman soldiers brought into Western Europe and Africa, the most powerful rival of Christianity. [Christianity, pp. 7 f.]

The Dynamic Ethic of Christianity

The ethic of Christianity is quite different from that of Greco-Oriental religions. The latter is concerned with liberation from the world only; it is not a dynamic ethic. Jesus, on the contrary, like the prophets and like Zarathustra, who has much in common with the prophets, demands that we should become free from the world, and at the same time that we should be active in the world. The only experience the religious mind of the Greco-Oriental type knows is the longing after the spiritual; but according to the teaching of Jesus men are to be gripped by God's will of love, and must help to carry out that will in this world, in small things as in great things, in saving as in pardoning. To be glad instruments of God's love in this imperfect world is the service to which men are called, and it forms a preparatory stage to the bliss that awaits them in the perfected world, the Kingdom of God. [Christianity, pp. 13 f.]

Eschatology and Immortality

Without its intense eschatological hope the Gospel would have perished from the earth, crushed by the weight of historic catastrophes. But, as it was, by the mighty power of evoking faith which lay in it, eschatology made good in the darkest times Jesus' sayings about the imperishability of His words, and died as soon as these sayings had brought forth new life upon a new soil. Why then make such a complaint against it?

The tragedy does not consist in the modification of primitive Christianity by eschatology, but in the fate of eschatology itself, which has preserved for us all that is most precious in Jesus, but must itself wither, because He died upon the cross with a loud cry, despairing of bringing in the new heaven and the new earth—that is the real tragedy. And not a tragedy to be dismissed with a theologian's sigh, but a liberating and life-giving influence, like every great tragedy. For in its death pangs eschatology bore to the Greek genius a wonder child, the mystic, sensuous, early Christian doctrine of immortality, and consecrated Christianity as the religion of immortality to take the place of the slowly dying civilization of the ancient world. [Quest, p. 254]

The Inconsistency of Christianity

Christianity is not consistent. In the bedrock of its pessimism there are optimistic veins, for it is not only the religion of redemption but of the Kingdom of God. Therefore, it wishes and hopes for a transformation of the world. [Christianity, p. 13]

The Optimism and Pessimism of Christianity

Christianity cannot definitely choose between pessimism and optimism. It is pessimistic, not only because, like Brahmanism and Buddhism, it realizes that imperfection, pain, and sorrow are essential features of the natural world, but for this additional and still more important reason, that in man it finds a will which does not answer to the will of the ethical God and which, therefore, is evil.

Again, Christianity is optimistic, because it does not abandon this world, does not, as do Brahmanism and Buddhism, withdraw from it in negation of life and of the world, but assigns to man a place in this world and commands him to live in it and to work in it in the spirit of the ethical God. Further, Christianity gives him the assurance that thereby God's purpose for the world and for man is being fulfilled; it cannot, however, explain how. For what significance have the ethical character and the ethical activity of the religious individual in the infinite happenings of the universe? What do they accomplish? We must admit that the only answer we have to this question is, that thereby the will of God is fulfilled. [Christianity, pp. 73 f.]

The Chaotic Greatness of Christianity

The religious philosophy of Jesus is not unified. His judgment of the natural world, it is true, is pessimistic; but to Him God is other than the sum-total of the forces at work in the world, other than a pure spirituality, of which part was lost into the world and has to be restored. He is a dynamic Power for good, a mysterious Will, distinct from the world and superior to the world. To Him we yield our will; to Him we leave the future of the world. In the contrast between the world and God, who is an ethical Personality, and in the peculiar tension between pessimism and optimism lies the uniqueness of the religion of Jesus. The fact that it is not a unified system constitutes its greatness, its truth, its depth, its strength. [Christianity, pp. 15 f.]

The Humility of Christianity

How does the Gospel of Jesus compare with Brahmanism
and Buddhism? When meeting them, it becomes first of all
conscious of its own simplicity. Brahmanism and Buddhism
believe that they have lifted the curtain and found the
solution of the riddles of the world and of human life.
This arrogance of those who "know," we find in Indian
literature. Those who work in India find it in the men
with whom they have to do. It is an important feature in
the character of the Indian religion. Jesus does not lead us
into such presumption, but into humility. He wakens in us
a longing to get a glimpse of the mystery of the Kingdom
of God. In I Cor. xiii the apostle Paul uses powerful words
to express the thought that at best "we know in part."
[Christianity, pp. 33 f.]

Freedom from the World

The Gospel of Jesus deals with man as such, and teaches
him how, though living and working in this world, he
should be inwardly free from it. Paul, speaking as a man
mighty in the spirit, says in that wonderful word in I Cor.
vii that we should "weep as though we wept not, rejoice
as though we rejoiced not, and buy as though we possessed
not." In the striving after spiritual liberty from the world
lies the solution of the problem. To obtain freedom from
the world in a spiritual sense is open to everyone. To obtain
freedom in an outward sense will always be the privilege
of the few who can afford to step outside the ordinary circumstances of life and to create exceptional conditions for
themselves. In so doing they will always depend on the
help of those who live the natural life. What would become
of the holy monks of Buddha, if they could not beg food
of the men who continue to till the ground? [Christi-
anity, pp. 42 f.]

Christianity Lacks Inwardness

The Indian religions train men to recollectedness. There is something besides arrogance in the attitude of their representatives towards us, the poor Westerners. They are aware of the peculiar weakness of the modern Christian piety. We are too much inclined to imagine that Christianity is merely activity. We do not have enough inwardness, we are not sufficiently preoccupied with our own spiritual life, we lack quietness; and this not only because in our exacting, busy existence it is difficult to obtain, but because, ignoring its importance, we do not take pains to secure it, being too easily contented with living our lives as unrecollected men who merely aim at being good. [Christianity, p. 43]

A Twofold Liberation

Redemption through Jesus is experienced by him as a two-fold liberation; his view of the world is purged of the previously dominant element of fear, and it becomes ethical instead of unethical. Never have I felt so strongly the victorious power of what is simplest in the teaching of Jesus as when, in the big schoolroom at Lambaréné, which serves as a church as well, I have been explaining the Sermon on the Mount, the parables of the Master, and the sayings of St. Paul about the new life in which we live. [Edge, pp. 155 f.]

Redemption

The redemption to be realized through a merging into spirituality has something grand about it. This idea, so complete in itself, attracts thoughtful men in an almost uncanny way. We, however, have a longing for another kind of union with God. We desire our union with God to result in living ethical spirituality, in activity in the power of God. Such a redemption from the world is the only kind of redemption that can satisfy the longing of the heart. Thus, although we know the charm of the logical religion, we stand by Christianity with all its simplicity and all its antinomies. It is indeed true and valuable, for it answers to the deepest stirrings of our inner will-to-live.   [Christianity, pp. 44 f.]

Faith in the Future

The great weakness of all doctrines of redemption since the primitive Christian is that they represent a man as wholly concerned with his own individual redemption, and not equally with the coming of the Kingdom of God. The one thing needful is that we should work for the establishment of a Christianity, which does not permit those who allow their lives to be determined by Christ to be "of little faith" in regard to the future of the world. However much circumstances may suggest to them this want of faith, Christianity must compel them to realize that to be a Christian means to be possessed and dominated by a hope of the Kingdom of God, and a will to work for it, which bids defiance to external reality. Until this comes about Christianity will stand before the world like a wood in the barrenness of winter.   [Mysticism, p. 384]

Illogical Christianity

Compared with the logical religions of the East, the Gospel of Jesus is illogical. It presupposes a God who is an ethical Personality, and who is, therefore, so to speak, outside the world. When trying to answer questions as to the relation between this ethical Personality and the forces at work in the world, Christianity cannot rise above the mist. It must hold fast the belief that God is the sum-total of the forces working in the world—that all that is, is in God. So far, therefore, Christianity, too, is obliged to think on monistic and pantheistic lines. And yet does not rest satisfied with conceiving God as the sum-total of the forces that are active in the world, for the God of monism and of pantheism—the God of Nature philosophies—is impersonal and has no ethical character. For this reason, Christianity accepts all the difficulties of the dualistic view; it is ethical theism and apprehends God as a Will that is distinct from the world and compels us not to conform to the world.

Again and again, in the course of the centuries, Christianity has sought to harmonize the philosophical and the ethical conceptions of God, but it has never succeeded. It carries within itself, unresolved, the antinomy between monism and dualism, between logical and ethical religion. [Christianity, pp. 72 f.]

Theism and Pantheism

Every form of living Christianity is pantheistic in that it is bound to envisage everything that exists as having its being in the great First Cause of all being. But at the same time all ethical piety is higher than any pantheistic mysticism, in that it does not find the God of Love in Nature, but knows about Him only from the fact that He announces Himself in us as Will-to-Love. The First Cause of Being, as He manifests Himself in Nature, is to us always something impersonal. But to the First Cause of Being, who becomes revealed to us as Will-to-Love, we relate ourselves as to an ethical Personality. Theism does not stand in opposition to pantheism, but emerges from it as the ethically determined out of what is natural and undetermined. [Life, p. 278]

The Knowledge of God

We, as Christians, have ceased to imagine that a living, ethical religion can be the logical outcome of "knowing the world." We are convinced that from the world we cannot gain our knowledge of God, who is an ethical Personality. Facing the terrible problem which the world presents, we strive hard not to despair of God. We dare to admit that the forces at work in nature are in so many ways different from what we should expect them to be in a world which owes its origin to a perfect creative Will. We dare to admit that in nature and in ourselves we find much that we feel to be evil. We are far more deeply conscious of what sin is than are the religious minds of China; and much more deeply than they do, do we feel that God cannot be "known," but must be grasped by that faith which says: "Nevertheless, I am continually with thee." [Christianity, pp. 54 f.]

Profound Naïveté

Christianity has had to give up one piece after another of what it still imagined it possessed in the way of explanations of the universe. In this development it grows more and more into an expression of what constitutes its real nature. In a remarkable process of spiritualization it advances further and further from naïve naïveté into the region of profound naïveté. The greater the number of explanations that slip from its hands, the more is the first of the Beatitudes, which may indeed be regarded as a prophetic word concerning Christianity, fulfilled: "Blessed are the poor in spirit; for theirs is the Kingdom of Heaven."

When Christianity becomes conscious of its innermost nature, it realizes that it is godliness rising out of inward constraint. The highest knowledge is to know that we are

THE STRENGTH OF CHRISTIANITY

surrounded by mystery. Neither knowledge nor hope for the future can be the pivot of our life or determine its direction. It is intended to be solely determined by our allowing ourselves to be gripped by the ethical God, who reveals Himself in us, and by our yielding our will to His. [Christianity, pp. 77 f.]

Christianity Does Not Explain Everything

When you preach the Gospel, beware of preaching it as the religion which explains everything. I suppose that in England, as on the Continent, thousands and thousands of men have despaired of Christianity, because they have seen and experienced the atrocities of the War. Confronted with the inexplicable, the religion which they believed to have an explanation for everything has collapsed.

For ten years, before I left for Africa, I prepared boys in the parish of St. Nicolas, in Strassburg, for confirmation. After the War some of them came to see me and thanked me for having taught them so definitely that religion was not a formula for explaining everything. They said it had been that teaching which had kept them from discarding Christianity, whereas so many others in the trenches discarded it, not being prepared to meet the inexplicable. [Christianity, pp. 80 f.]

Christianity and Primitive Man

The Negro lives with a general view of things which is innocent of history, and he has no means of measuring and appreciating the time interval between Jesus and ourselves. Similarly, the doctrinal statements which explain how the divine plan of redemption was prepared and effected, are not easily made intelligible to him, even though he has an elementary consciousness of what redemption is. Christi-

anity is for him the light that shines amid the darkness of
his fears; it assures him that he is not in the power of nature
spirits, ancestral spirits, or fetishes, and that no human being
has any sinister power over another, since the will of God
really controls everything that goes on in the world.

> "I lay in cruel bondage,
> Thou cam'st and mad'st me free!"

These words from Paul Gerhardt's Advent hymn express
better than any others what Christianity means for primitive man. [Edge, p. 154]

No Fear of Death

It is well known that hopes and fears about a world beyond
play no part in the religion of primitive man; the child of
nature does not fear death, but regards it merely as something natural. The more medieval form of Christianity
which keeps anxiety about a judgment to come in the fore-
ground, has fewer points of contact with his mentality
than the more ethical form. To him Christianity is the
moral view of life and the world, which was revealed by
Jesus; it is a body of teaching about the Kingdom of God
and the grace of God.   [Edge, pp. 154 f.]

Ethical Conversion

The ethical conversion is often incomplete with a Negro,
but in order to be just to such a convert one must distinguish between the real morality which springs from the
heart, and the respectable morality of society; it is wonderful how faithful he often is to the former. One must live
among them to know how much it means when a man,
because he is a Christian, will not wreak the vengeance
which he is expected to take, or even the blood revenge

which is thought to be an obligation on him. On the whole
I feel that the primitive man is much more good-natured
than we Europeans are; with Christianity added to his good
qualities wonderfully noble characters can result. I expect
I am not the only white man who feels himself put to
shame by the natives.   [Edge, pp. 156 f.]

Missionary Rivalry

The most difficult problem in the mission field arises from
the fact that evangelistic work has to be done under two
banners, the Catholic and the Protestant. How much grander
would be the work undertaken in the name of Jesus if this
distinction did not exist, and there were never two churches
working in competition. On the Ogowe, indeed, the missionaries of both bodies live in quite correct, sometimes in
even friendly, relations with one another, but that does not
remove the rivalry which confuses the native and hinders
the spread of the Gospel.   [Edge, p. 166]

Protestant and Catholic Missions

I often visit the Catholic mission stations in my capacity of
doctor and so have been able to gather a fairly clear idea
of the way in which they conduct their evangelistic work
and their education. As to organization, their missions seem
to me to be better managed than ours in several ways. If I
had to distinguish between the aims which the two keep
before them, I should say the Protestant mission puts in the
first place the building up of Christian personalities, while
the Catholic has in mind before all else the establishment on
solid foundations of a church. The former object is the
higher one, but it does not take sufficient account of reali-
ties. To make the work of training permanently successful,
a firmly established church, which grows in a natural way

with the increase in the number of Christian families, is
necessary. The church history of every period teaches this.
Is it not the weakness as well as the greatness of Protestantism that it means personal religion too much and church
too little?   [Edge, pp. 166 f.]

The Weakness of Christianity

To make up to itself for the fact that it does so little to
prove the reality of its spiritual and ethical nature, the
Christianity of today cheats itself with the delusion that it
is making its position as a church stronger year by year.
It is accommodating itself to the spirit of the age by adopt-
ing a kind of modern worldliness. Like other organized
bodies it is at work to make good, by ever stronger and
more uniform organization, its claim to be a body justified
by history and practical success. But just in proportion as it
gains in external power, it loses in spiritual.   [Life, p. 276]

Religion Is Not a Force

"Is religion a force in the spiritual life of our age?" I answer
in your name and mine, "No!" There is still religion in the
world; there is much religion in the church; there are many
pious people among us. Christianity can still point to works
of love and to social works of which it can be proud.
There is a longing for religion among many who no longer
belong to the churches. I rejoice to concede this. And yet
we must hold fast to the fact that religion is not a force.
The proof? The war!   [Religion, p. 1483]

What Christianity Needs

What Christianity needs is that it shall be filled to over-
flowing with the spirit of Jesus, and in the strength of that

shall spiritualize itself into a living religion of inwardness and love, such as its destined purpose should make it. Only as such can it become the leaven in the spiritual life of mankind. What has been passing for Christianity during these nineteen centuries is merely a beginning, full of weakness and mistakes, not a full-grown Christianity springing from the spirit of Jesus. [Life, pp. 278 f.]

Logical and Ethical Religion

Christianity must, clearly and definitely, put before men the necessity of a choice between logical religion and ethical religion, and it must insist on the fact that the ethical is the highest type of spirituality, and that it alone is living spirituality. Thus Christianity shows itself as the religion which, penetrating and transcending all knowledge, reaches forward to the ethical, living God, who cannot be found through contemplation of the world, but reveals Himself in man only. And it is thus that Christianity speaks with all the authority of its inherent truth. [Christianity, p. 83]

The Renewing of Christianity

The renewing of Christianity which must come will be a return to the immediacy and intensity of the faith of early Christianity. No doubt a reintegration of primitive Christian faith as such is impossible, because it was embodied in temporally conditioned conceptions to which it is impossible for us to return. But the spiritual essence of them we can make ours. This we can do in proportion as we toilfully win for ourselves a living faith in the Kingdom of God, and realize ourselves within this as men redeemed by Christ. [Mysticism, p. 384]

GOD AND HIS KINGDOM

The Great Problem of Religion

All problems of religion, ultimately, go back to this one —the experience I have of God within myself differs from the knowledge concerning Him which I derive from the world. In the world He appears to me as the mysterious, marvellous creative Force; within me He reveals Himself as ethical Will. In the world He is impersonal Force, within me He reveals Himself as Personality. The God who is known through philosophy and the God whom I experience as ethical Will do not coincide. They are one; but how they are one, I do not understand. [Christianity, p. 74]

The Vital Knowledge of God

Now, which is the more vital knowledge of God? The knowledge derived from my experience of Him as ethical Will. The knowledge concerning God which is derived from nature is always imperfect and inadequate, because we perceive the things in the world from without only. I see the tree grow, and I see it cover itself with leaves and blossoms; but I do not understand the forces which effect this; their generative power remains a mystery to me. In myself, on the other hand, I know things from within. The creative force which produces and sustains all that is, reveals itself in me in a way in which I do not get to know it elsewhere, namely, as ethical Will, as something which desires to be creative within me. This mystery, which I have experienced, is the decisive factor in my thinking, my willing and my understanding. All the mysteries of the world and of my existence in the world may ultimately be left on one side unsolved and insoluble. My life is completely and unmistakably determined by the mysterious experience of God revealing Himself within me as ethical Will and desiring to take hold of my life.   [Christianity, pp. 75 f.]

God in the Universe

There is an ocean—cold water without motion. In this ocean, however, is the Gulf Stream, hot water flowing from the equator towards the Pole. Inquire of all scientists how it is physically imaginable that a stream of hot water flows between the waters of the ocean, which, so to speak, form its banks, the moving within the motionless, the hot within the cold: no scientist can explain it. Similarly, there is the God of love within the God of the forces of the universe—one with Him, and yet so totally different. We let ourselves be seized and carried away by that vital stream.   [Christianity, p. 76]

Union with God

All profound religion is mystical. To be freed from the world by being in God: that is the longing we have within us, so long as we do not numb ourselves in thoughtlessness. A union with God, however, which is realized through the intellectual act of "knowing," as conceived in the Eastern religions, must always remain a dead spirituality. It does not effect a rebirth, in God, into living spirituality. Living spirituality, real redemption from the world, cannot come but

from that union with God which is ethically determined.
The religions of the East are logical mysticism, Christianity
alone is ethical mysticism.

Thus we go on our way through the world, not troubled
about knowledge, but committing to God what we hope
for, for ourselves and the world, and possessing all in all
through being apprehended by the living, ethical God.
[Christianity, pp. 78 f.]

The Active God

In the Greco-Oriental religion there is no living conception of God. To it God is nothing but pure spirituality.
The God of Jesus is an active God, who works in man.
Therefore, the religion of Jesus is not consistent pessimism,
completely systematized, but it is a chaotic mixture of pessimism and optimism.   [Christianity, p. 15]

Dogmatic Religion

Dogmatic religion is based on the creeds, the early church
and the reformation. It has no relations with thinking, but
emphasizes the difference between thinking and believing.
This religion further is more dominated by the thought of
redemption than by that of the Kingdom of God. It has no
wish to influence the world. That is characteristic of all the
ancient creeds—that the idea of the Kingdom of God finds
no expression in them.   [Religion, p. 1483]

The Idea of the Kingdom

The teaching of Jesus and of Paul concerning the Kingdom of God is, briefly, as follows: The end of this world
and the dawn of the supernatural world are regarded as
near at hand. The "Saints," not being conformed to this

GOD AND HIS KINGDOM

world, have thereby proved their election to God's Kingdom, and they will live in that Kingdom together with the Messiah, in transfigured bodies, until the end comes and all things return unto God, so that God may be all in all, as in the beginning (I Cor. xv:28).

Of such an eschatological hope—that is, an expectation of the end of the world, and of its transfiguration—nothing is to be found in the Greco-Oriental mystery religions. Where there is any kind of expectation of the end of the world, and of the Kingdom of God, we certainly have to do with a type of religious thinking which cannot be traced back to those mystery religions, but which is derived from that Jewish outlook we find in the prophets. Amos and Isaiah have created the conception of the Kingdom of God. Late Judaism developed it in fantastic ways, no doubt partly under the influence of ideas from Zarathustra's religion, with which the exile made the Jews acquainted. Jesus brings the Kingdom idea to its ethical perfection, without inveighing against its late-Jewish form. [Christianity, pp. 9 f.]

Manifesting the Power of the Kingdom

Paul does not urge those who have been redeemed by Christ to withdraw from the world; he bids them take their place in it, that they may make use of the powers derived from their being in the Kingdom of God. His extraordinary realism preserves him from all extravagance. Inasmuch as the conception of dying and rising again with Christ has its roots in the belief in the Kingdom of God, the world-negation which it involves does not urge to asceticism or to withdrawal from the world. Consequently this religious ethic, which, moreover, arose out of the world-view incident to an expectation of the imminent end of the world is, for all its glowing ardor, sound and

natural. Out of a deep necessity, and with an amazing
naturalness, it makes the experience of redemption through
union with Christ become actual as a manifestation of the
Spirit of being-in the Kingdom of God. [Mysticism,
p. 388]

The Kingdom Must be within Us

Paul's Kingdom-of-God belief does not take into account
the possibility of a development of this natural world into
the Kingdom of God. But though he gives up this world
he nevertheless expects the redeemed man to manifest in it
the Spirit of the Kingdom of God which is in him. Purely
from inner necessity, not with the view to success, there
arises an activity which is determined by the Kingdom of
God. As a star, by the inner law of the light which is in it,
shines over a dark world, even when there is no prospect
of heralding a morning which is to dawn upon it, so the
elect must radiate the light of the Kingdom in the world.
This manifestation of the Kingdom of God from inner
necessity must be the core and kernel of the matter; to this
any work deliberately directed to the realization of the
Kingdom is merely the outer envelope. We have constantly
to remember the inexorable law, that we can only bring
so much of the Kingdom of God into the world as we
possess within us.   [Mysticism, pp. 388 f.]

Religion and Civilization

Why did the idea of the Kingdom of God have no significance in the early church? It was closely connected with
the expectation of the end of the world. And when hope of
the coming of the end of the world had faded, the idea of
the Kingdom of God lost its force as well. So it came about
that the creeds were not at the same time preoccupied with

the idea of redemption. Only after the reformation did the idea gradually arise that we men and women in our own age must so understand the religion of Jesus that we endeavor to make the Kingdom of God a reality in this world. It is only through the idea of the Kingdom of God that religion enters into relationship with civilization. [Religion, p. 1484]

The Kingdom of God in Chinese Thought

Before Chinese religious thinkers, as before modern Christians, there hovered a vision of the Kingdom of God, expected to be realized on earth through love. Let us not minimize what we thus find of Christian ideals among non-Christians of remote centuries in a far-off country. To do so would not be in accordance with the spirit of Jesus. Let us rejoice in the truth, wherever we find its lamp burning. [Christianity, p. 51]

God Alone Brings the Kingdom

We modern men are inclined to interpret the thoughts of Jesus in a modern way. We are familiar with the idea that by the active ethical conduct of individuals the Kingdom of God may be realized on earth. Finding that Jesus speaks of ethical activity and also of the Kingdom of God, we think that He, too, connected the two in the way which seems so natural to us. In reality, however, Jesus does not speak of the Kingdom of God as of something that comes into existence in this world and through a development of human society, but as of something which is brought about by God when He transforms this imperfect world into a perfect one. In the thought of Jesus, the ethical activity of man is only like a powerful prayer to God, that He may cause the Kingdom to appear without delay. In this

sense we have to take the word of Jesus (Matt. xi:12) that
from the days of John the Baptist the Kingdom of God
has been suffering violence, and the violent have been
seizing it by force.   [Christianity, pp. 16 f.]

Religion Turns Its Back

In recent times a tendency has appeared in dogmatic religion which completely turns its back on thinking and at
the same time declares that religion has nothing to do with
the world and civilization. It is not its business to realize
the Kingdom of God on earth. This extreme tendency is
mainly represented by Karl Barth.   [Religion, p. 1484]

The Coming of the Kingdom

The first Christians expected the Kingdom of God to come
speedily, as a complete transformation of the natural world
into a perfect one. We have become more moderate in our
expectations. We no longer think of the Kingdom of God
as extending over the universe. We limit it to mankind
and look forward to it as to the miracle of God's spirit
bringing all human spirits into subjection.

The generations preceding ours wanted to believe, and
were able to believe, that the miracle would be performed
in a steady, slow development. We, however, having lived
through, and still living in, a time of appalling and meaningless events, feel as if a terrible tidal wave had flung us
back, far away from the harbor of the Kingdom of God,
towards which we now have to start out afresh, rowing
hard against storm and tide, without being certain of really
making headway. Thus we, too, like the early Christians,
are taught by God the awful discipline of the word: "My
thoughts are not your thoughts." He sets before us the
difficult task of being faithful to the Kingdom of God as

those who do not see and yet believe. We are able to accomplish that task, if we have been apprehended by Him.
[Christianity, pp. 79 f.]

Paul's Kingdom-of-God Religion

Our religion must renew itself by contact with Paul's Kingdom-of-God religion. As modern men we are in danger of confining ourselves to Kingdom-of-God propaganda and external Kingdom-of-God work. Modern Kingdom-of-God religion calls on men to do Kingdom-of-God work, as though anyone could do anything for the Kingdom of God who does not bear the Kingdom of God within him. Thus, with the best intentions, we are constantly in danger of giving our allegiance to an externalized Kingdom-of-God belief.   [Mysticism, p. 388]

By Works of Love

It constituted a great difficulty for the non-dogmatic religion when theological science at the end of the nineteenth century was forced to admit that the ethical religion of Jesus shared the supernatural ideas of late-Jewish belief in the Messianic kingdom, and indeed that it also shared with it its expectation of the approaching end of the world. Here it becomes clear that there is no purely historical foundation for religion. We must take the ethical religion of Jesus out of the setting of His world-view and put it in our own. Whereas He expected the Kingdom of God to come at the end of the world, we must endeavor, under the influence of the spirit of His ethical religion, to make the Kingdom of God a reality in this world by works of love.   [Religion, p. 1484]

The Miracle of the Spirit

A change has come over our belief in the Kingdom of God. We no longer look for a transformation of the natural circumstances of the world; we take the continuance of the evil and suffering, which belong to the nature of things, as something appointed by God for us to bear. Our hope of the Kingdom is directed to the essential and spiritual meaning of it, and we believe in that as a miracle wrought by the Spirit in making men obedient to the will of God. But we must cherish in our hearts this belief in the coming of the Kingdom through the miracle of the Spirit with the same ardor with which the primitive Christianity cherished its hope of the translation of the world into the supernatural condition. Christianity cannot get away from the fact that God has laid upon it the task of spiritualizing its faith. Our concern must be to see that the strength of our faith is not impaired by this transformation. It is time for our Christianity to examine itself and see whether we really still have faith in the Kingdom of God, or whether we merely retain it as a matter of traditional phraseology. There is a deep sense in which we may apply to the theological preoccupations of our day the saying of Jesus, "Seek ye first the Kingdom of God and His righteousness, and all these things shall be added unto you." [Mysticism, pp. 384 f.]

AFFIRMATION AND NEGATION

Affirmation and Negation

World- and life-affirmation consists in this: that man regards existence as he experiences it in himself and as it has developed in the world as something of value *per se* and accordingly strives to let it reach perfection in himself, whilst within his own sphere of influence he endeavors to preserve and to further it.

World- and life-negation on the other hand consists in his regarding existence as he experiences it in himself and as it is developed in the world as something meaningless and sorrowful, and he resolves accordingly (*a*) to bring life to a standstill in himself by mortifying his will-to-live, and (*b*) to renounce all activity which aims at improvement of the conditions of life in this world.

World- and life-affirmation unceasingly urges men to serve their fellows, society, the nation, mankind, and indeed all that lives, with their utmost will and in lively hope of realizable progress. World- and life-negation takes no interest in the world, but regards man's life on earth either merely as a stage play in which it is his duty to participate, or only as a puzzling pilgrimage through the land of time to his home in eternity.   [Indian, pp. 1 f.]

World- and Life-Affirmation

What is world- and life-affirmation?

To us Europeans and to people of European descent

everywhere the will-to-progress is something so natural and so much a matter of course that it never occurs to us to recognize that it is rooted in a world-view, and springs from an act of the spirit. But if we look about us in the world, we see at once that what is to us such a matter of course is in reality anything but that. To Indian thought all effort directed to triumphs in knowledge and power and to the improvement of man's outer life and of society as a whole is mere folly. It teaches that the only sensible line of conduct for a man is to withdraw entirely into himself and to concern himself solely with the deepening of his inner life. He has nothing to do with what may become of human society and of mankind. The deepening of one's inner life, as Indian thought interprets it, means that a man surrenders himself to the thought of "no more will to live," and by abstention from action and by every sort of life denial reduces his earthly existence to a condition of being which has no content beyond a waiting for the cessation of being.   [Life, pp. 177 f.]

World- and Life-Denial

It is interesting to trace the origin of this idea, so contrary to nature, of world- and life-denial. It had at first nothing whatever to do with any world-view, but was a magical conception of the Indian priests of early times. These believed that by detachment from the world and from life they could become in some measure supernatural beings, and obtain power over the gods. In accordance with this idea arises the custom that the Brahman, after living part of his life in the normal way and founding a family, terminated his life in complete renunciation of the world.

In the course of time this world- and life-negation which originally formed the Brahman's privilege was developed into a world-view which claimed to be valid for men as such. . . .

It depends on the world-view, then, whether there is any will-to-progress or not. The world-view of world- and life-negation excludes it; that of world- and life-affirmation demands it. Among primitive and half-primitive peoples too, whose unformed world-view has not yet reached the problem of world-affirmation or negation, there is no will-to-progress. The ideal is the simplest life with the least possible trouble. [Life, pp. 178 f.]

Ethics in the World-View

In modern European thought there is being enacted a tragedy, in that by a slow but irresistible process the bonds originally existing between world- and life-affirmation and the ethical are becoming slack and are finally being severed. The result that we are coming to is that European humanity is being guided by a will-to-progress that has become merely external and has lost its bearings.

World- and life-affirmation can produce of itself only a partial and imperfect civilization. Only if it becomes inward and ethical can the will-to-progress which results from it possess the requisite insight to distinguish the valuable from the less valuable, and strive after a civilization which does not consist only in achievements of knowledge and power, but before all else will make men, both individually and collectively, more spiritual and more ethical. [Life, pp. 181 f.]

Optimism in Religion

A religion is optimistic if it represents the conviction that the forces at work in the natural world have their origin in a perfect primal force, which leads all things towards perfection through a natural development. [Christianity, p. 24]

Pessimism in Religion

The religious mind is said to hold a pessimistic view, if it cannot conceive the forces at work in the world of sense as the expression of divine goodness and perfection. It, therefore, does not rest its hopes on possibilities of development within this physical world, but looks beyond into the world of pure, spiritual being.   [Christianity, p. 24]

The Evil in the World

To the question whether I am a pessimist or an optimist, I answer that my knowledge is pessimistic, but my willing and hoping are optimistic.

I am pessimistic in that I experience in its full weight what we conceive to be the absence of purpose in the course of world-happenings. Only at quite rare moments have I felt really glad to be alive. I could not but feel with a sympathy full of regret all the pain that I saw around me, not only that of men but that of the whole creation. From this community of suffering I have never tried to withdraw myself. It seemed to me a matter of course that we should all take our share of the burden of pain which lies upon the world. Even while I was a boy at school it was clear to me that no explanation of the evil in the world could ever satisfy me; all explanations, I felt, ended in sophistries, and at bottom had no other object than to make it possible for men to share in the misery around them, with less keen feelings. That a thinker like Leibnitz could reach the miserable conclusion that though this world is, indeed, not good, it is the best that was possible, I have never been able to understand.

But however much concerned I was at the problem of the misery in the world, I never let myself get lost in broodings over it; I always held firmly to the thought that each

one of us can do a little to bring some portion of it to an
end. Thus I came gradually to rest content in the knowledge that there is only one thing we can understand about
the problem, and that is that each of us has to go his own
way, but as one who means to help to bring about deliverance.   [Life, pp. 279 f.]

The Road to Ruin

In my judgment of the situation in which mankind finds
itself at the present time I am pessimistic. I cannot make
myself believe that that situation is not so bad as it seems
to be, but I am inwardly conscious that we are on a road
which, if we continue to tread it, will bring us into "Middle
Ages" of a new character. The spiritual and material misery
to which mankind of today is delivering itself through its
renunciation of thinking and of the ideals which spring
therefrom, I picture to myself in its utmost compass. And
yet I remain optimistic. One belief of my childhood I have
preserved with the certainty that I can never lose it: belief
in truth. I am confident that the spirit generated by truth
is stronger than the force of circumstances. In my view
no other destiny awaits mankind than that which, through
its mental and spiritual disposition, it prepares for itself.
Therefore I do not believe that it will have to tread the
road to ruin right to the end.   [Life, pp. 280 f.]

Willing the Ideal

Pessimism and optimism each go about masquerading in
the clothes of the other; this practice is, indeed, a characteristic attendant on the fact that both inhabit the same
dwelling. With us at the present time what is really pessimism gives itself out as optimism, and contrariwise what is
really optimism goes by the name of pessimism. What is

commonly called optimism in current speech is merely the natural or acquired ability to see things in the best possible light. Such a view can only exist because we have a degraded idea both of what ought to be now and of our future. The poisonous germs of phthisis induce in the sufferer the so-called *euphory*, that is, a subjective feeling of well-being and of energy. Similarly, a superficial and externalized optimism comes to view amongst the masses of men when individuals and society have been injected with pessimism without being conscious of the fact. True optimism has no connection whatever with over-indulgent judgments of any kind. It consists in conceiving and willing the ideal, as this is inspired by profound and self-consistent affirmation of life and of the world.   [Ethics, pp. 16 f.]

The Precipice of Pessimism

The battle between optimism and pessimism which goes on in us is necessarily endless. We are always walking on loose stones which overhang the precipice of pessimism. When that which we experience, either in our own existence or in the history of humanity, acts on us so as to depress our will-to-live, and to take away our freshness and our conviction, then we are liable to lose our foothold and to be dragged down into the depths, together with the rock which gives way under us.

But since we know that death awaits us there we drag ourselves painfully up again to the path above. . . . Or it may be that a wave of pessimism comes over us like the longing for rest which takes hold of those who, wearied with travel, sit down in the snow. Oh, to renounce once for all the obligation to hope and to will all that which the ideals imposed on us by the deepened will-to-live demand from us! Oh, to have no more unrest since here we could attain rest by renouncing the struggle! . . . The intellect whispers gently to our will and would fain persuade it to resign itself to the logic of objective tasks. . . .

This is the fatal resignation into which educated men and civilized humanity in general are too apt to sink and thus to die.   [Ethics, pp. 224 f.]

The Battle for Affirmation

People commonly speak of an optimistic and a pessimistic world-view. But these expressions do not define the distinction in its essential nature. What determines a man's world-view is not whether, according to his disposition, he takes things more or less lightly or whether he has been gifted with or denied the capacity to have confidence; what is decisive is his inner attitude towards Being, his affirmation or negation of life. World-view consists in a determination of the will. The question is not so much what man expects or does not expect from existence, but what use he aims at making of it. Naturally the attitude toward existence determined by the will can be influenced by a more optimistic or more pessimistic disposition just as it may be by favorable or unfavorable events. But it is not simply the result of that. The most profound world- and life-affirmation is that which has been hard won from an estimate of things unbiased by illusion and even wrested from misfortune, whilst the most profound world- and life-negation is that which is developed in theory in despite of a naturally serene disposition and happy outward circumstances.

The battle for world- and life-affirmation and world- and life-negation must be constantly fought and won afresh.   [Indian, pp. 2 f.]

The Impossibility of World-Negation

The difficulty of the world-view of world- and life-negation consists in the fact that it is impracticable. It is compelled to make concessions to world- and life-affirmation.

It really ought to demand of man that, as soon as he reaches the conviction that non-Being is to be regarded as higher than Being, he shall quit existence by a self-chosen death. It gives a reason for not demanding this of him by explaining that it is not so important to make an end of life as soon as possible as it is to mortify as thoroughly as we can the will-to-live in our hearts. The world-view of world- and life-negation is therefore in contradiction with itself in that it does want to be lived. With this desire it enters on the path of concession to world- and life-affirmation which it must then follow to the end.

To remain alive, even in the most miserable fashion, presupposes some activity conducive to the maintenance of life. Even the hermit, who is most strict of all men in his world- and life-negation, cannot escape from that. He picks berries, goes to the spring, fills his drinking cup, perhaps even washes himself now and then, and feeds his companions the birds and the deer as a proper hermit should.   [Indian, pp. 7 f.]

The Meaning of Life

The impossibility of the attempt to understand the meaning of life in the meaning of the world, faces us immediately when we reflect that in objective facts no purposive element is apparent with which the action of men and of humanity can have any possible connection. The human race has been in existence for a relatively infinitesimal space of time on one of the smaller among the myriads of heavenly bodies. For how long will it continue? Any raising or lowering of the earth's temperature, the slightest eccentric motion of a star or planet, any elevation of the ocean's surface, or any alteration of the composition of the atmosphere would make an end of its existence; or the earth itself may become a victim of some cosmic catastrophe as has happened to many another heavenly body. We do not know what our own importance is from the point of view of the earth. How much less, then, are we able to estimate our own value or attempt to attribute to the eternal universe a meaning in which we ourselves are an end, or which is to be explained by reference to our existence. [Ethics, p. 211]

The Enigma of Nature

It is not merely the monstrous disproportion of unknown infinite quantity between the universe and man which makes it impossible for us to find a logical foundation in the universe for the aims of humanity. Such an attempt is condemned to failure at the outset by the fact that we have not succeeded in discovering a general all-embracing purposiveness in the courses of the objective world. The only purposiveness apparent to us in the world is always entirely isolated. It is true that nature shows herself at times magnificently purposive in the way in which she originates and maintains certain forms of life, but she never seems concerned to unite all these purposive lines directed toward individual aims in one great universal purposiveness. She does not undertake to unite with life in one great common life. She is a force at once wonderfully creative and senselessly destructive. In nature we are faced, it seems, by an insoluble enigma. The essence of the universe is full of meaning in its meaninglessness, meaningless in its fulness of meaning. [Ethics, pp. 211 f.]

Our Rightful Place in the Universe

The knowledge that results from the recording of single manifestations of Being remains ever incomplete and unsatisfying so far as it is unable to give the final answer to

the great question of what we are in the universe, and to
what purpose we exist in it. We can find our right place
in the Being that envelops us only if we experience in our
individual lives the universal life which wills and rules
within it. The nature of the living Being without me I can
understand only through the living Being which is within
me. It is to this reflective knowledge of the universal Being
and of the relation to it of the individual human being that
the Humanities seek to attain. The results they reach contain truth so far as the spirit which is creatively active in
this direction possesses a sense of reality, and has passed
through the stage of gaining a knowledge of facts about
Being to reflection about the nature of Being. [Life,
pp. 127 f.]

This Vale of Tears

Dissatisfaction is always present somewhere even amidst
our gains. Disappointment and sorrow are our lot in the
short space of time which lies between birth and death.
The spiritual element in us exists in a grizzly kind of dependence on the physical. Our very existence is the prey
of meaningless events, and may be put an end to by such
at any moment. The will-to-live affords me an impulse to
activity. But this very activity is as if I should plough the
sea and sow in the furrows of it. What have my predecessors attained? What significance, if any, has that for which
they strove in the eternal courses of the world? Is the will-
to-live only intent, in all the dreams of fancy which it
conjures up, on persuading me to delay my existence here
a little longer and to bring into being other creatures destined to the same wretched heritage as myself, so that the
play may still continue?

The theories against which the will-to-live dashes itself
when it begins to reflect are thus pessimistic through and

through. It is thus not accidental that all the religious world-views, with the exception of the Chinese, have a pessimistic tinge. From this earthly existence, they tell us, we have nothing to expect. Who will secure for us the power to cast from us the bonds of actuality? Every reflecting man comes face to face with this thought. . . .

What is it that determines us, so long as we are in some measure in our right senses, to put aside the thought of ending our existence? An instinctive impulse against such an act. The will-to-live is stronger than the pessimistic intellect. There is in us an instinctive awe in the presence of life, for we ourselves are sparks of the will-to-live. [Ethics, pp. 218 f.]

The Sacrifice of Life

In the profoundest form of world- and life-affirmation, in which man lives his life on the loftiest spiritual and ethical plane, he attains to inner freedom from the world and becomes capable of sacrificing his life for some end. This profoundest world- and life-affirmation can assume the appearance of world- and life-negation. But that does not make it world- and life-negation: it remains what it is—the loftiest form of world- and life-affirmation. He who sacrifices his life to achieve any purpose for an individual or for humanity is practising life-affirmation. He is taking an interest in the things of this world and by offering his own life wants to bring about in the world something which he regards as necessary. The sacrifice of life for a purpose is not life-negation, but the profoundest form of life-affirmation placing itself at the service of world-affirmation. World- and life-negation is only present when man takes no interest whatever in any realizable purpose nor in the improvement of conditions in this world. As soon as he in any way withdraws from this standpoint, whether he admits it to

himself or not, he is already under the influence of world-
and life-affirmation.   [Indian, pp. 6 f.]

The Ideal of Perfection

We modern Europeans are so much occupied with our activity within the world that we give little or no heed to
the question of our spiritual future. But the world-view of
world- and life-negation sets the question of man becoming spiritually more perfect at the center of all reflection and deliberation. It holds before man as the highest aim
that he should endeavor to attain to the right composure,
the right inwardness, the right ethical attitude of mind and
to true peace of soul. Although the ideal set up by Indian
world- and life-negation of becoming spiritually more and
more perfect is of necessity one-sided and inadequate,
nevertheless it has great significance for us in affording an
insight into a system of thought which is occupied with a
great problem of which we take far too little notice.
[Indian, pp. 9 f.]

THE DIGNITY OF THE INDIVIDUAL

The Foolishness of God

One day, in my despair, I threw myself into a chair in the consulting-room and groaned out: "What a blockhead I was to come out here to doctor savages like these!" Whereupon Joseph quietly remarked: "Yes, Doctor, here on earth you are a great blockhead, but not in heaven." [Hospital, p. 118]

Life's Enthusiasms

The ideas which determine our character and life are implanted in mysterious fashion. When we are leaving childhood behind us, they begin to shoot out. When we are seized by youth's enthusiasm for the good and the true, they burst into flower, and the fruit begins to set. In the development which follows the one really important thing is—how much there still remains of the fruit, the buds of which were put out in its springtime by the tree of our life.

The conviction that in after life we must struggle to remain thinking as freely and feeling as deeply as we did in our youth, has accompanied me on my road through life as a faithful advisor.   [Childhood, p. 97]

Lost Youth

The epithet "ripe" applied to persons always did, and does still, convey to me the idea of something depressing. I

hear with it, like musical discords, the words, impoverish-
ment, stunted growth, blunted feelings. What we are usually invited to contemplate as "ripeness" in a man is the re-
signing of ourselves to an almost exclusive use of the reason.
One acquires it by copying others and getting rid, one by
one, of the thoughts and convictions which were dear in the
days of one's youth. We believed once in the victory of
truth; but we do not now. We believed in our fellow men;
we do not now. We believed in goodness; we do not now.
We were zealous for justice; but we are not so now. We
trusted in the power of kindness and peaceableness; we do
not now. We were capable of enthusiasm; but we are not
so now. To get through the shoals and storms of life more
easily we have lightened our craft, throwing overboard
what we thought could be spared. But it was really our
stock of food and drink of which we deprived ourselves;
our craft is now easier to manage, but we ourselves are in a
decline.

I listened, in my youth, to conversations between grown-
up people through which there breathed a tone of sorrowful regret which oppressed the heart. The speakers looked
back at the idealism and capacity for enthusiasm of their
youth as something precious to which they ought to have
held fast, and yet at the same time they regarded it as almost a law of nature that no one should be able to do so.
This woke in me a dread of having ever, even once, to look
back on my own past with such a feeling; I resolved never
to let myself become subject to this tragic domination of
mere reason, and what I thus vowed in almost boyish defiance I have tried to carry out.   [Childhood, pp. 97 ff.]

Youthful Idealism

Grown-up people reconcile themselves too willingly to
a supposed duty of preparing young ones for the time

when they will regard as illusion what now is an inspiration to heart and mind. Deeper experience of life, however, advises their inexperience differently. It exhorts them to hold fast, their whole life through, to the thoughts which inspire them. It is through the idealism of youth that man catches sight of truth, and in that idealism he possesses a wealth which he must never exchange for anything else. We must all be prepared to find that life tries to take from us our belief in the good and the true, and our enthusiasm for them, but we need not surrender them. That ideals, when they are brought into contact with reality, are usually crushed by facts does not mean that they are bound from the very beginning to capitulate to the facts, but merely that our ideals are not strong enough; and they are not strong enough because they are not pure and strong and stable enough in ourselves.   [Childhood, pp. 99 f.]

Full-Grown Idealism

The ripeness that our development must aim at is one which makes us simpler, more truthful, purer, more peace loving, meeker, kinder, more sympathetic. That is the only way in which we are to sober down with age. That is the process in which the soft iron of youthful idealism hardens into the steel of a full-grown idealism which can never be lost.   [Childhood, p. 100]

The Power of Ideals

The power of ideals is incalculable. We see no power in a drop of water. But let it get into a crack in the rock and be turned to ice, and it splits the rock; turned into steam, it drives the pistons of the most powerful engines. Something has happened to it which makes active and effective the power that is latent in it.

So it is with ideals. Ideals are thoughts. So long as they exist merely as thoughts, the power latent in them remains ineffective, however great the enthusiasm, and however strong the conviction with which the thought is held. Their power only becomes effective when they are taken up into some refined human personality.   [Childhood, p. 100]

Grow into Your Ideals

The knowledge of life which we grownups have to pass on to the younger generation will not be expressed thus: "Reality will soon give way before your ideals," but "Grow into your ideals, so that life can never rob you of them." If all of us could become what we were at fourteen, what a different place the world would be!   [Childhood, p. 102]

The Secret of Success

The great secret of success is to go through life as a man who never gets used up. That is possible for him who never argues and strives with men and facts, but in all experiences retires upon himself, and looks for the ultimate cause of things in himself.   [Childhood, p. 101]

Ethical Enthusiasm

The Gospel of Jesus knows nothing of a cold superiority with which to look upon things, but creates enthusiasm for activity within God's will of love. In its very essence it aims at being the supreme ethical enthusiasm.   [Christianity, p. 40]

Human Values

Man today is in danger not only through his lack of freedom, of the power of mental concentration, and of the opportunity for all-round development: he is in danger of losing his humanity. . . .

As a matter of fact, the most utterly inhuman thoughts have been current among us for two generations past in all the ugly clearness of language and with the authority of logical principles. There has been created a social mentality which discourages humanity in individuals. The courtesy produced by natural feeling disappears, and in its place comes a behavior which shows entire indifference, even though it is decked out more or less thoroughly in a code of manners. The stand-offishness and want of sympathy which are shown so clearly in every way to strangers are no longer felt as being really rudeness, but pass for the behavior of the man of the world. Our society has also ceased to allow to all men, as such, a human value and a human dignity; many sections of the human race have become merely raw material and property in human form. We have talked for decades with ever increasing light-mindedness about war and conquest, as if these were merely operations on a chessboard; how was this possible save as the result of a tone of mind which no longer pictured to itself the fate of individuals, but thought of them only as figures or objects belonging to the material world? When the War broke out the inhumanity within us had a free course. And what an amount of insulting stuff, some decently veiled, some openly coarse, about the colored races, has made its appearance during the last decades, and passed for truth and reason, in our colonial literature and our parliaments, and so become an element in general public opinion!   [Decay, pp. 23 ff.]

The Duty of Humanity

In the education and the school books of today the duty of humanity is relegated to an obscure corner, as though it were no longer true that it is the first thing necessary in the training of personality, and as if it were not a matter of great importance to maintain it as a strong influence in our human race against the influence of outer circumstances. It has not been so always. There was a time when it was a ruling influence not only in schools, but in literature, even down to the book of adventures. Defoe's hero, Robinson Crusoe, is continually reflecting on the subject of humane conduct, and he feels himself so responsible for loyalty to this duty that when defending himself he is continually thinking how he can sacrifice the smallest number of human lives; he is so faithful, indeed, to this duty of humanity, that the story of his adventures acquires thereby quite a peculiar character. Is there among works of this kind today a single one in which we shall find anything like it?   [Decay, pp. 26 f.]

Thought and Discipline

Our whole spiritual life nowadays has its course within organizations. From childhood up the man of today has his mind so full of the thought of discipline that he loses the sense of his own individuality and can only see himself as thinking in the spirit of some group or other of his fellows. A thorough discussion between one idea and another or between one man and another, such as constituted the greatness of the eighteenth century, is never met with now. But at that time fear of public opinion was a thing unknown. All ideas had then to justify themselves to the individual reason. Today it is the rule—and no one questions it—always to take into account the views which prevail in organized society. The individual starts by taking it for granted that both for himself and his neighbors there are certain views already established which they cannot hope to alter, views which are determined by nationality, creed, political party, social position, and other elements in one's surroundings. These views are protected by a kind of taboo, and are not only kept sacred from criticism, but are not a legitimate subject of conversation. This kind of intercourse, in which we mutually abjure our natural quality as thinking beings, is euphemistically described as respect for other people's convictions, as if there could be any convictions at all where there is no thought.   [Decay, pp. 28 f.]

The Individual and the Masses

The modern man is lost in the mass in a way which is without precedent in history, and this is perhaps the most characteristic trait in him. His diminished concern about his own nature makes him as it were susceptible, to an extent that is almost pathological, to the views which society and its organs of expression have put, ready made, into circulation. Since, over and above this, society, with its well-constructed organization, has become a power of as yet unknown strength in the spiritual life, man's want of independence in the face of it has become so serious that he is almost ceasing to claim a spiritual existence of his own. He is like a rubber ball which has lost its elasticity, and preserves indefinitely every impression that is made upon it. He is under the thumb of the mass, and he draws from it the opinions on which he lives, whether the question at issue is national or political or one of his own belief or unbelief.   [Decay, pp. 29 f.]

Man Is Always Man

All that thought in which a man embraces, not simply the people of a single age, but humanity itself, composed of individual human beings . . . has something superior to every age in it. Society is something temporal and ephemeral; man, however, is always man.   [Gedenkrede, p. 43]

Strive for True Humanity

Goethe's message to the men of today is the same as to the men of his time and to the men of all times: "Strive for true humanity! Become a man who is true to his inner nature, a man whose deed is in tune with his character."   [Gedenkrede, p. 43]

Remain Men

To the individual Goethe says: Do not abandon the ideal of personality, even when it runs counter to developing circumstances. Do not give it up for lost even when it seems no longer tenable in the presence of opportunistic theories which would make the spiritual conform only to the material. Remain men in possession of your own souls! Do not become human things which have given entrance to a soul which conforms to the will of the masses and beats in time with it.   [Gedenkrede, pp. 48 f.]

Human Personality May Endure

Not everything in history is ordained to be overthrown in the process of constant change, as it seems to superficial observers; on the contrary ideals that carry within themselves enduring worth will adjust themselves to changing circumstances and grow stronger and deeper in the midst of them. Such an ideal is that of human personality. If it is given up, then the human spirit will be destroyed, which will mean the end of civilization, and even of humanity. [Gedenkrede, p. 49]

The Ethics of Materialism

The ethics of materialism is unnecessary. Society has no need that the individual should serve it. Society does not need his morality; it can force upon him the sociology which it holds to be best. Herbert Spencer was not only a great thinker but a great prophet. He expressed anxiety lest the state should by violence force the individual to submit to it. He was right. The ethics of materialism has not triumphed, for in our days we have experienced the state destroying the individual in order to make the individual its servant. Therefore, the ethics of materialism is no religion.   [Religion, p. 1519]

The Demoralization of the Modern Man

Not only in the intellectual sphere, but in the moral also, the relation between the individual and the community has been upset. With the surrender of his own personal opinion the modern man surrenders also his personal moral judgment. In order that he may find good what the mass declares to be such, whether in word or deed, and may condemn what it declares to be bad, he suppresses the scruples which stir in him. He does not allow them to find utterance either with others or with himself. There are no stumbling-blocks which his feeling of unity with the herd does not enable him to surmount, and thus he loses his judgment in that of the mass, and his own morality in theirs.

Above all he is thus made capable of excusing everything that is meaningless, cruel, unjust, or bad in the behavior of his nation. Unconsciously to themselves, the majority of the members of our barbarian civilized states give less and less time to reflection as moral personalities, so that they may not be continually coming into inner conflict with their fellows as a body, and continually having to get over things which they feel to be wrong.

Public opinion helps them by popularizing the idea that the actions of the community are not to be judged so much by the standards of morality as by those of expediency. But they suffer injury to their souls. If we find among men of today only too few whose human and moral sensibility is still undamaged, the chief reason is that the majority have offered up their personal morality on the altar of their country, instead of remaining at variance with the mass and acting as a force which impels the latter along the road to perfection.   [Decay, pp. 32 f.]

A Time of Darkness

The man of today pursues his dark journey in a time of darkness, as one who has no freedom, no mental collectedness, no all-round development, as one who loses himself in an atmosphere of inhumanity, who surrenders his spiritual independence and his moral judgment to the organized society in which he lives, and who finds himself in every direction up against hindrances to the temper of true civilization. Of the dangerous position in which he is placed philosophy has no understanding, and therefore makes no attempt to help him. She does not even urge him to reflection on what is happening to himself.

The terrible truth that with the progress of history and the economic development of the world it is becoming not easier, but harder, to develop true civilization, has never found utterance.   [Decay, p. 34]

Mutual Knowledge

After all, is there not much more mystery in the relations of man to man than we generally recognize? None of us can truly assert that he really knows someone else, even if he has lived with him for years. Of that which constitutes

our inner life we can impart even to those most intimate
with us only fragments; the whole of it we cannot give, nor
would they be able to comprehend it. We wander through
life together in a semi-darkness in which none of us can
distinguish exactly the features of his neighbor; only from
time to time, through some experience that we have of our
companion, or through some remark that he passes he stands
for a moment close to us, as though illumined by a flash of
lightning. Then we see him as he really is. After that we
again walk on together in the darkness, perhaps for a long
time, and try in vain to make out our fellow traveler's features.   [Childhood, pp. 91 f.]

We Are a Secret to Each Other

To this fact, that we are each a secret to the other, we
have to reconcile ourselves. To know one another cannot
mean to know everything about each other; it means to
feel mutual affection and confidence, and to believe in
one another. A man must not try to force his way into the
personality of another. To analyze others—unless it be
to help back to a sound mind someone who is in spiritual
or intellectual confusion—is a rude commencement, for
there is a modesty of the soul which we must recognize,
just as we do that of the body. The soul, too, has its clothing
of which we must not deprive it, and no one has a right
to say to another: "Because we belong to each other as we
do, I have a right to know all your thoughts." Not even
a mother may treat her child in that way. All demands of
this sort are foolish and unwholesome. In this matter giving is the only valuable process; it is only giving that stimu-
lates. Impart as much as you can of your spiritual being
to those who are on the road with you, and accept as something precious what comes back to you from them.
[Childhood, p. 92]

Have Light in Yourself

No one should compel himself to show to others more of his inner life than he feels it natural to show. We can do no more than let others judge for themselves what we inwardly and really are, and do the same ourselves with them. The one essential thing is that we strive to have light in ourselves. Our strivings will be recognized by others, and when people have light in themselves, it will shine out from them. Then we get to know each other as we walk together in the darkness, without needing to pass our hands over each other's faces, or to intrude into each other's hearts.   [Childhood, pp. 93 f.]

Reserve

It was perhaps a result of my inherited reserve that from my youth up reverence for the personality of others was to me something natural and a matter of course. Since then I have become more and more confirmed in this view through seeing how much sorrow, pain, and mutual estrangement come from people claiming the right to read the souls of others, as they might a book that belonged to them, and from wishing to know and understand where they ought to believe. We must all beware of reproaching those we love with want of confidence in us if they are not always ready to let us look into all the corners of their heart. We might almost say that the better we get to know each other, the more mystery we see in each other. Only those who respect the personality of others can be of real use to them.   [Childhood, p. 93]

Man Belongs to Man

We must take care to be tactful, and not mix ourselves up uninvited in other people's business. On the other hand we must not forget the danger lurking in the reserve which our practical daily life forces on us. We cannot possibly let ourselves get frozen into regarding everyone we do not know as an absolute stranger. No man is ever completely and permanently a stranger to his fellow man. Man belongs to man. Man has claims on man. Circumstances great or small may arise which make impossible the aloofness which we have to practice in daily life, and bring us into active relations with each other, as men to men. The law of reserve is condemned to be broken down by the claims of the heart, and thus we all get into a position where we must step outside our aloofness, and to one of our fellow men become ourselves a man.   [Childhood, pp. 95 f.]

Mastering Violence

As one who tries to remain youthful in his thinking and feeling, I have struggled against facts and experience on behalf of belief in the good and the true. At the present time when violence, clothed in life, dominates the world more cruelly than it ever has before, I still remain convinced that truth, love, peaceableness, meekness, and kindness are the violence which can master all other violence. The world will be theirs as soon as ever a sufficient number of men with purity of heart, with strength, and with perseverance, think and live out the thoughts of love and truth, of meekness and peaceableness.   [Childhood, pp. 102 f.]

The Strength of Kindness

All ordinary violence produces its own limitations, for it calls forth an answering violence which sooner or later becomes its equal or its superior. But kindness works simply and perseveringly; it produces no strained relations which prejudice its working; strained relations which already exist it relaxes. Mistrust and misunderstanding it puts to flight, and it strengthens itself by calling forth answering kindness. Hence it is the furthest-reaching and the most effective of all forces.

All the kindness which a man puts out into the world works on the heart and the thoughts of mankind, but we are so foolishly indifferent that we are never in earnest in the matter of kindness. We want to topple a great load over, and yet will not avail ourselves of a lever which would multiply our power a hundredfold.   [Childhood, p. 103]

Passive Resistance

Passive resistance is a non-violent use of force. The idea is that by circumstances brought about without violence pressure is brought to bear on the opponent and he is forced to yield. Being an attack that is more difficult to parry than an active attack, passive resistance may be the more successful method. But there is also a danger that this concealed application of force may cause more bitterness than an open use of violence. In any case the difference between passive and active resistance is only quite relative.   [Indian, pp. 231 f.]

This Is a Harzreise

At the end of my student days I reread, almost by chance, the account of his [Goethe's] Harzreise [trip into the Harz Mountains] in the winter of 1777, and it made a wonderful impression on me that this man, whom we regarded as an Olympian, set out amid November rain and mist to visit a minister's son who was in great spiritual difficulties, to give him suitable help. A second time there was revealed to me behind the Olympian the deep but homely man. I was learning to love Goethe. And so whenever it

happened in my own life that I had to take upon me some
work or other in order to do for some fellow man the
human service that he needed, I would say to myself, "This
is a *Harzreise* for you."   [Goethe, pp. 685 f.]

The Dignity of Work

I came on the real Goethe when it struck me in connection
with his activities that he could not think of any intellectual
employment without practical work side by side with it,
and that the two were not held together by their character and object being similar, but were quite distinct and
only united through his personality. It gripped me deeply
that for this giant among the intellectuals there was no work
which he held to be beneath his dignity, no practical employment of which he ever said that others on account
of their natural gifts and of their profession could do it
better than he, and that he was always ready to prove
the unity of his personality by the union of practical work
with intellectual activity.   [Goethe, p. 686]

Work and Intellect

I was already a minister when I first had to arrange my daily
work, and when I sighed over the fact that through the
much walking and the manifold duties entailed by my new
office—which I had persisted in taking upon me to satisfy
an inward need—I lost time which would have been available for intellectual labor, I comforted myself with Goethe,
who, as we know, with mighty plans of intellectual activity
in his head, would sit studying accounts and trying to set
in order the finances of a small principality, examining
plans so that streets and bridges should be constructed in the
most practical way, and exerting himself year in, year out,
to get disused mines at work again. And so this union of

homely employment with intellectual activity comforted
me concerning my own existence.   [Goethe, p. 686]

Quixotic Activity

When the life-course I had chosen led me to the point
where I was compelled to embrace an activity which lay
far from the natural endowment in which I had hitherto
proved myself—far, too, from the employment for which I
had prepared myself—then Goethe was the comforter who
provided the words which helped me through. When
other people, and even those who knew me best, found
fault with my decision and tormented me with reproaches
for wanting to study medicine, a subject for which (they
said) I was not suited, declaring it to be a quixotic adven-
ture, then I was able to reflect that this quixotic proceeding would perhaps not have been for him, the great man,
so entirely quixotic, seeing that he finally allows his Wilhelm Meister, little prepared as he seemed to be for it, to
become a surgeon in order that he may be able to serve.
And at this point it struck me what a meaning it has for
us all that Goethe in his search for the final destiny of man
allows those characters in which he has depicted himself,
viz. Faust and Wilhelm Meister, to end their days in a quite
insignificant activity that they may thereby become men
in the fullest sense in which, according to his ideals, they
can become so.   [Goethe, pp. 686 f.]

On through Reality

For my medical course I had to busy myself with natural science, though as a learner, not, like him [Goethe], as an in-
vestigator. And how far removed, alas! lay natural science
from what I hoped to complete in the way of intellectual
production before I became immersed in practical work!

But I was able to reflect that Goethe too had left intellectual work to return to the natural sciences. It had almost excited me that, at a time when he ought to have been bringing to its final shape so much that was stirring within him, he lost himself in the natural sciences. And now I myself, who had hitherto been engaged only in intellectual work, was compelled to occupy myself with them. It deepened my nature, and it became clear to me why Goethe devoted himself to them and would not give them up. It was because it means for everyone who produces intellectually, enlightenment and enormous gain, if he who has hitherto created facts now has to face facts, which are something, not because one has imagined them, but because they exist. Every kind of thinking is helped, if at any particular moment it can no longer occupy itself with what is imagined, but has to find its way through reality. And when I found myself under this "On through reality!" compulsion, I could look back at the man who had done it all before us.   [Goethe, p. 687]

The Meaning of Toil

When my laborious years of study had ended, and I left them behind as a qualified doctor, I met Goethe, seeming even to converse with him in the primeval forest. I had always supposed that I went out there as a doctor, and in the first years, whenever there was building or similar work to be done, I took care to put it on the shoulders of those who seemed to me to be specially adapted for it, or who had been engaged for it. But I had to acknowledge that this would not do. Either they did not turn up or they were so ill-suited for the work that no progress was made. So I accommodated myself to the work, far removed though it was from my duties as a doctor. But the worst came last. When at the end of 1925, owing to a severe famine which endangered the existence of my hospital, I was compelled to get a plantation made for it, so that during any famine in the future we might be able to keep our heads above water to some extent through our own resources, I was obliged to superintend the clearing of the forest myself. The very miscellaneous body of workers which the chance of the moment produced from among the willing ones of the friends of our patients would bow to no authority but that of "the old Doctor," as I was called. So I stood for weeks and months in the forest, worrying over refractory laborers, in order to wrest from it land that would produce food for us. Whenever I got reduced to despair I thought how Goethe had devised for the final activities of his Faust the task of winning from the sea, land on which men could live and feed themselves. And thus Goethe stood at my side in the swampy forest as my smiling comforter, and the man who really understood.   [Goethe, pp. 687 f.]

Justice

There is one point which I should like to mention of Goethe's influence on me, and it is this: that I found him everywhere haunted by anxiety about justice. When about the end of the last century the theory began to prevail that whatever is to be realized must be realized without regard to right, without regard to the fate of those who are hard hit by the change, and I myself did not know how these theories should be met, it was to me a real experience to find everywhere in Goethe the longing to avoid realizing any design at the cost of right. And I have again and again with real emotion turned over the final pages of *Faust* (which both in Europe and in Africa I always reread at Easter) where Goethe represents as the last experience of Faust, and that in which he is for the last time guilty of wrongdoing, his attempt to remove the hut which disturbs him in his possession—by a slight and well-intentioned act of violence

—being, as he himself says, tired of righteousness. But in the execution of it this well-intentioned act of violence becomes a cruel act of violence in which more than one person loses his life, and the hut goes up in flames. That Goethe at the conclusion of his *Faust* should insert this episode which holds up the action of the poem gives us a deep insight into the way in which there worked within him anxiety about justice, and the strong desire to realize any plan that has to be carried out without causing any kind of injury.   [Goethe, p. 688]

Sharing the Life of the Age

My final lasting contact with Goethe arose out of my recognition of the living and vigorous way in which he shared the life of his age in its thought and in its activity. Its billows were ever surging within him. That is what impresses one, not only in the young and in the fully ripe Goethe, but in the aged Goethe also. When the mail coach was still crawling along the high road, and we should have thought that the industrial age could be announcing its arrival merely by uncertain shadows cast in advance, it was for him already there. He was already concerning himself with the problem it put before the world, viz. that the machine was now taking the place of the man. If in his *Wilhelm Meister* he is no longer master of his material, it is not because the old man no longer has the power to shape it which he formerly had at his command, but because the material had grown till it could be neither measured nor molded; it was because the old man was putting into it the whole of his experience and of his anxiety about the future; it was because this old man was so concerned about being among the men of his age as one who understands the new age and has grown to be a part of it. That is what impresses one so deeply in the aging Goethe.   [Goethe, pp. 688 f.]

The Struggle with Conditions, with Men, with Ourselves

A spirit like Goethe's lays upon us three obligations. We have to wrestle with conditions so as to secure that men who are imprisoned in work and are being worn out by it may nevertheless preserve the possibility of a spiritual existence. We have to wrestle with men so that in spite of being continually drawn aside to the external things which are provided so abundantly for our age, they may find the road to inwardness and keep in it. We have to wrestle with ourselves and with all and everything around us, so that in a time of confused ideals which ignore all the claims of humanity we may remain faithful to the great humane ideals of the eighteenth century, translating them into the thought of our own age, and attempting to realize them today. That is what we have to do, each of us in his life, each of us in his profession, in the spirit of the great Frankfort child whose birthday we are celebrating today in his birthplace. [The City of Frankfort awarded the Goethe Prize to Schweitzer on Goethe's birthday.] I myself think that this Frankfort child does not move further away from us with the course of time, but comes nearer to us. The further we travel forward the more certainly we recognize Goethe to be the man who, as our own duty is, amid the deep and widely varied experiences of his age, cared for his age and labored for it; the man who would become a man who understood his age and grew to be a part of it. He did this with the abounding talents which were laid in his cradle here by destiny. We have to do it as men who have received only one small pound, but who in our trading with that pound wish to be found faithful. So may it be!   [Goethe, p. 690]

Fondness for the Natives

It seems to me incomprehensible that I am leaving the natives for months. How fond of them one becomes, in spite

of all the trouble they give one! How many beautiful
traits of character we can discover in them, if we refuse
to let the many and varied follies of the child of nature
prevent us from looking for the man in him! How they
disclose to us their real selves, if we have love and patience
enough to understand them!   [Hospital, p. 186]

Superiority of the Negro

A white timber trader, a thoroughly kind but somewhat
irritable man, once said to me, "What a good thing it is
that the Negroes have better characters than we have."
There was a grain of truth in the saying. Every one of us
has at some time been put to shame by the way the natives
have put up with our impetuous rudeness. They quietly
went on with their work and remained as friendly as if
they had never had to endure our probably not unjustified,
but still, and not for the first time, very excessive abuse.
[Notebook, p. 134]

The Intellectual

In the middle of September we get the first rains, and the
cry is to bring all building timber under cover. As we have
in the hospital hardly a man capable of work, I begin, assisted by two loyal helpers, to haul beams and planks about
myself. Suddenly I catch sight of a Negro in a white suit
sitting by a patient whom he has come to visit. "Hullo!
friend," I call out, "won't you lend us a hand?" "I am an
intellectual and don't drag wood about," came the answer.
"You're lucky," I reply. "I too wanted to become an intellectual, but I didn't succeed."   [Hospital, p. 119]

The Negro's Notion of Goodness

There slumbers within him [the Negro] an ethical rationalist. He has a natural responsiveness to the notion of good-

ness and all that is connected with it in religion. Certainly, Rousseau and the illuminati of that age idealized the child of nature, but there was nevertheless truth in their views about him—in their belief, that is, in his possession of high moral and rational capacities. No one must think that he has described the thought-world of the Negro when he has made a full list of all the superstitious ideas which he has taken over, and the traditional legal rules of his tribe. They do not form his whole universe, although he is controlled by them. There lives within him a dim suspicion that a correct view of what is truly good must be attainable as the result of reflection. In proportion as he becomes familiar with the higher moral ideas of the religion of Jesus, he finds utterance for something in himself that has hitherto been dumb, and something that has been tightly bound up finds release. The longer I live among the Ogowe Negroes, the clearer this becomes to me.   [Edge, p. 155]

Coals of Fire

A European in the Samkita district was engaged in a dispute with the inhabitants of a village lower down the river. As he could not induce them to give him the satisfaction he demanded, he determined to bring a charge against them before the district officer at Lambaréné. When he set out on his journey, he had not noticed the approach of a tornado, and was surprised by it just above the village of his opponents. He and his men, clinging to the capsized boat, were being carried past the village. When the people heard their shouts, in spite of the dangerous storm and in spite of the fact that they knew who it was, they hastened to the rescue. They not only brought the men to shore, but saved as much of the boat's cargo as was whirling about on the surface of the river. Although they knew why the white man was on his way down to Lambaréné, they did not

utter a word to remind him that he had been obliged to
have recourse to the help of people against whom he was
about to take legal proceedings.   [Notebook, pp. 134 f.]

Influence

One thing stirs me when I look back at my youthful days,
viz. the fact that so many people gave me something or
were something to me without knowing it. Such people,
with whom I have, perhaps, never exchanged a word, yes,
and others about whom I have merely heard things by re-
port, have had a decisive influence upon me; they entered
into my life and became powers within me. Much that I
should otherwise not have felt so clearly or done so effec-
tively was felt or done as it was, because I stand, as it were,
under the sway of these people. Hence I always think that
we all live, spiritually, by what others have given us in
the significant hours of our life. These significant hours
do not announce themselves as coming, but arrive un-
expected. Nor do they make a great show of themselves;
they pass almost unperceived. Often, indeed, their significance comes home to us first as we look back, just as the
beauty of a piece of music or of a landscape often strikes
us first in our recollection of it. Much that has become
our own in gentleness, modesty, kindness, willingness to
forgive, in veracity, loyalty, resignation under suffering, we
owe to people in whom we have seen or experienced these
virtues at work, sometimes in a great matter, sometimes in a
small. A thought which had become act sprang into us like
a spark, and lighted a new flame within us.   [Childhood,
pp. 89 f.]

Ingratitude

When I look back upon my early days I am stirred by the
thought of the number of people whom I have to thank for

what they gave me or for what they were to me. At the same time I am haunted by an oppressive consciousness of the little gratitude I really showed them while I was young. How many of them have said farewell to life without my having made clear to them what it meant to me to receive from them so much kindness or so much care! Many a time have I, with a feeling of shame, said quietly to myself over a grave the words which my mouth ought to have spoken to the departed, while he was still in the flesh.

For all that, I think I can say with truth that I am not ungrateful, I did occasionally wake up out of that youthful thoughtlessness which accepted as a matter of course all the care and kindness that I experienced from others, and I believe I became sensitive to my duty in this matter just as early as I did to the prevalence of suffering in the world. But down to my twentieth year, and even later still, I did not exert myself sufficiently to express the gratitude which was really in my heart. I valued too low the pleasure felt at receiving real proofs of gratitude. Often, too, shyness prevented me from expressing the gratitude that I really felt.   [Childhood, pp. 87 f.]

The Ten Lepers

I refuse to think that there is as much ingratitude in the world as is commonly maintained: I have never interpreted the parable of the Ten Lepers to mean that only one was grateful. All the ten, surely, were grateful, but nine of them hurried home first, so as to greet their friends and attend to their business as soon as possible, intending to go to Jesus soon afterwards and thank him. But things turned out otherwise; they were kept at home longer than they meant to be, and in the meanwhile Jesus was put to death. One of them, however, had a disposition which made him act at once as his feelings bade him; he sought out the person who had helped him, and refreshed his soul with the assurance of his gratitude.   [Childhood, p. 88]

Unspoken Gratitude

We ought all to make an effort to act on our first thoughts and let our unspoken gratitude find expression. Then there will be more sunshine in the world, and more power to work for what is good. But as concerns ourselves we must all of us take care not to adopt as part of our theory of life all people's bitter sayings about the ingratitude of the world. A great deal of water is flowing underground which never comes up as a spring. In that thought we may find comfort. But we ourselves must try to be the water which does find its way up; we must become a spring at which men can quench their thirst for gratitude.   [Childhood, pp. 88 f.]

The Spark from Outside

I do not believe that we can put into anyone ideas which are not in him already. As a rule there are in everyone all sorts of good ideas, ready like tinder. But much of this tinder catches fire, or catches it successfully, only when it meets some flame or spark from outside, i.e., from some other person. Often, too, our own light goes out, and is rekindled by some experience we go through with a fellow-man. Thus we have each of us cause to think with deep gratitude of those who have lighted the flames within us. If we had before us those who have thus been a blessing to us, and could tell them how it came about, they would be amazed to learn what passed over from their life into ours.   [Childhood, pp. 90 f.]

The Right to Happiness

The thought that I had been granted such a specially
happy youth was ever in my mind; I felt it even as something oppressive, and ever more clearly there presented itself to me the question whether this happiness was a thing
that I might accept as a matter of course. Here, then, was
the second great experience of my life, viz. this question
about the right to happiness. As an experience it joined itself
to that other one which had accompanied me from my
childhood up; I mean my deep sympathy with the pain
which prevails in the world around us. These two experiences slowly melted into one another, and thence came
definiteness to my interpretation of life as a whole, and a
decision as to the future of my own life in particular.

It became steadily clearer to me that I had not the inward right to take as a matter of course my happy youth,
my good health, and my power of work. Out of the depths
of my feeling of happiness there grew up gradually within
me an understanding of the saying of Jesus that we must
not treat our lives as being for ourselves alone. Whoever
is spared personal pain must feel himself called to help in
diminishing the pain of others. We must all carry our
share of the misery which lies upon the world. Darkly and
confusedly this thought worked in me, and sometimes it left
me, so that I breathed freely and fancied once more that I
was to become completely the lord of my own life. But the
little cloud had risen above the horizon. I could, indeed,
sometimes look away and lose sight of it, but it was growing nevertheless; slowly but unceasingly it grew, and at last
it hid the whole sky.   [Childhood, pp. 81 f.]

"Whosoever Shall Lose His Life"

The plan which I meant now to put into execution had
been in my mind for a long time, having been conceived so

long ago as my student days. It struck me as incomprehensible that I should be allowed to lead such a happy life, while I saw so many people around me wrestling with care and suffering. Even at school I had felt stirred whenever I got a glimpse of the miserable home surroundings of some of my schoolfellows and compared them with the absolutely ideal conditions in which we children of the parsonage of Günsbach [Schweitzer's childhood home in the Münster Valley, Upper Alsace] lived. While at the University and enjoying the happiness of being able to study and even to produce some results in science and art, I could not help thinking continually of others who were denied that happiness by their material circumstances or their health. Then one brilliant summer morning at Günsbach, during the Whitsuntide holidays—it was in 1896—there came to me, as I awoke, the thought that I must not accept this happiness as a matter of course, but must give something in return for it. Proceeding to think the matter out at once with calm deliberation, while the birds were singing outside, I settled with myself before I got up, that I would consider myself justified in living till I was thirty for science and art, in order to devote myself from that time forward to the direct service of humanity. Many a time already had I tried to settle what meaning lay hidden for me in the saying of Jesus, "Whosoever would save his life shall lose it, and whosoever shall lose his life for My sake and the Gospels shall save it." Now the answer was found. In addition to the outward, I now had inward happiness.   [Life, pp. 102 f.]

The Threefold Sacrifice

When I first went to Africa I prepared to make three sacrifices: to abandon the organ, to renounce the academic teaching activities to which I had given my heart, and to lose my financial independence, relying for the rest of my life on the help of friends.

These three sacrifices I had begun to make, and only my intimate friends knew what they cost me.

But now there happened to me, what happened to Abraham when he prepared to sacrifice his son. I, like him, was spared the sacrifice. The piano with pedal attachment, built for the tropics, which the Paris Bach Society had presented to me, and the triumph of my own health over the tropical climate had allowed me to keep up my skill on the organ. During the many quiet hours which I was able to spend with Bach during my four and a half years of loneliness in the jungle I had penetrated deeper into the spirit of his works. I returned to Europe, therefore, not as an artist who had become an amateur, but in full possession of my technique and privileged to find that, as an artist, I was more esteemed than before.

For the renunciation of my teaching activities in Strassburg University I found compensation in opportunities of lecturing in very many others.

And if I did for a time lose my financial independence, I was able now to win it again by means of organ and pen.

That I was let off the threefold sacrifice I had already offered was for me the encouraging experience which in all the difficulties brought upon me, and upon so many others, by the fateful postwar period has buoyed me up, and made me ready for every effort and every renunciation.   [Life, pp. 230 f.]

"Lord, I Am Coming"

One morning in the autumn of 1904 I found on my writing table in the College one of the green-covered magazines in which the Paris Missionary Society reported every month on its activities. . . . That evening, in the very act of

putting it aside that I might go on with my work, I me-
chanically opened this magazine, which had been laid on
my table during my absence. As I did so, my eye caught the
title of an article: "Les besoins de la Mission du Congo"
("The needs of the Congo Mission").

It was by Alfred Boegner, the President of the Paris
Missionary Society, an Alsatian, and contained a complaint
that the Mission had not enough workers to carry on its
work in the Gaboon, the northern province of the Congo
Colony. The writer expressed his hope that his appeal
would bring some of those "on whom the Master's eyes already rested" to a decision to offer themselves for this
urgent work. The conclusion ran: "Men and women who
can reply simply to the Master's call, 'Lord, I am coming,'
those are the people whom the Church needs." The article
finished, I quietly began my work. My search was over.
[Life, pp. 106 f.]

Heroes of Renunciation

Only a person who can find a value in every sort of activity and devote himself to each one with full consciousness of duty, has the inward right to take as his object some
extraordinary activity instead of that which falls naturally
to his lot. Only a person who feels his preference to be a
matter of course, not something out of the ordinary, and
who has no thought of heroism, but just recognizes a duty
undertaken with sober enthusiasm is capable of becoming
a spiritual adventurer such as the world needs. There are
no heroes of action: only heroes of renunciation and suffering. Of such there are plenty. But few of them are known,
and even these not to the crowd, but to the few.

Carlyle's *Heroes and Hero Worship* is not a profound
book. [Life, pp. 110 f.]

The Responsibility of Self-Sacrifice

The idea that men should ever be condemned to or favored by being free from the responsibilities of self-sacrifice as men for men, is foreign to the ethic of reverence for life. It requires that in some way or other and in something or other we should all live as men for men. To those who have no opportunity for human relations in their ordinary work, and who have nothing else to give, it suggests that they should sacrifice some of their own time and leisure even when they have but very little of either. Take up some side line, it says to them, some quite insignificant, perhaps even secret, side line. Open your eyes and look for some man, or some work for the sake of men, which needs a little time, a little friendship, a little sympathy, a little sociability, a little human toil. Perhaps it is a lonely person, or an embittered person, or an invalid, or some unfortunate inefficient, to whom you can be something. It may be an old man or it may be a child. Or some good work is in want of volunteers who will devote a free evening to it or will run on errands for it. Who can reckon up all the ways in which that priceless fund of impulse, man, is capable of exploitation! He is needed in every nook and corner. Therefore search and see if there is not some place where you may invest your humanity. Do not be put off if you find that you have to wait and to experiment. Be sure that you will have disappointments to endure. But do not be satisfied without some side line in which you may give yourself out as a man to men. There is one waiting for you if only you are willing to take it up in the right spirit. . . .

So speaks the true ethic to those who have nothing to give but some time and some human kindness. Well for them if they listen to it and thus remain secure against becoming self-centered and disgruntled men because of missed opportunities for self-sacrifice.   [Ethics, pp. 268 f.]

Spiritual Self-Surrender

Only an infinitesimal part of infinite being can ever be
affected by my personality. All the rest floats past me
utterly indifferent to my existence, like faraway ships to
which I make futile signals. But in giving myself for the
sake of that which comes into my tiny circle of influence,
and which has need of my help, I realize the inner spiritual
self-surrender to eternal being and thus lend meaning and
richness to my own poor existence. The river has rejoined its
ocean.   [Ethics, p. 249]

The Hidden Forces of Goodness

Of all the will for the ideal which exists in mankind only
a small part can be manifested in action. All the rest is
destined to realize itself in unseen effects, which represent,
however, a value exceeding a thousandfold and more, that
of the activity which attracts the notice of the world. Its
relation to the latter is like that of the deep sea to the waves
which stir its surface. The hidden forces of goodness are
embodied in those persons who carry on as a secondary
pursuit the immediate personal service which they cannot
make their lifework. The lot of the many is to have as a
profession, for the earning of their living and the satisfaction of society's claim on them, a more or less soulless
labor in which they can give out little or nothing of their
human qualities, because in that labor they have to be little
better than human machines. Yet no one finds himself in
the position of having no possible opportunity of giving
himself to others as a human being. The problem produced
by the fact of labor being today so thoroughly organized,
specialized, and mechanized depends only in part for its
solution of society's not merely removing the conditions
thus produced, but doing its very best to guard the rights

of human personality. What is even more important is that sufferers shall not simply bow to their fate, but shall try with all their energy to assert their human personality amid their unfavorable conditions by spiritual activity. Anyone can rescue his human life, in spite of his professional life, who seizes every opportunity of being a man by means of personal action, however unpretending, for the good of fellow men who need the help of a fellow man. Such a man enlists in the service of the spiritual and good. No fate can prevent a man from giving to others this direct human service side by side with his lifework. If so much of such service remains unrealized, it is because the opportunities are missed.   [Life, pp. 112 f.]

Underground Idealism

That everyone shall exert himself in that state of life in which he is placed, to practise true humanity towards his fellow men, on that depends the future of mankind. Enormous values come to nothing every moment through the missing of opportunities, but the values which do get turned into will and deed mean wealth which must not be undervalued. Our humanity is by no means so materialistic as foolish talk is continually asserting it to be. Judging by what I have learned about men and women, I am convinced that there is far more in them of idealist will power than ever comes to the surface of the world. Just as the water of the streams we see is small in amount, compared to that which flows underground, so the idealism which becomes visible is small in amount, compared with what men and women bear locked in their hearts, unreleased or scarcely released. To unbind what is bound, to bring the underground waters to the surface: mankind is waiting and longing for such as can do that.   [Life, pp. 113 f.]

Tolerance

One thing more I have taken with me into life from this little church, that was Protestant and Catholic at the same time, I mean religious tolerance. These Catholico-Protestant churches, which had their origin in the irresponsible edict of a ruler, are for me something more than a historical phenomenon. They are a symbol to show that the differences which separate churches today are things which are destined ultimately to disappear. When I was still merely a child, I felt it to be something beautiful that in our village Catholics and Protestants worshipped in the same building, and my heart fills with joy today whenever I set foot inside it. I should like all the churches in Alsace which are still used by both confessions to remain so, as a prophecy of, and an exhortation to, a future of religious unity, upon which we must ever keep our thoughts fixed if we are really and truly Christians.   [Childhood, pp. 66 f.]

Forgiveness

Why do I forgive my fellow man? The current ethic says that it is because I sympathize with him. It presents men as impossibly good when they forgive, and allows them to practise a kind of forgiveness which is really humiliating to the person forgiven. Thus it turns forgiveness into a sort of sweetened triumph of self-sacrifice.

The ethic of reverence for life clears away these obscure and misty notions. All forbearance and forgiveness is for it an act to which it is compelled by sincerity towards itself. I am obliged to exercise unlimited forgiveness because, if I did not forgive, I should be untrue to myself, in that I should thus act as if I were not guilty in the same way as the other has been guilty with regard to me. I must forgive the lies directed against myself, because my own life has been so many times blotted by lies; I must forgive the lovelessness, the hatred, the slander, the fraud, the arrogance which I encounter, since I myself have so often lacked love, hated, slandered, defrauded, and been arrogant. I must forgive without noise or fuss. In general I do not forgive, I do not even get as far as being merely just. [Ethics, p. 260]

Dealing with Disappointment

The most valuable knowledge we can have is how to deal with disappointments. All acts and facts are a product of spiritual power, the successful ones of power which is strong enough; the unsuccessful ones of power which is too weak. Does my behavior in respect of love effect nothing? That is because there is not enough love in me. Am I powerless against the untruthfulness and the lies which have their being all around me? The reason is that I myself am not truthful enough. Have I to watch dislike and ill will carrying on their sad game? That means that I myself have not yet completely laid aside small-mindedness and envy. Is my love of peace misunderstood and scorned? That means that I am not yet sufficiently peace-loving. [Childhood, p. 101]

Work Done in Faith

No one who is always striving to refine his character can ever be robbed of his idealism, for he experiences in himself the power of the ideas of the good and the true. When he sees far too little of the external results at which he is aiming, he knows nevertheless that he is producing as much as his character allows; it is only that success has not yet begun, or that it is as yet hidden from him. Where there is power, there, some result or other is produced. No ray of sunlight is ever lost, but the green which it wakes into existence needs time to sprout, and it is not always granted to the sower to live to see the harvest. All work that is worth anything is done in faith.   [Childhood, pp. 101 f.]

Free Personal Activity

Those who are so favored as to be able to embark on a course of free personal activity must accept this good fortune in a spirit of humility. They must often think of those who, though willing and capable, were never in a position to do the same. And as a rule they must temper their own strong determination with humility. They are almost always destined to have to seek and wait till they find a road open for the activity they long for. Happy are those to whom the years of work are allotted in richer measure than those of seeking and waiting! Happy those who in the end are able to give themselves really and completely!   [Life, pp. 111 f.]

Love and Knowledge

Anyone who has recognized that the idea of love is the spiritual beam of light which reaches us from the Infinite, ceases to demand from religion that it shall offer him complete knowledge of the suprasensible. He ponders, indeed, on the great questions: what the meaning is of the evil in the world; how in God, the great First Cause, the will-to-create and the will-to-love are one; in what relation the spiritual and the material life stand to one another, and in what way our existence is transitory and yet eternal. But he is able to leave these questions on one side, however painful it may be to give up all hope of answers to them. In the knowledge of spiritual existence in God through love he possesses the one thing needful.

"Love never faileth: but . . . whether there be knowledge it shall be done away," says St. Paul.   [Life, p. 277]

The Proof of the Spirit Is Love

While for other believers ecstatic discourses and convulsive raptures mean the surest proof of the possession of the Spirit, St. Paul turns the doctrine of the Spirit into ethical channels. According to him the Spirit which believers possess is the Spirit of Jesus, in which they have become participators because of the mysterious fellowship with Him which they enjoy. This Spirit of Jesus is the heavenly life-force which is preparing them for existence in the post-resurrection condition, just as it effected the resurrection itself in Him. At the same time it is the power which compels them, through their being different from the world, to approve themselves as men who have ceased to belong to this world. The highest proof of the Spirit is love. Love is the eternal thing which men can already on earth possess as it really is.   [Life, p. 249]

The Strength That Conquers

Anyone who proposes to do good must not expect people to roll stones out of his way, but must accept his lot calmly if they even roll a few more upon it. A strength which becomes clearer and stronger through its experience of such obstacles is the only strength that can conquer them. Resistance is only a waste of strength.   [Life, p. 112]

The Mystery of Power

Not one of us knows what effect his life produces, and what he gives to others; that is hidden from us and must remain so, though we are often allowed to see some little fraction of it, so that we may not lose courage. The way in which power works is a mystery.   [Childhood, p. 91]

THE TRANSFORMATION OF SOCIETY

The Indestructible Rights of Man

It is our task to unearth and proclaim once more the indestructible rights of man, rights which afford the individual the utmost possible freedom for his individuality in his own human group; human rights which guarantee protection to his existence and his personal dignity against every alien power to which he may become subject. [Ethics, p. xx]

Stable and Unstable Societies

The idea of the rights of man was formed and developed in the eighteenth century, when society was an organized and stable thing. Whatever the fundamental rights of men are, they can only be fully secured in a stable and well-ordered society. In a disordered society the very well-being of man himself often demands that his fundamental rights should be abridged.   [Races, p. 65]

The Rights of Man

The fundamental rights of man are, first, the right to habitation; secondly, the right to move freely; thirdly, the right to the soil and subsoil, and to the use of it; fourthly, the right to freedom of labor and of exchange; fifthly, the right to justice; sixthly, the right to live within a natural. na-

tional organization; and, seventhly, the right to education.
[Races, p. 65]

The Right to Habitation

Man has the right to live where his life has been developed,
and not to be displaced. This is a burning point in primitive
society. Yet in colonization the right is constantly menaced;
often not by ill well in any degree, but by the sheer force
of facts. For instance, a large, modern white city grows up
round a small, primitive village, or the creation and development of an arterial road on which the very lives of
the inhabitants depends, involves living by that road. The
future development of the good of the people may neces-
sitate the movement of villages, yet, if it is done without
long foresight, careful planning and adequate warning, with
provision for the creation of new plantations, and if any
violence enters into it, a fatal impression will be created
in the mind of the native that he is delivered up to the
working of an arbitrary will. Any movement that is ordered
must always be on a rational basis and for the future good.
[Races, p. 66]

The Right to Circulate Freely

The right of emigration and immigration is today surrounded by every kind of difficulty. For instance, vast
cocoa plantations exercise a very strong economic pull for
labor on the plantations of the neighboring territories. To
allow that economic pull to have free play would rob
neighboring colonies of the essential labor. Therefore there
is restriction on movement. In the collection of taxes again,
there is a strong temptation to the natives to disappear into
the forest and move to another area to escape taxes. So the
administration insists that he stay in his own canton. From

the state's point of view and from that of the development of the country this is reasonable; but the right to circulate is limited.   [Races, p. 66]

The Right to the Soil

There is a right to the natural riches of the soil and subsoil; and to dispose of it as one will. But here, again, two very strong factors enter in. First, the development of the value of the whole land by enterprises from without. Few things are more difficult to foresee on a long view than what lands and subsoils should remain in the hand of the native, and how much should be placed in the hands of enterprises that will develop their values.

Again, on the other hand, a chief is offered money to sell his land. The money is put into his hands. He spends it on clothes, and trinkets, and tools and other things for himself and his wives. The land is gone and the money is gone; and his descendants find themselves pariahs—landless laborers. It is, therefore, in the interests of the people themselves to restrict the right of the chief to dispose of his land. [Races, pp. 66 f.]

The Right to Free Work

No right is more fundamental or more essential than that of the free disposal by a man of his labor. In the present condition of things, however, we are confronted from time to time by circumstances and conditions that seem to make it essential for the state to demand labor. The state has the right to impose taxes to be collected in money or in kind. Has it also the right to collect service in actual labor? . . . A famine occurs in a certain area to which food must be transported if life is to be saved. The men will not carry that food for simple payment. (Payment, of course, is always made whether labor is forced or not.) Is it not then essential actually to command labor?   [Races, p. 67]

The Right to Justice

Primitive tribal justice has the great quality that it is justice for everybody face to face with his adversary, administered locally and swiftly by the chief. Attempts to administer justice by Europeans, with a judge either infrequently there or at a long distance, not knowing the language or the people individually, and unable to penetrate behind the lives of the witnesses, is often long, slow, difficult and inefficient. Furthermore, the natives' own law (often more severe than ours) has been developed to meet their own conditions. Therefore in order to secure the great need for a settlement on the spot at a man's own door, we must have traveling judges or administrators who will move from place to place giving justice on the spot, in cooperation with the authority of the chiefs. . . . To do away with that authority is to destroy your one intermediary between the administration and the multitude. In Europe the intermediary between government and the people is the office. That process is impossible with primitive peoples. It is always the man that matters. We have to do not with peoples but with tribes; not with organized governments, but with chiefs.   [Races, pp. 68 f.]

The Right to Natural Social Organization

The only way to defend other rights is to develop a new stable social organization. To go back to the very beginning of what I have here said—the rights of man are a direct function of the normal organization of society. We have, therefore, to create a social organization and economic conditions in which the natives can flourish face to face with

Western commerce. To do this, we need a stable population, possessing houses, fields, orchards, workshops, and the requisite capacity to create and use them. This can only be achieved by the exercise of the right to education.   [Races, p. 69]

The Right to Education

The education so far undertaken has been incomplete—in fact, usually the only educational work yet done has been that contributed by the missionaries. If, for instance, I want (or any man wants) an artisan—someone who can really work skillfully with his hands, a carpenter, for instance—I cannot find any save those educated by the missionary societies. When the modern state talks about doing an educational work among the natives, I say to it: "Do not make phrases; show me your work. How many educators have you in fact exported to your colony?"   [Races, pp. 69 f.]

Overwork

An excessive amount of labor is the rule today in every circle of society, with the result that the laborer's spiritual element cannot possibly thrive. This overwork hits him indirectly even in his childhood, for his parents, caught in the inexorable toils of work, cannot devote themselves to his upbringing as they should. Thus his development is robbed of something which can never be made good, and later in life, when he himself is the slave of over-long hours, he feels more and more the need of external distractions. To spend the time left to him for leisure in self-cultivation, or in serious intercourse with his fellows or with books, requires a mental collectedness and a self-control which he finds very difficult. Complete idleness, forgetfulness, and diversion from his usual activities are a physical necessity. He does not

want to think, and seeks not self-improvement, but entertainment, that kind of entertainment, moreover, which
makes least demand upon his spiritual faculties. [Decay,
pp. 18 f.]

Education and the Essentials of Life

The work of education among a primitive people must be a
blend of the intellectual and the manual adapted to the needs
of citizenship in a primitive society. We must send out to
such areas not only ordinary teachers, but artisan educators;
in fact, a central problem of education there is how to make
a craft loved and practised among primitive peoples. The
native is in danger of cutting out the stage between primitive
life and professional. That is, he tends to eliminate the stages
of agriculture and handicraft. He has a certain antagonism
to the use of tools, and a desire to sit in an office with a
cigarette in his mouth and a pen in his hand. I am constantly
hearing the phrase "I want to be a writer." At my hospital
recently I was helping to carry things to the garden, partly
in order to create this impression of the dignity of labor. I
saw a native in white clothes standing by the fence, and
asked him to join in and help. His reply was—"No, I am an
intellectual; a brain-worker." I went to a store, run by a
native for natives, and could not get a single tool that I
wanted, but found masses of silk stockings. We cannot,
therefore, build a proper social organization until the native
himself is skilled in making the essentials of his life—that is,
growing his food and building his habitation. All independence, and therefore all capacity to face economic stress
and to secure justice, is rooted there. [Races, p. 70]

Independence

The independence of primitive or semi-primitive peoples is
lost at the moment when the first white man's boat arrives

with powder or rum, salt or fabrics. The social, economic and political situation at that moment begins to be turned upside down. The chiefs begin to sell their subjects for goods. From that point the political work of a state in colonizing is to correct, by its action, the evils developed through unrestrained economic advance.   [Races, p. 65]

Colonization and Its Responsibilities

Independence is not lost by primitive peoples from the moment when a Protectorate or other form of government is proclaimed; but has already been lost in the commercial advance of which the political colonization must be a corrective. The question for us, therefore, is not—"Have we a right there?"—the question is simply one of alternatives. Are we, on the one hand, the masters of these folk and lands, simply as raw material for our industries; or are we, on the other hand, responsible for developing a new social order, so as to create the possibility among those peoples of resisting the evils, and of developing themselves a new political organization? We have, I hold, the right to colonize if we have the moral authority to exercise this influence.   [Races, p. 65]

Colonization and Civilization

The tragic fact is that the interests of colonization and those of civilization do not always run parallel, but are often in direct opposition to each other. The best thing for primitive peoples would be that, in such seclusion from world trade as is possible, and under an intelligent administration, they should rise by slow development from being nomads and semi-nomads to be agriculturists and artisans, permanently settled on the soil. That, however, is rendered impossible by

the fact that these peoples themselves will not let themselves
be withheld from the chance of earning money by selling
goods to world trade, just as on the other hand world trade
will not abstain from purchasing native products from them
and depositing manufactured goods in exchange. Thus it
becomes very hard to carry to completion a colonization
which means at the same time true civilization. The real
wealth of these peoples would consist in their coming to
produce for themselves by agriculture and handicrafts as far
as possible all the necessities of their life. Instead of that they
are exclusively bent on providing the materials which world
trade requires, and for which it pays them good prices.
With the money thus obtained they procure from it manufactured goods and prepared foodstuffs, thereby making
home industry impossible, and often even endangering the
stability of their own agriculture. This is the condition in
which all primitive and semi-primitive peoples find themselves who can offer to world trade rice, cotton, coffee,
cocoa, minerals, timber, and similar things. [Life, pp.
223 f.]

Where Nature Is Everything

Newspapers one can hardly bear to look at. The printed
string of words, written with a view to the single, quickly
passing day, seems here, where time is, so to say, standing
still, positively grotesque. Whether we will or no, all of us
here live under the influence of the daily repeated experience that nature is everything and man is nothing. This
brings into our general view of life—and this even in case of
the less educated—something which makes us conscious of
the feverishness and vanity of the life of Europe; it seems
almost something abnormal that over a portion of the earth's
surface nature should be nothing and man everything!
[Edge, p. 150]

The Child of Nature

In return for very little work nature supplies the native with nearly everything that he requires for his support in his village. The forest gives him wood, bamboos, raffia leaves, and bast for the building of a hut to shelter him from sun and rain. He has only to plant some bananas and manioc, to do a little fishing and shooting, in order to have by him all that he really needs, without having to hire himself out as a laborer and to earn regular wages. If he does take a situation, it is because he needs money for some particular object; he wishes to buy a wife, or his wife, or his wives, want some fine dress material, or sugar, or tobacco; he himself wants a new axe, or hankers after rum or cheap spirits, or would like to wear boots and a suit of khaki.

There are, then, various needs differing in number with the individual, but all lying outside the regular struggle for existence, which bring the child of nature to hire himself out for work. If he has no definite object in view for which to earn money he stays in his village. If he is at work anywhere and finds that he has earned enough to supply his heart's desires, he has no reason for troubling himself any further, and he returns to his village, where he can always find board and lodging.   [Edge, pp. 112 f.]

Social Problems in the Forest

Are there really social problems in the forest? Yes; one has only to listen for ten minutes to conversation between any two white men, and one will certainly hear them touch on the most difficult of them all, viz. the labor problem. People imagine in Europe that as many laborers as are wanted can always be found among the savages, and secured for very small wages. The real fact is the very opposite. Laborers are nowhere more difficult to find than among primitive races, and nowhere are they paid so well in proportion to the work they do in return. This comes from their laziness, people say; but is the Negro really so lazy? Must we go a little deeper into the problem?

Any one who has seen the population of a native village at work, when they have to clear a piece of virgin forest in order to make a new plantation, knows that they are able to work enthusiastically, and with all their might, for weeks together. This hardest of all work, I may say in passing, is forced upon every village triennially. The banana exhausts the soil with extraordinary rapidity, so that every three years they must lay out a new plantation, manured by the ashes of the jungle, which they cut down and burn. For my part I can no longer talk ingenuously of the laziness of the Negro after seeing fifteen of them spend some thirty-six hours in almost uninterrupted rowing in order to bring up the river to me a white man who was seriously ill.

The Negro, then, under certain circumstances works well, but—only so long as circumstances require it. The child of nature—here is the answer to the puzzle—is always a casual worker.   [Edge, pp. 111 f.]

The Negro Is a Free Man

The Negro is not idle, but he is a free man; hence he is always a casual worker, with whose labor no regular industry can be carried on. This is what the missionary finds to be the case on the mission station and in his own house on a small scale, and the planter or merchant on a large one. When my cook has accumulated money enough to let him gratify the wishes of his wife and his mother-in-law, he goes off without any consideration of whether we still want his services or not. The plantation owner is left in the lurch by his laborers just at the critical time when he must wage war on the insects that damage the cocoa plant. Just when there comes from Europe message after message about timber, the timber merchant cannot find a soul to go and fell it, because the village happens at the moment to be out on a fishing expedition, or is laying out a new banana plot. So we are all filled with righteous indignation at the lazy Negroes, though the real reason why we cannot get them is that they have not yet learnt to understand what we really mean by continuous work.   [Edge, pp. 113 f.]

Conflicting Interests

The tragic element in this question [Negro labor] is that the interests of civilization and of colonization do not coincide, but are largely antagonistic to each other. The former would be promoted best by the natives being left in their villages and there trained to various industries, to lay out plantations, to grow a little coffee or cocoa for themselves or even for sale, to build themselves houses of timber or brick instead of huts of bamboo, and so to live a steady and worthy life. Colonization, however, demands that as much of the population as possible shall be made available in every possible way for utilizing to the utmost the natural wealth of the country. Its watch word is "Production," so that the capital invested in the colonies may pay its interest, and that the motherland may get her needs supplied through her connection with them. For the unsuspected incompatibilities which show themselves here, no individual is responsible; they arise out of the circumstances themselves, and the lower the level of the natives and the thinner the population, the harder is the problem.   [Edge, p. 117]

Compulsory Labor

What is the real educational value of the much discussed compulsory labor as enforced by the state? What is meant by labor compulsion?

It means that every native who has not some permanent industry of his own must, by order of the state, spend so many days in the year in the service of either a trader or a planter. On the Ogowe we have no labor compulsion. The French colonial administration tries, on principle, to get on without any such measure. In German Africa, where labor compulsion was enforced in a humane but effective manner, the results were, according to some critics, good; according to others, bad. I myself hold labor compulsion to be not wrong in principle, but impossible to carry through in practice. The average colony cannot get on without having it on a small scale. If I were an official and a planter came to tell me that his laborers had left him just as the cocoa crop had to be gathered, and that the men in the neighboring villages refused to come to his help at this critical time, I should think I had a right, and that it was even my duty, to secure him the labor of these men so long as he needed it for the saving of his crop, on payment, of course, of the wages usual in the locality. But the enforcement of general labor compulsion is complicated by the fact that under it men have practically always to leave their village and their family and go to work many miles away. Who provides their food on the journey? What becomes of them if they fall ill? Who will guarantee that the white man does not call on them for their labor just when their village has set about its own planting, or when it is the best time for fishing expeditions? Will he not, perhaps, keep them longer than he is entitled to, on the plea that they have done no work? Will he treat them properly? There is always the danger that compulsory labor may become, secretly but really, a kind of slavery.   [Edge, pp. 118 f.]

At the Expense of the Future

In the Cameroons the forest has been pierced with a network of roads, which are kept in splendid condition and are the admiration of all visitors from other colonies. But has not this great achievement been brought about at the cost of the native population and their vital interests? One is forced to ask questions when things have gone so far that women are impressed for the maintenance of the roads. It is impossible to acquiesce when, as is often the case, the colony itself prospers, while the native population diminishes year by year. Then the present is living at the expense of the future, and the obvious fatal result is only a question of time. The maintenance of the native population must be the first object of any sound colonial policy.   [Edge, p. 122]

Education and Industry

Close on the problem of labor comes that of the educated native. Taken by itself, a thorough school education is, in my opinion, by no means necessary for these primitive peoples. The beginning of civilization with them is not knowledge, but industry and agriculture, through which alone can be secured the economic conditions of higher civilization. But both government and trade require natives with extensive knowledge whom they can employ in administration and in the stores. The schools, therefore, must set their aims higher than is natural, and produce people who understand complicated figures and can write the white man's language perfectly. Many a native has such ability that the results of this attempt are, so far as intellectual knowledge goes, astounding. Not long ago there came to me a native government clerk, just at the time that there was also a missionary staying with me. When the clerk went away, the missionary and I said to each other: "Well, we could hardly compete with him in essay writing!" His chief gives him documents of the most difficult sort to draw up and most complicated statistics to work out, and he does it all faultlessly.

But what becomes of these people? They have been up-
rooted from their villages, just like those who go off to work
for strangers. They live at the store, continually exposed to
the dangers which haunt every native so closely, the tempta-
tions to defraud and to drink. They earn good wages, indeed, but as they have to buy all their necessaries at high
prices, and are a prey to the black man's innate love of
spending, they often find themselves in financial difficulties
and even in want. They do not now belong to the ordinary
Negroes, nor do they belong to the whites either; they are a
tertium quid between the two. Quite recently the above-
mentioned government clerk said to the wife of a missionary: "We Negro intellectuals are in a very uncomfortable
position. The women in these parts are too uneducated to
be good wives for us. They should import wives for us from
the higher tribes in Madagascar." This loss of class position
in an upwards direction is the misfortune which comes to
many of the best of the natives.   [Edge, pp. 122 ff.]

Social Problems Produced by Imports

Social problems are also produced by imports from Europe.
Formerly the Negroes practised a number of small industries; they carved good household utensils out of wood;
they manufactured excellent cord out of bark fiber and
similar substances; they got salt from the sea. But these and
other primitive industries have been destroyed by the goods
which European trade has introduced into the forest. The
cheap enameled ware has driven out the solid, homemade
wooden bucket, and round every Negro village there are
heaps of such things rusting in the grass. Many minor crafts
which they once practised are now almost forgotten; it is
now only the old women who know how to make cord out
of bark, and sewing cotton out of the fibers of the pineapple
leaves. Even the art of canoe-making is dying out. Thus
native industries are going backwards instead of forwards,

just when the rise of a solid industrial class would be the first and surest step towards civilization.   [Edge, p. 124]

Rum and Deficits

One first gets a clear idea of the real meaning of the social danger produced by the importation of cheap spirits, when one reads how much rum per head of the population comes every year to the port towns, and when one has seen in the villages how the children drink with their elders. Here on the Ogowe officials and traders, missionaries and chiefs are all unanimous that the importation of cheap spirits should be stopped. Why, then, is it not stopped? Because it is so profitable to the revenue. The import duty on rum produces one of the biggest items in the receipts of the colony, and if it ceased there would be a deficit. The financial position of the African colonies is well known to be anything but brilliant, and the duty on spirits has a second advantage, that it can be increased every year without diminishing by a liter the quantity consumed. The position here as in other colonies is that the Government says: "Abolish cheap spirits? Willingly—today rather than tomorrow; but tell us first what we can find to cover the deficit which that will cause in the budget." And the strongest opponents of alcohol have not been able to make any practicable proposal. When shall we find some way out of this idiotic dilemma? The one hope is that some day a governor will come who will put the future of the colony above the financial worries of the present, and have the courage to banish rum at the price of having to carry on for some years with a deficit. [Edge, pp. 124 f.]

The Problem of Polygamy

Polygamy is another difficult social problem. We Europeans come here with our ideal of monogamy, and missionaries contend with all their resources against polygamy, in some places even urging the Government to suppress it by law. On the other hand, all of us here must allow that it is closely bound up with the existing economic and social conditions. Where the population lives in bamboo huts, and society is not so organized that a woman can earn her own living, there is no room for the unmarried woman, and if all women are to be married, polygamy is a necessary condition. Moreover, there are in the forest neither cows nor nanny goats, so that a mother must suckle her child for a long time if it is to be reared. Polygamy safeguards the claims of the child, for after its birth the woman has the right, and the duty, of living only for her child; she is now no longer a wife, but only a mother, and she often spends the greater part of this time with her parents. At the end of three years comes the weaning, which is marked by a festival, and then she returns to her husband's hut to be a wife once more. But this living for her child is not to be thought of unless the man has another wife, or other wives, to make a home for him and look after his banana plots.

Here is another point for consideration. Among these nature peoples there are no widows unprovided for and no neglected orphans. The nearest male relative inherits the dead man's widow, and must maintain her and her children. She enters into enjoyment of all the rights of his other wives, even though she can later, with his consent, take another husband.

To agitate, therefore, against polygamy among primitive peoples, is to undermine the whole structure of their society. Have we the right to do this if we are not also in a position to give them a new social order which suits their own circumstances? Were the agitation successful, would not polygamy still continue to exist, with the single difference that the later wives would be illegitimate ones? These questions naturally cause missionaries much anxious thought.

But, as a matter of fact, the more developed the economic condition of a people becomes, the easier becomes the contest with polygamy. When men begin to live in permanent houses, and to practise the rearing of cattle, and agriculture, it disappears of itself because it is no longer demanded by their circumstances, and is no longer even consistent with them. Among the Israelites, as their civilization advanced, monogamy peacefully drove out polygamy. During the prophetic period they were both practised side by side; the teaching of Jesus does not even hint at the existence of the latter.   [Edge, pp. 126 f.]

Polygamy and Immorality

Certainly mission teaching should put forward monogamy as the ideal and as what Christianity demands, but it would be a mistake for the state to make it compulsory. It is also a mistake, so far as I can judge, to identify the fight against immorality with that against polygamy. Under this system the relation of the wives to each other is unusually good. A Negress does not in fact like being the only wife, because then she has the care of the banana plot, which always falls to the wives, all to herself, and this is a laborious duty, as the plots are usually at a distance from the village in some well-concealed part of the forest.

What I have seen in my hospital of life with many wives has not shown me, at any rate, the ugly side of the system. An elderly chief once came as a patient and brought two young wives with him. When his condition began to cause anxiety, a third appeared who was considerably older than the first two; this was his first wife. From the day of her arrival she sat continually on his bed, held his head in her lap, and gave him what he wanted to drink. The two young ones behaved respectfully to her, took orders from her, and looked after the cooking.

One can have the experience in this land of a fourteen-year-old boy announcing himself as a *paterfamilias*. It comes about in the following way. He has inherited from some deceased relative a wife with children, and though the woman has contracted a marriage with another man, that does not touch his rights over the children nor his duty towards them. If they are boys, he will some day have to buy wives for them; if they are girls, he will get the customary purchase price from those who wish to marry them.

Should one declaim against the custom of wife-purchase, or tolerate it? If it is a case of a young woman being promised, without being herself consulted, to the man who bids most for her, it is obviously right to protest. If it merely means that in accordance with local custom the man who is courting a girl must, if she is willing to marry him, pay to the family a sum mutually agreed upon, there is no more reason for objecting than there is in the matter of the dowery, customary in Europe. Whether the man, if the marriage comes off, pays money to the family or receives money from it, is in principle the same thing; in either case there is a definite money transaction which has its origin in the social views of the period. What has to be insisted on, both among ourselves and among "natives," is that the money transaction must remain subordinate, and not so influence the personal choice that either the wife is bought, as in Africa, or the husband, as in Europe. What we have to do, then, is not to fight against the custom of wife-purchase, but to educate the natives up to seeing that they must not give the girl to the highest bidder, but to the suitor who can make her happy, and whom she is herself inclined to take. As a rule, indeed, the Negro girls are not so wanting in independence as to let themselves be sold to any one who offers. Love, it is true, does not play the same part in marriage here as with us, for the child of nature knows nothing of the romantic, and marriages are usually decided on in the family council; they do, however, as a rule, turn out happily.

Most girls are married when they are fifteen, even those in the girl's schools. Those in our mission school are mostly already engaged to some husband, and marry as soon as they leave school. They can even be promised to a husband before they are born, as I learnt through a case of most unprincipled wife-purchase, which took place at Samkita, and was related to me by a missionary. A man owed one of his neighbors 400 fr., but, instead of repaying it, he bought a wife and married her with the usual ceremonies. While they were at the wedding feast, the creditor made his appearance, and overwhelmed the bridegroom with abuse for having bought a wife instead of paying his debt. A palaver began which ended in an agreement that the debtor should give his creditor the first girl born of the marriage for a wife, on which the latter joined the guests and took his part in the festivities. Sixteen years later he came as a wooer, and so the debt was paid!

My opinion is, and I have formed it after conversation with all the best and most experienced of the white men in this district, that we should accept, but try to improve and refine the rights and customs which we find in existence, and make no alterations which are not absolutely necessary. [Edge, pp. 127 ff.]

The Rule of the Whites

Have we white people the right to impose our rule on primitive and semi-primitive peoples—my experience has been gathered among such only? No, if we only want to rule over them and draw material advantage from their country. Yes, if we seriously desire to educate them and help them to attain to a condition of well-being. If there were any sort of possibility that these peoples could live really by and for themselves, we could leave them to themselves. But as things are, the world trade which has reached them is a fact against which both we and they are powerless. They have already through it lost their freedom. Their economic and social relations are shaken by it. An inevitable development brought it about that the chiefs, with the weapons and money which commerce placed at their disposal, reduced the mass of the natives to servitude and turned them into slaves who had to work for the export of trade to make a few select people rich. It sometimes happened too that, as in the days of the slave trade, the people themselves became merchandise, and were exchanged for money, lead, gunpowder, tobacco, and brandy. In view of the state of things produced by world trade there can be no question with these peoples of real independence, but only whether it is better for them to be delivered over to the mercies, tender or otherwise, of rapacious native tyrants or to be governed by officials of European states.

That of those who were commissioned to carry out in our name the seizure of our colonial territories many were guilty of injustice, violence, and cruelty as bad as those of the native chiefs, and so brought on our heads a load of guilt, is only too true. Nor of the sins committed against the natives today must anything be suppressed or whitewashed. But willingness to give these primitive and semi-primitive people of our colonies an independence which would inevitably end in enslavement to their fellows, is no way of making up for our failure to treat them properly. Our only possible course is to exercise for the benefit of the natives the power we actually possess, and thus provide a moral justification for it.   [Life, pp. 222 f.]

The Elder Brother

A word about the relations between the whites and the blacks. What must be the general character of the intercourse between them? Am I to treat the black man as my equal or as my inferior? I must show him that I can respect the dignity of human personality in everyone, and this attitude in me he must be able to see for himself; but the essential thing is that there shall be a real feeling of brotherliness. How far this is to find complete expression in the sayings and doings of daily life must be settled by circumstances. The Negro is a child, and with children nothing can be done without the use of authority. We must, therefore, so arrange the circumstances of daily life that my natural authority can find expression. With regard to the Negroes, then, I have coined the formula: "I am your brother, it is true, but your elder brother."   [Edge, pp. 130 f.]

Friendliness with Authority

The combination of friendliness with authority is the great secret of successful intercourse. One of our missionaries, Mr. Robert, left the staff some years ago to live among the Negroes as their brother absolutely. He built himself a small house near a village between Lambaréné and N'Gomo, and wished to be recognized as a member of the village. From that day his life became a misery. With his abandonment of the social interval between white and black he lost all his influence; his word was no longer taken as the "white man's word," but he had to argue every point with them as if he were merely their equal.   [Edge, p. 131]

Moral Authority

A white man can only have real authority if the native respects him. No one must imagine that the child of nature looks up to us merely because we know more, or can do more, than he can. This superiority is so obvious to him that it ceases to be taken into account. It is by no means the case that the white man is to the Negro an imposing person because he possesses railways and steamers, can fly in the air, or travel under water. "White people are clever and can do anything they want to," says Joseph. The Negro is not in a position to estimate what these technical conquests of nature mean as proofs of mental and spiritual superiority, but on one point he has an unerring intuition, and that is on the question whether any particular white man is a real, moral personality or not. If the native feels that he is this, moral authority is possible; if not, it is simply impossible to create it. The child of nature, not having been artificialized and spoiled as we have been, has only elementary standards of judgment, and he measures us by the most elementary of them all, the moral standard. Where he finds goodness, justice, and genuineness of character, real worth and dignity, that is, behind the external dignity given by social circumstances, he bows and acknowledges his master; where he does not find them he remains really defiant in spite of all appearance of submission, and says to himself: "This white is no more of a man than I am, for he is not a better one than I am." [Edge, pp. 132 f.]

The Danger of Moral Ruin

Even the morally best and the idealists find it difficult out here to be what they wish to be. We all get exhausted in the terrible contest between the European worker who bears the responsibility and is always in a hurry, and the child of nature who does not know what responsibility is and is never in a hurry. The Government official has to record at the end of the year so much work done by the native in building and in road maintenance, in service as carrier or boatman, and so much money paid in taxes; the trader and the planter are expected by their companies to provide so much profit for the capital invested in the enterprise. But in all this they are forever dependent on men who cannot share the responsibility that weighs on them, who only give just so much return of labor as the others can force out of them, and who if there is the slightest failure in superintendence, do exactly as they like without any regard for the loss that may be caused to their employers. In this daily and hourly contest with the child of nature every white man is continually in danger of gradual moral ruin.

My wife and I were once very much delighted with a newly arrived trader, because in the conversations we had with him he was always insisting on kindness towards the natives, and would not allow the slightest ill-treatment of them by his foremen. The next spring, however, he had the following experience. Lying in a pond some sixty miles from here he had a large quantity of okoumé, but he was summoned to Lambaréné to clear off some urgent correspondence just as the water began to rise. He ordered his foremen and laborers to be sure to use the two or three days of high water to get all the timber, if possible, into the river. When the water had fallen he went back to the place and found that nothing whatever had been done! They had smoked, and drunk, and danced; the timber which had already lain too long in the pond was almost completely ruined, and he was responsible to his company for the loss. His men had been thoughtless and indifferent because they did not fear him enough. This experience changed him entirely, and now he laughs at those who think it is possible to do anything with the natives without employing relentless severity.

Not long ago the termites, or white ants, got into a box which stood on our verandah. I emptied the box and broke it up, and gave the pieces to the Negro who had been helping me. "Look," I said to him, "the ants have got into it; you mustn't put the wood with the rest of the firewood or the ants will get into the framework of the hospital building.

Go down to the river and throw it into the water. Do you understand?" "Yes, yes, you need not worry." It was late in the day, and being too tired to go down the hill again, I was inclined to break my general rule and trust a black—one who was in fact on the whole intelligent and handy. But about ten o'clock I felt so uneasy that I took the lantern and went down to the hospital. There was the wood with the ants in it lying with the rest of the firewood. To save himself the trouble of going the twenty yards down to the river the Negro had endangered all my buildings!

The greater the responsibility that rests on a white man, the greater the danger of his becoming hard toward the natives. We on a mission staff are too easily inclined to become self-righteous with regard to the other whites. We have not got to obtain such and such results from the natives by the end of the year, as officials and traders have, and therefore this exhausting contest is not so hard a one for us as for them. I no longer venture to judge my fellows after learning something of the soul of the white man who is in business from those who lay as patients under my roof, and whose talk has led me to suspect that those who now speak savagely about the natives may have come out to Africa full of idealism, but in the daily contest have become weary and hopeless, losing little by little what they once possessed of spirituality. That it is so hard to keep oneself really humane, and so to be a standard-bearer of civilization, that is the tragic element in the problem of the relations between white and colored men in Equatorial Africa. [Edge, pp. 133 ff.]

Moral Controls

The Negro is worth something only so long as he is in his village and under the moral control of intercourse with his family and other relatives; away from these surroundings he

easily goes to the bad, both morally and physically. Colonies
of Negro laborers away from their families are, in fact,
centers of demoralization, and yet such colonies are required for trade and for the cultivation of the soil, both of
which would be impossible without them.   [Edge, p. 117]

The Spirit of True Law

We are living in a period characterized by lack of any real
feeling for law. Our parliaments light-heartedly produce
statutes which are contrary to the spirit of true law. States
deal with their subjects arbitrarily, without regard to the
maintenance of any sort of legal conscience, whilst men who
fall into the clutches of a foreign nation find themselves
practically outlawed. We do not respect their natural claim
either to a home, or to freedom, or to a dwelling place, or to
property, or to wages, or to sustenance, or, in short, to anything whatever. Our faith in law has vanished absolutely
and completely.   [Ethics, p. xix]

The Cause of the World War

In the last resort it is machinery and world commerce which
are responsible for the World War; and the inventions
which gave such mighty destructive power into our hands
have given such a form of devastation to the war that it has
ruined conquered and conquerors together in an incon-
ceivably short space of time. And, again, it was our technical
progress which made it possible for us to kill, as it were, at a
distance and to annihilate men in great masses, so that we
came to lay aside the ultimate rules of humanity and to be
nothing but blind wills, the servants of perfected instruments of slaughter, unable in their annihilating activity to

recognize any longer the difference between combatants and noncombatants.   [Ethics, p. 5]

War and the Gospel of Love

We are, all of us, conscious that many natives are puzzling over the question how it can be possible that the whites, who brought them the Gospel of Love, are now murdering each other, and throwing to the winds the commands of the Lord Jesus. When they put the question to us we are helpless. If I am questioned on the subject by Negroes who think, I make no attempt to explain or to extenuate, but say that we are in "front" of something terrible and incomprehensible. How far the ethical and religious authority of the white man among these children of nature is impaired by this war we shall only be able to measure later on. I fear that the damage done will be very considerable.

In my own house I take care that the blacks learn as little as possible of the horrors of war. The illustrated papers we receive—for the post has begun to work again fairly regularly—I must not leave about, lest the boys, who can read, should absorb both text and pictures and retail them to others.

Meanwhile the medical work goes on as usual. Every morning when I go down to the hospital I feel it as an inexpressible mercy that, while so many men find it their duty to inflict suffering and death on others, I can be doing good and helping to save human life. This feeling supports me through all my weariness.   [Edge, p. 138]

The Traveler Ant

Another serious enemy is the traveler ant, which belongs to the genus *Dorylus*, and from it we suffer a great deal. On their great migrations they march five or six abreast in perfect order, and I once watched a column near my house which took thirty-six hours to march past. If their course is over open ground and they have to cross a path, the warriors form up in several rows on either side and with their large jaws form a kind of palisade to protect the procession in which the ordinary traveler ants are carrying the young ones with them. In forming the palisade the warriors turn their backs to the procession—like the Cossacks when protecting the Czar—and in that position they remain for hours at a time.

As a rule there are three or four columns marching abreast of each other, but independently, from five to fifty yards apart. All at once they break up the column and disperse, though how the word of command is given we do not yet know. Anyhow, in the twinkling of an eye a huge area is covered with a quivering, black mass, and every living thing upon it is doomed. Even the great spiders in the trees cannot escape, for these terrible ravagers creep after them in crowds up to the very highest twigs; and if the spiders, in despair, jump from the trees, they fall victims to the ants on the ground. It is a horrible sight. The militarism of the forest will very nearly bear comparison with that of Europe! [Edge, pp. 143 f.]

Ten Men Killed Already

About this time [during the first World War] it became known that of the whites who had gone home to fulfil their military duties ten had already been killed, and it made a great impression on the natives. "Ten men killed already in this war!" said an old Pahouin. "Why, then, don't the tribes meet for a palaver? How can they pay for all these dead men?" For, with the natives, it is a rule that all who fall in a war, whether on the victorious or on the defeated side, must be paid for by the other side. [Edge, p. 151]

War As It Really Is

About that time I read a magazine article which maintained that there would always be wars, because a noble thirst for glory is an ineradicable element in the heart of man. These champions of militarism think of war only as idealized by ignorant enthusiasm or the necessity of self-defense. They would probably reconsider their opinions if they spent a day in one of the African theaters of war, walking along the paths in the virgin forest between lines of corpses of carriers who had sunk under their load and found a solitary death by the roadside, and if, with these innocent and unwilling victims before them, they were to meditate in the gloomy stillness of the forest on war as it really is.   [Edge, p. 170]

Truth Knows No Arrogance

Profound truth knows no arrogance. Moreover, bitter humiliation awaits all of us who preach the Gospel in distant lands. "Where, indeed, is your ethical religion?"— that is the question we are asked, no matter whether we are among more primitive peoples in out-of-the-way places or among the educated classes in the large centers of Eastern and African civilization. What Christianity has accomplished as the religion of love is believed to have been blotted out by the fact that it failed to educate the Christian nations to peaceableness, and that in the War it associated itself with so much worldliness and hatred, from which to this day it has not yet broken away. It has been so terribly unfaithful to the spirit of Jesus. When preaching the Gospel in the mission field, let us not minimize this deplorable fact in any way nor try to gloss it over. And why have we fallen so low? Because we fancied it an easy thing to have the spirit of Jesus. Henceforward we must strive after that spirit much more seriously. [Christianity, pp. 84 f.]

Property

Regarding the question of property, the ethic of reverence for life is outspokenly individualist in the sense that goods earned or inherited are to be placed at the disposition of the community, not according to any standards whatever laid down by society, but according to the absolutely free decision of the individual. It places all its hopes on the enhancement of the feeling of responsibility in men. It defines possessions as the property of the community, of which the individual is sovereign steward. One serves society by conducting a business from which a certain number of employees draw their means of sustenance; another, by giving away his property in order to help his fellow men. Each one will decide on his own course somewhere between these two extreme cases according to the sense of responsibility which is determined for him by the particular circumstances of his own life. No one is to judge others. It is a question of individual responsibility; each is to value his possessions as instruments with which he is to work. It makes no difference whether the work is done by keeping and increasing, or by giving up, the property. Possessions must belong to the community in the most various ways, if they are to be used to the best advantage in its service.   [Ethics, p. 266]

The Machine and Social Problems

Because he has power over the forces of nature, man built machines which took work away from man, and this makes social problems of such magnitude that no one would have dreamed of them forty years ago. In some cities now air raid practices are held, with sirens shrieking and all lights out. People shove something over their heads which makes them look like beasts, and rush into cellars, while flying through the air appears the superman, possessing endless power for destruction.   [Religion, p. 1520]

The Least Faithful

Those who have very little that they can call their own are in most danger of becoming purely egoistic. A deep truth lies in the parable of Jesus, which makes the servant who had received least the least faithful of all.   [Ethics, p. 266]

What Is Nationalism?

What is nationalism? It is an ignoble patriotism, exaggerated till it had lost all meaning, which bears the same relation to the noble and healthy kind as the fixed idea of an imbecile does to normal conviction.   [Decay, p. 48]

The Transformation of Society

The collapse of civilization has come about because we left the whole question of ethics to society. An ethical revival will only be possible when ethics again becomes the business of thinking men and when individuals seek to maintain themselves in the community as ethical personalities. According to the measure in which we succeed in securing this, will society be transformed from what it is now from top to bottom, a purely natural body, into an ethical organism. The generations which preceded us have made the dire mistake of idealizing society in an ethical sense. We, on the contrary, do our duty by the community by judging it critically and seeking to make it, as far as we are able, more ethical. Having now an *absolute* ethical criterion we no longer allow principles of purposiveness or even, as previously, the most blatantly vulgar opportunism, to pose as ethical without protest on our part. Neither do we linger in the crassly stupid position where we permit ideals of brute force, of passion, or of nationalism, set up by paltry politicians and kept before the public by mind-deafening propaganda, to continue any longer to pose as ethical. With a sort of splendid pedantry we measure all the principles, mental dispositions and ideals which arise among us with the rule gauged for us by the absolute ethic of reverence for life. We can only allow as genuine that which is compatible with humanitarianism. We again exalt the standard of regard for the life and happiness of the individual. We proclaim the sacred rights of humanity; not those which political bigwigs extol at banquets, and trample under foot in the sphere of real action, but the true and genuine rights. We again demand justice, not that substitute for it which purblind authorities have elaborated in juridical scholasticism, nor that about which demagogues of all colors and complexions shriek themselves hoarse, but that which is inspired by a sense of the value of every human existence.   [Ethics, pp. 275 f.]

The Advance Guard

Preaching the Gospel in foreign lands today we are the advance guard of an army that has suffered a defeat and needs to be made fit again. Let us be courageous advance guards. The truth which the Gospel of Jesus carries within itself cannot be impaired by men's errors nor by their lack of faithfulness. And if only our lives, in genuine non-conformity to the world, reveal something of what it means to be apprehended by the living, ethical God, then something of the truth of Jesus goes out from us.

A word of Scripture which resounds with special meaning for us is the following, written by Paul the apostle of the Gentiles: "The Kingdom of God is not in words but in power." That word makes us humble and at the same time fills our hearts with joy. [Christianity, p. 85]

THE IDEALS OF CIVILIZATION

Solitude

Strange, indeed, are the surroundings amid which I study; my table stands inside the lattice door which leads on to the verandah, so that I may snatch as much as possible of the light evening breeze. The palms rustle an *obbligato* to the loud music of the crickets and the toads, and from the forest come harsh and terrifying cries of all sorts. Caramba, my faithful dog, growls gently on the verandah, to let me know that he is there, and at my feet, under the table, lies a small dwarf antelope. In this solitude I try to set in order thoughts which have been stirring in me since 1900, in the hope of giving some little help to the restoration of civilization. Solitude of the primeval forest, how can I ever thank you enough for what you have been to me?   [Edge, pp. 148 f.]

A Definition of Civilization

Civilization I define in quite general terms as spiritual and material progress in all spheres of activity, accompanied by an ethical development of individuals and of mankind. [Life, p. 232]

Civilization Is Progress

What is civilization? This question ought to have been pressing itself on the attention of all men who consider themselves civilized, but it is remarkable that in the world's literature generally one hardly finds that it has been put at all until today, and still more rarely is any answer given. It was supposed that there was no need for a definition of civilization, since we already possessed the thing itself. If the question was ever touched upon, it was considered to be sufficiently settled with references to history and the present day. But now, when events are bringing us inexorably to the consciousness that we live in a dangerous medley of civilization and barbarism, we must, whether we wish to or not, try to determine the nature of true civilization.

For a quite general definition we may say that civilization is progress, material and spiritual progress, on the part of individuals as of the mass.

In what does it consist? First of all in a lessening of the strain imposed on individuals and on the mass by the struggle for existence. The establishment of as favorable conditions of living as possible for all is a demand which must be made partly for its own sake, partly with a view to the spiritual and moral perfecting of individuals, which is the ultimate object of civilization.

The struggle for existence is a double one: man has to assert himself in nature and against nature, and similarly also among his fellow men and against them.

A diminution of the struggle is secured by strengthening the supremacy of reason over both external nature and human nature, and making it subserve as accurately as possible the ends proposed.

Civilization is then twofold in its nature: it realizes itself in the supremacy of reason, first, over the forces of nature, and secondly, over the dispositions of men. [Decay, pp. 35 f.]

Does Everything Serve Progress?

Hegel dares to say that everything serves progress. The passions of rulers and of peoples—all are the servants of progress. One can only say that Hegel did not know the passions of people as we know them, or he would not have dared to write that!   [Religion, p. 1483]

Civilization without Ethics

In the movement of civilization which began with the Renaissance, there were both material and spiritual-ethical forces of progress at work side by side, as though in rivalry with each other, and this continued down to the beginning of the nineteenth century. Then, however, something unprecedented happened: man's ethical energy died away, while the conquests achieved by his spirit in the material sphere increased by leaps and bounds. Thus, for several decades our civilization enjoyed the great advantages of its material progress while as yet it hardly felt the consequences of the dying down of the ethical movement. People lived on in the conditions produced by that movement without seeing clearly that their position was no longer a tenable one and preparing to face the storm that was brewing in the relations between the nations and within the nations themselves. In this way our own age, having never taken the trouble to reflect, arrived at the opinion that civilization consists primarily in scientific, technical and artistic achievements, and that it can reach its goal without ethics, or, at any rate, with a minimum of them.   [Decay, p. 40]

The Crisis of Civilization

Our civilization is passing through a grave crisis.

People usually imagine that this crisis has been brought on by the war. This is erroneous. The war, with all that pertains to it, is itself only one phenomenon of the *debacle* of civilization in which we find ourselves living, for civi-

lization is wavering and tottering even in states which have
not taken part in the war and which the war has not affected
directly. The only difference is that in these cases the
debacle is not so apparent as in those countries which
have been hit directly by the consequences of the uniquely
terrible spiritual and material events of the war.

But is there any sign of living reflection about the fall
of civilization and about the possibility of finding a way
out of it by earnest toil? Scarcely. Ingenious people
blunder around in seven-league boots through the history
of civilization, and will have us to understand that it is
purely a natural growth which blossoms in definite races
at definite periods and then inevitably fades away, so that
fresh civilized peoples must arise to replace those which are
worn out. It is true that if they were obliged, at the finish
of this demonstration, to show what races are destined to
enter on our heritage, they would be in a difficult strait,
for in fact we cannot point out any people to whom we
could entrust such a legacy, even only in partial measure.
All the races of the earth have been powerfully affected by
our civilization as well as by our lack of it. They share our
fate more or less. Nowhere do we come across lines of
thought which can lead to a significant and original wave
of civilization.   [Ethics, pp. 1 f.]

Our Doomed Civilization

One elementary point emerges which we must make clear
to ourselves. Our civilization is doomed because it has
developed with much greater vigor materially than it has
spiritually. Its equilibrium has been destroyed. Through
the discoveries which subject the powers of nature to us in
such a remarkable way the living conditions of individuals,
of groups, and of states have been completely revolution-

ized. Our knowledge and consequent power are enriched
and enhanced to an unbelievable extent; and thus we are
in a position to frame the conditions of man's existence
incomparably more favorably in many respects than was
previously possible. But in our enthusiasm for knowledge
and power we have arrived at a mistaken conception of
what civilization is. We over value the material gains
wrung from nature, and have no longer present in our
minds the true significance of the spiritual clement in life.
And now come the stern matters of fact which call us to
reflect. They teach us in terms of awful severity that a
civilization which develops itself on the material, and not
in a corresponding degree on the spiritual, side is like a
ship with defective steering gear, which becomes more un-
steerable from moment to moment, and so rushes on to
catastrophe.   [Ethics, p. 2]

Our Degeneration

Our degeneration, when it is traced back to its origin in
our view of the world, really consists in the fact that true
optimism has vanished unperceived from our midst. We
are not a race weakened and exhausted by luxury whose
task is to rouse itself once more, amid the storms of history,
to a condition of efficiency and of idealism. On the contrary, we are hindered and embarrassed in our spiritual
conflict by the very efficiency which we have attained in
most of the realms of direct objective activity. Our whole
notion of life, together with everything which derives from
it, has been lowered and degraded alike for the individual
and for men in the mass. The higher powers of volition
and creation are becoming exhausted because the optimism
from which they ought to draw their life energy has been
gradually and unconsciously sapped by the pessimism which
has interpenetrated its substance.   [Ethics, p. 16]

The Drama of Faust

After all, what is now taking place in this terrible epoch of ours except a gigantic repetition of the drama of *Faust* upon the stage of the world? The cottage of Philemon and Baucis burns with a thousand tongues of flame! In deeds of violence and murders a thousandfold a brutalized humanity enacts its cruel play! Mephistopheles leers at us with a thousand grimaces! In a thousand different ways mankind has been persuaded to give up its natural relations with reality, and to seek its welfare in the magic formulas of some kind of economic and social witchcraft, by which the possibility of freeing itself from economic and social misery is only still further removed!   [Gedenkrede, pp. 44 f.]

Cities and Civilization

The conditions of life for the inhabitants of our big cities are as unfavorable as they could be. Naturally, then, those inhabitants are in most danger on their spiritual side. It is doubtful whether big cities have ever been foci of civilization in the sense that in them there has arisen the ideal of a man well and truly developed as a spiritual personality; today, at any rate, the conditions of things are such that true civilization needs to be rescued from the spirit that issues from them and their inhabitants. [Decay, pp. 20 f.]

The Senility of Civilization

Where is the road that can bring us back from barbarism to civilization? Is there such a road at all?

The unethical conception of civilization answers: "No." To it all symptoms of decay are symptoms of old age, and civilization, just like any other natural process of growth, must after a certain period of time reach its final end. There is nothing, therefore, for us to do, so it says, but to take the causes of this as quite natural, and do our best at any rate to find interesting the unedifying phenomena of its senility, which testify to the gradual loss of the ethical character of civilization.   [Decay, p. 62]

There Are No Reserve Civilizations

Those who regard the decay of civilization as something quite normal and natural console themselves with the thought that it is not civilization, but *a* civilization, which is falling a prey to dissolution; that there will be a new age and a new race in which there will blossom a new civilization. But that is a mistake. The earth no longer has in reserve, as it had once, gifted peoples as yet unused, who can relieve us and take our place in some distant future as leaders of the spiritual life. We already know all those which the earth has to dispose of. There is not one among them which is not already taking such a part in our civilization that its spiritual fate is determined by our own. All of them, the gifted and the ungifted, the distant and the near, have felt the influence of those forces of barbarism which are at work among us. All of them are, like ourselves, diseased, and only as we recover can they recover.

It is not the civilization of a race, but that of mankind, present and future alike, that we must give up as lost, if belief in a rebirth of our civilization is a vain thing. [Decay, pp. 63 f.]

Christianity and Civilization

In modern times, under the influence of the Renaissance, the Reformation, and the thinkers of the Age of Enlightenment (Aufklärung), Christianity laid aside the world- and life-denial which clung to it as a survival from the primitive Christian expectation of the end to the world, and allowed room within itself for world- and life-affirmation. It thus changed into a religion which could work for a realization of civilization.

As such a religion it took part in the struggle against ignorance, want of purpose, cruelty, and injustice out of which in modern times a new world emerged. It was only because the powerful ethical energies of Christianity allied themselves with the will-to-progress which characterized the world- and life-affirmation of the modern world, and worked in the service of the modern age that the seventeenth and eighteenth centuries were capable of doing the work for civilization for which we have to thank them.

In proportion, however, to the extent to which the world- and life-negation which had been repressed in the eighteenth century begins to acquire importance in it again through medieval and later tendencies, Christianity ceases to be a force making for civilization and begins to attract attention as a hindrance to it, as is amply shown by the history of our own time.   [Life, p. 216]

External or Internal Regeneration

One great difficulty in the way of the regeneration of our civilization lies in the fact that it must be an internal process, and not an external as well, and that, therefore, there is no place for healthy cooperation between the material and the spiritual. From the Renaissance to the middle of the nineteenth century the men who carried on the work of civilization could expect help towards spiritual progress from achievements in the sphere of external organization. Demands in each of these spheres stood side by side in their program and were pushed on simultaneously. They were convinced that while working to transform the institutions of public life they were producing results which would call forth the development of the new spiritual life. Success in one sphere strengthened at once the hopes and the energies that were at work in the other. They labored for the progressive democratization of the state with the idea of thereby spreading through the world the rule of grace and justice.

We, who have lived to see the spiritual bankruptcy of all the institutions which they created, can no longer work in this way simultaneously at the reform of institutions and the revival of the spiritual element. The help which such cooperation would give is denied us.   [Decay, pp. 70 f.]

The Will-to-Progress

The striving for material and spiritual progress, which characterizes the peoples of modern Europe, has its source in the world-view to which these peoples have come. As a result of the Renaissance and the spiritual and religious movements bound up with it, men have entered on a new relation to themselves and to the world, and this has aroused in them a need to create by their own activities spiritual and material values which shall help to a higher development of individuals and of mankind. It is not the case that the man of modern Europe is enthusiastic for progress because he may hope to get some personal advantage from it. He is less concerned about his own condition than about the happiness which he hopes will be the lot of coming generations. Enthusiasm for progress has taken possession of him. Impressed by his great experience of finding the world revealed to him as constituted and maintained by forces which carry out a definite design, he himself wills to become an active, purposeful force in the world. He looks with confidence toward new and better times which shall dawn for mankind, and learns by experience that the ideals which are held and acted upon by the mass of people do win power over circumstances and remold them.

It is on his will to material progress, acting in union with the will to ethical progress, that the foundations of modern civilization are being laid.   [Life, p. 180]

A True Course

The question of how many or how few material conquests we have to record is not the decisive question for civilization. Its fate hangs on the possession or lack of possession, by convictions and dispositions, of power over matters of fact. The result of the voyage does not depend on the speed of the ship, whether it be a fast sailer or somewhat slower, nor on the method of propulsion, whether by sails or by steam, but on whether or not it keeps a true course and whether or not its steering gear remains in order. [Ethics, p. 3]

The Ideals of True Civilization

We may take as the essential element in civilization the ethical perfecting of the individual and of society as well. But at the same time, every spiritual and every material step in advance has a significance for civilization. The will-to-civilization is then the universal will-to-progress which is conscious of the ethical as the highest value for all. In spite of the great importance we attach to the triumphs of knowledge and achievement, it is nevertheless obvious that only a humanity which is striving after ethical ends can in full measure share in the blessings brought by material progress and become master of the dangers which accompany it. To the generation which had adopted a belief in an imminent power of progress realizing itself, in some measure, naturally and automatically, and which thought that it no longer needed any ethical ideals but could advance to its goal by means of knowledge and achievement alone, terrible proof was being given by its present position of the error into which it had sunk.

The only possible way out of the present chaos is for us to adopt a world-view which will bring us once more under the control of the ideals of true civilization which are contained in it.

But what is the nature of the world-view on which the universal will-to-progress and the ethical alike are founded and in which they are linked together each with the other?

It consists in an ethical affirmation of the world and of life. [Life, pp. 176 f.]

Reconstruction

The ideals of civilization which our age needs are not new and strange to it. They have been in the possession of mankind already, and are to be found in many an antiquated formula. We have fundamentally nothing else to do than to restore to them the respect in which they were once held, and again regard them seriously as we bring them into relation with the reality which lies before us for treatment.

To make what is used up usable—is there a harder task? "It is an impossible one," says history. "Never hitherto have worn-out ideas risen to new power among the peoples who have worn them out. Their disappearance has always been a final one."

That is true. In the history of civilization we find nothing but discouragement for our task. Anyone who finds history speaking optimistically lends her a language which is not her own.

Yet from the history of the past we can infer only what has been, not what will be. Even if it proves that no single people has ever lived through the decay of its civilization and a rebirth of it, we know at once that this, which has never happened yet, must happen with us, and therefore we cannot be content to say that the reasoned ethical ideals on which civilization rests get worn out in the course of history, and console ourselves with the reflection that this is exactly in accordance with the ordinary processes of nature. We require to know why it has so happened hitherto, and to draw an explanation, not from the analogy of nature, but from the laws of spiritual life. We want to get into our hands the key of the secret, so that we may with it unlock the new age, the age in which the worn-out becomes again unworn and the spiritual and ethical can no longer get worn-out. We must study the history of civilization otherwise than as our predecessors did, or we shall be finally lost.   [Decay, pp. 65 ff.]

THE RELIGION OF THE SPIRIT

What Am I in the World?

In religion we try to find an answer to the elementary question with which each one of us is newly confronted every morning, namely, what meaning and what value is to be ascribed to our life. What am I in the world? What is my purpose in it? What may I hope for in this world? I do not want to consider my existence merely as one which rises and perishes among the billions of billions of beings which constitute the universe, but as a life which has a value, if I comprehend it and live it according to true knowledge. [Christianity, p. 26]

The Purpose of Life

Religion has not only to explain the world. It has also to respond to the need I feel of giving my life a purpose. The question on which ultimately the decisive judgment must be based is, whether a religion is truly and vitally ethical or not. When it comes to this final test, the logical religions of the East fail. They strive for an ethic. They stretch out towards it in thought; but in the end they sink back exhausted. The branch which they pulled down breaks in their hand and springs back, depriving them of the possibility to take hold of the fruit they had longed to pluck. [Christianity, p. 69]

The Inclusive Question in Religion

All questions of religion tend towards the one which comprises them all: How can I conceive of myself as being in the world and at the same time in God? All the questions of Christian theology, too, in all the centuries, go back to this one.   [Christianity, pp. 26 f.]

Incentives to Perfection

The great question which each religion must be asked is, how far it produces permanent and profound incentives to the inward perfecting of personality and to ethical activity. [Christianity, p. 26]

More than Negation

Religion is more than negation of life and of the world. [Christianity, p. 45]

Naïveté

Every rational faith has to choose between two things: either to be an ethical religion or to be a religion that explains the world. We Christians choose the former, as that which is of higher value. We turn away from the logical, self-contained religion. To the question, how a man can be in the world and in God at one and the same time, we find this answer in the Gospel of Jesus: "By living and working in this world as one who is not *of* the world."

Thus we no longer rely on the bridges formed by ordinary logical thought. Our path leads into the region of naïveté and of paradox. We tread it resolutely and with confidence. We hold to the absolutely and profoundly ethical religion as to the one thing needful, though philosophy may go to rack and ruin. That which appears to be naïveté in Christianity is in reality its profundity.

There are two kinds of naïveté: one which is not yet aware of all the problems and has not yet knocked at all the doors of knowledge; and another, a higher kind, which is the result of philosophy having looked into all problems, having sought counsel in all the spheres of knowledge, and then having come to see that we cannot explain anything but have to follow convictions whose inherent value appeals to us in an irresistible way.   [Christianity, pp. 70 ff.]

Chinese Piety

Chinese piety is built on sand. It is based on the assumption that in the working of the forces of nature we may read all that we believe and affirm in the religion of love, and that, therefore, meditation on the nature of the universe leads us to that religion. Thus, they attempt to pretend that the essence of the religion of love is knowledge of the world. It is an illusion. Knowledge of the world does not lead so far.   [Christianity, p. 51]

Monism in Religion

A religion is monistic if it considers God to be the sum total of all the forces at work in the universe, and, therefore, believes that in the knowledge of the universe we can attain to perfect knowledge of God. Thus, in its very nature, monism is pantheistic.   [Christianity, pp. 24 f.]

Dualism in Religion

A religion is dualistic if it does not make any attempt to arrive at a full knowledge of the nature of God by examining the forces which are active in the natural world, but

seeks to realize Him in accordance with the ideal conceptions of Him that we carry within us. Of necessity this
leads to the idea that this God stands to a certain extent
in contrast with the forces of nature, however great may
be the difficulties which this involves for human reasoning.
The God whom we have within us as an ideal is an ethical
Personality; on the other hand, the happenings due to the
forces at work in the universe bear no ethical character.
Thus, the dualistic religion is theistic. [Christianity,
p. 25]

From Finite to Infinite

The Catholic chancel, into which I used to gaze, was to
my childish imagination the *ne plus ultra* of magnificence.
There was first an altar painted to look like gold, with
huge bunches of artificial flowers upon it; then tall candle-
sticks of metal with majestic wax candles in them; on the
wall, above the altar and between the two windows, was
a pair of large gilt statues, which to me were Joseph and
the Virgin Mary; and all these objects were flooded with
the light which came through the chancel windows. Then
through the windows themselves one looked out over trees,
roofs, clouds, and blue sky on a world, in short, which
continued the chancel of the church into an infinity of
distance, and was, in its turn, flooded with a kind of trans-
figuring glory imparted to it by the chancel. Thus my gaze
wandered from the finite to the infinite, and my soul was
wrapped in peace and quiet.   [Childhood, p. 65]

The Contagion of Devotion

From the services in which I joined as a child I have taken
with me into life a feeling for what is solemn, and a need
for quiet and self-recollection, without which I cannot

realize the meaning of my life. I cannot, therefore, support the opinion of those who would not let children take
part in grown-up people's services till they to some extent
understand them. The important thing is not that they shall
understand, but that they shall feel something of what is
serious and solemn. The fact that the child sees his elders
full of devotion, and has to feel something of their devotion himself, that is what gives the service its meaning for
him.   [Childhood, p. 62]

The Church a Place for Worship

When I see churches in which modern architects have tried
to embody the ideal of "a preacher's church," I feel a
sinking of the heart. A church is much more than a building
in which one listens to sermons; it is a place for devotions,
and merely as a building it ought to keep people at a devo-
tional level. But it can never do that if in every direction
the worshiper's eye is brought up short by walls. There is
need of distance, of a background, which lends itself to the
mood of the worshiper, so that the outward gaze can change
to the inner one. The chancel, therefore, is not something
exclusively Catholic; it is part of the church as a church,
and if Protestant services are from their very nature defective, there is no need for the building to be so as well. The
building ought to make the service a complete whole, and
become as much an element in the soul's experience as the
words heard, the singing, and the prayers.   [Childhood,
pp. 65 f.]

When Thinking Was Religious

The religion of our age gives the same impression as an
African river in the dry season—a great river bed, sand
banks, and between, a small stream which seeks its way. One
tries to imagine that a river once filled that bed; that there
were no sand banks but that the river flowed majestically

on its way; and that it will someday be like that again. Is it possible, you say, that once a river filled this bed? Was there a time when ethical religion was a force in the spiritual life of the time? Yes, in the eighteenth century. Then ethical religion and thinking formed one unity. Thinking was religious, and religion was a thinking religion. Because it was conditioned by ethical religious ideas, the thinking of that period undertook to represent reality to itself as it should be. It possessed ethical ideals in accordance with which it transformed reality.   [Religion, p. 1483]

Eighteenth Century Religion

The religion of the eighteenth century undertook a great work of reform. It waged war against superstition and ignorance. It obtained recognition for humanity in the eyes of the law. Torture was abolished, first in Prussia in the year 1740 through a cabinet order of Frederick the Great. It was demanded of the individual that he should place himself at the service of the community. English emigrants formulated in America for the first time the rights of man. The idea of humanity began to gain in significance. People dared to grasp the thought that lasting peace must reign on earth. Kant wrote a book on *Everlasting Peace* (1795), and in it represented the thought that even politics must submit to the principles of ethics. Finally, an achievement which the spirit of the eighteenth century brought about in the nineteenth century, came the abolition of slavery.

The religious-ethical spirit of the eighteenth century desired then to make the Kingdom of God a reality on earth. [Religion, p. 1483]

The Spiritual Advance of Mankind

The men of the Renaissance and the Illuminati of the eighteenth century drew courage to desire the renewal of

the world through ideas from their conviction of the absolute indefensibility of the material and spiritual conditions
under which they lived. Unless with us, too, the many
come to some such conviction, we must continue incapable
of taking in hand this work, in which we must imitate
them. But the many obstinately refuse to see things as they
are, and hold with all their might to the most optimistic
view of them that is possible. For this power, however,
of idealizing with continually lowering ideals the reality
which is felt to be ever less and less satisfying, pessimism
also is partly responsible. Our generation, though so proud
of its many achievements, no longer believes in the one
thing which is all-essential: the spiritual advance of mankind. Having given up the expectation of this, it can put
up with the present age without feeling such suffering as
would compel it, for very pain, to long for a new one.
What a task it will be to break the fetters of unthinking
optimism and unthinking pessimism which hold us prisoners,
and so to do what will pave the way for the renewal of
civilization!   [Decay, p. 65]

When Our Age Began

In the nineteenth century the spirit of realism rose against
the spirit of idealism. The first personality in which it was
realized was Napoleon I. The first thinker in whom it
announced itself was the German philosopher Hegel. Men
have not, Hegel maintained, to transform reality in order
to bring it into accord with ideals devised by thinking.
Progress takes place automatically in the natural course of
events. The passions of ruling personalities and of peoples
in some way or other are in the service of progress—even
war is. The view that ethical idealism is a form of sentimentality of which no use can be made in the world of
reality, began with Hegel. He was first to formulate the

theory of rationalism. He wrote: "What is reasonable is real, and what is real is reasonable." On the night of June 25, 1820, when that sentence was written, our age began, the age which moved on to the World War—and which perhaps someday will end civilization!   [Religion, p. 1483]

Two Currents in Religion

In religion there are two different currents: one free from dogma and one that is dogmatic. That which is free from dogma bases itself on the preaching of Jesus; the dogmatic bases itself on the creeds of the early church and the reformation. The religion free from dogma is to some extent the heir of rationalistic religion. It is ethical, limits itself to the fundamental ethical verities, and endeavors, so far as is in its power, to remain on good terms with thinking. It wants to realize something of the Kingdom of God in the world. It believes itself identical with the religion of Jesus. All the efforts of historical-theological science in the nineteenth century are aimed at proving that Christian dogma began with St. Paul and that the religion of Jesus is non-dogmatic, so that it can be adopted in any age.   [Religion, p. 1484]

A Religion That Utters No Commands

The ethical religion of the philosophers of the second half of the nineteenth century is not firmly grounded. Its idea of God is quite incomplete. What is ethical in such teaching has no force. It lacks compulsive power and enthusiasm, and so this fine philosophical religion has had no significance for the thinking of the world in general. It is something which cannot be placed in the center of things; it is too delicate, too cautious, it utters no commands.   [Religion, p. 1519]

We Face Reality Powerless

How did it come about that ethical ideals could not oppose the inhuman ideals of the war? It was due to the spirit of practical realism. I place at opposite extremes the spirit of idealism and the spirit of realism. The spirit of idealism means that men and women of the period arrive at ethical ideals through thinking, and that these ideals are so powerful that men say: We will use them to control reality. We will transform reality in accordance with these ideals. The spirit of idealism desires to have power over the spirit of realism. The spirit of practical realism, however, holds it false to apply ideals to what is happening. The spirit of realism has no power over reality. If a generation lives with these ideas, it is subject to reality. This is the tragedy which is being enacted in our age. For what is characteristic of our age is that we no longer really believe in social or spiritual progress, but face reality powerless.   [Religion, p. 1483]

The Defeat of Religion

Religion was powerless to resist the spirit through which we entered the war. It was overcome by this spirit. It could bring no force against the ideals of inhumanity and unreasonableness which gave birth to the war, and when war had broken out, religion capitulated. It became mobilized. It had to join in helping to keep up the courage of the peoples. To give each people courage to go on fighting, one had to explain that they were fighting for their existence and for the spiritual treasures of humanity. Religion helped to give this conviction. It is easy to understand why it did this. It seemed a necessity. It remains true, however, that in the war religion lost its purity and lost its authority. It joined forces with the spirit of the world. The one victim of defeat was religion. And that religion *was* defeated is apparent in our time. For it lifts up its voice, but only to protest. It cannot command. The spirit of the age does not listen. It goes its own way.   [Religion, p. 1483]

Vital Spirituality

Facts call us to reflect, even as the tossings of a capsizing vessel cause the crew to rush on deck and to climb the masts. Faith in the spiritual progress of man and of humanity has already become almost impossible for us. We must force ourselves to it with the courage of desperation. We must turn together to will the spiritual progress of men and of humanity in mutual accord and to base our hopes on it once more. This is the putting of the helm hard to port which must be accomplished if our vessel is to be brought head to wind again, even now at the last moment.

We shall only be capable of this as the result of intelligent reverence for life. Let reverence for life begin to work somehow or other on thought and conviction, and then the miracle will be possible. The power of the elemental and vital spirituality implicit in it is incalculable.   [Ethics, p. 286]

Knowledge and Power May Prove Fatal

All our advances in knowledge and power will prove fatal to us in the end unless we retain control over them by a corresponding advance in our spirituality. Through the power which we win over the forces of nature we get also a gruesome kind of power over our fellow human beings. With the possession of a hundred machines a single man, or a small group of men, are given control over the lives of all those who run these machines. Through a new invention it becomes possible for one man with a single movement to kill not only a hundred but ten thousand other men. It is not

possible in any battle to avoid the destruction of economic
and physical values on both sides. Generally what happens
is that conqueror and conquered are involved in the same
fate. The only way out is that we should mutually renounce
the power to injure each other which we now possess. But
this is necessarily a spiritual act.   [Ethics, pp. 285 f.]

Spiritual Harmony

As we know life in ourselves, we want to understand life
in the universe, in order to enter into harmony with it.
Physically we are always trying to do this. But that is not
the primary matter; for the great issue is that we shall
achieve a spiritual harmony. Just to recognize this fact is to
have begun to see a part of life clearly.   [Reverence,
p. 225]

The Tasks of the Spirit

How heavy the tasks that the spirit has to take in hand! It
has to create the power of understanding the truth that is
really true where at present nothing is current but propa-
gandist truth. It has to depose ignoble patriotism, and en-
throne the noble kind of patriotism which aims at ends that
are worthy of the whole of mankind, in circles where the
hopeless issues of past and present political activities keep
nationalist passions aglow even among those who in their
hearts would fain be free from them. It has to get the fact
that civilization is an interest of all men and of humanity
as a whole recognized again in places where national civilization is today worshiped as an idol, and the notion of a
humanity with a common civilization lies broken to fragments. It has to maintain our faith in the civilized state, even
though our modern states, spiritually and economically
ruined by the war, have no time to think about the tasks of

civilization, and dare not devote their attention to anything but how to use every possible means, even those which undermine the conception of justice, to collect money with which to prolong their own existence. It has to unite us by giving us a single ideal of civilized man, and this in a world where one nation has robbed its neighbor of all faith in humanity, idealism, righteousness, reasonableness, and truthfulness, and all alike have come under the domination of powers which are plunging us ever deeper into barbarism. It has to get attention concentrated on civilization while the growing difficulty of making a living absorbs the masses more and more in material cares, and makes all other things seem to them to be mere shadows. It has to give us faith in the possibility of progress while the reaction of the economic on the spiritual becomes more pernicious every day and contributes to an ever growing demoralization. It has to provide us with reasons for hope at a time when not only secular and religious institutions and associations, but the men, too, who are looked upon as leaders, continually fail us, when artists and men of learning show themselves as supporters of barbarism, and notabilities who pass for thinkers, and behave outwardly as such, are revealed, when crises come, as being nothing more than writers and members of academies.

All these hindrances stand in the path of the will to civilization.   [Decay, pp. 76 ff.]

Spiritual Self-Reliance

Spiritual freedom we shall recover only when the majority of individuals become once more spiritually independent and self-reliant, and discover their natural and proper relation to those organizations in which their souls have been entangled. But liberation from the Middle Ages of today will be a much more difficult process than that which freed the peoples of Europe from the first Middle Ages. The struggle then was against external authority established in the course of history. Today the task is to get the mass of individuals to work themselves out of the condition of spiritual weakness and dependence to which they have brought themselves. Could there be a harder task?   [Decay, p. 31]

Shall We Make or Suffer History?

One truth stands firm. All that happens in world history rests on something spiritual. If the spiritual is strong, it creates world history. If it is weak, it suffers world history. The question is, shall we make world history or only suffer it passively? Will our thinking again become ethical-religious? Shall we again win ideals that will have power over reality? This is the question before us today.   [Religion, pp. 1483 f.]

THE MYSTICAL WORLD–VIEW

What Is Mysticism?

We are always in the presence of mysticism when we find a human being looking upon the division between earthly and super-earthly, temporal and eternal, as transcended, and feeling himself, while still externally amid the earthly and temporal, to belong to the super-earthly and eternal. [Mysticism, p. 1]

The Perfect World-View

Mysticism is the perfected form of world-view. In his world-view man endeavors to arrive at a spiritual relationship to the infinite Being to which he belongs as a part of nature. He studies the universe to discover whether he can apprehend and become one with the mysterious will which governs it. Only in spiritual unity with infinite Being can he give meaning to his life and find strength to suffer and to act.

And if in the last resort the aim of a world-view is our spiritual unity with infinite Being, then the perfect world-view is of necessity mysticism. It is in mysticism that man realizes spiritual union with infinite Being.

Mysticism alone corresponds to the ideal of a world-view. All other world-views are in their nature incomplete, and fail to correspond with the facts. Instead of providing a solution of the fundamental question how man is to become

spiritually one with infinite Being and from this solution as
a beginning deciding in detail what is to be his attitude to
himself and to all things in the universe, these other forms
of world-view lay down precepts about the universe to in-
struct man about what part he ought to play in it. [Indian,
pp. 10 f.]

The Mystery of the Universe

Modern thinkers emancipated from Kant . . . want to get
at religion by saying: All this knowledge of the world
through science is only a description of the world, from
which man derives nothing. What we must know is the
essential nature of the universe. The thing we must be preoccupied with is the mystery of our life. How we understand the mystery of our life is the mystery of the universe.
They say: We know the universe by intuition, not by
reason. Our life knows the life in the world, and through
our life we become one with the life of the universe. This
thinking therefore is mysticism.

But ethics plays no part in this form of thought. The
great problem of what man is aiming at plays no part in it.
[Religion, p. 1520]

Mystical Knowledge and Faith

The mystical knowledge does not depreciate faith, but com-
pletes it. For those who through the Spirit have attained
fullness of knowledge the whole panorama to its furthest
ranges lies in clear daylight; for those who are "babes in
Christ" only the nearest hills are visible; for those who are
wise "with the wisdom of this world" all is still veiled in
cloud. [Mysticism, pp. 24 f.]

Mysticism and Reason

Why assume that the road of thought must suddenly stop at the frontier of mysticism? It is true that pure reason has hitherto called a halt whenever it came into that neighborhood, for it was unwilling to go beyond the point at which it could still exhibit everything as part of a smooth, logical plan. Mysticism, on its side, always depreciated pure reason as much as it could, to prevent at all costs the idea from gaining currency that it was in any way bound to give an account to reason. And yet, although they refuse to recognize each other, the two belong to each other.   [Decay, pp. 90 f.]

Christian Mysticism

Even into Christianity, naïvely dualistic as it is, distinguishing strictly between the present and the future, the here and the hereafter, this mysticism penetrates. Not indeed unopposed; but whenever in the great thinkers or under the influence of great movements of thought Christianity endeavors to attain to clarity regarding the relation of God and the world, it cannot help opening the door to mysticism. Mysticism finds expression in the Hellenistic theology of Ignatius and the Johannine Gospel, in the writings of Augustine and in those attributed to Dionysius the Areopagite; it is found in Hugo of St. Victor and other scholastics, in Francis of Assisi, in Meister Eckhart, in Suso, in Tauler and the other fathers of the German theological mysticism; it speaks in the language of Jakob Böhme and other mystical heretics of Protestantism; there is mysticism in the hymns of Tersteegen, Angelus Silesius, and Novalis; and in the writings of Schleiermacher mysticism seeks to express itself in the language of the church.   [Mysticism, p. 2]

Two Kinds of Mysticism

There are two kinds of mysticism: the one kind resulting from the assumption that the World-Spirit and the spirit of man are identical, and the other of ethical origin.   [Indian, p. 262]

The Mysticism of Identity

The mysticism of identity, whether Indian or European, is not ethical either in origin or in nature and cannot become so. Ethical thoughts can only be found in it and developed from it insofar as an ethical nature is attributed to the World-Spirit. But as soon as thinking even in the very least degree leaves the position that the World-Spirit and the world events are an unfathomable secret, that thinking is no longer in harmony with reality.

In measure as the ethical element in Indian thought develops and gains recognition, so does that thought see itself compelled to attempt the impossible task of comprehending its mysticism of identity as ethical. But it can no more succeed than did Meister Eckhart succeed in making his mysticism become ethical. The attempt invariably consists in nothing more than adding an ethical element to mysticism by means of inadmissible explanations.   [Indian, pp. 262 f.]

Ethical Mysticism

The mysticism which derives from ethics is completely in touch with reality. It can reconcile itself to the fact that the World-Spirit and world events remain to us incomprehensible. Since it need not make trial of any kind of explanation of the universe, it engages in no conflict with the knowledge gained by experience. Whilst the other mysticism regards this knowledge with contempt and appeals in face of it to an intuitive knowledge of the universe, this ethical mysticism recognizes the importance of that knowledge. It knows that all knowledge grounded in experience only leads deeper and deeper into the great mystery that all that is is will-to-live. [Indian, p. 263]

Knowing Ignorance

Ethical mysticism is completely in earnest about that "knowing ignorance" (*docta ignorantia*) talked of by medieval mystics. Only for ethical mysticism this is not, as for the other mysticism, something alongside and above the knowledge drawn from experience, but is what results from that knowledge.

The enlightened ignorance of ethical mysticism is ignorance in so far as it admits how absolutely mysterious and unfathomable are the world and life. It is knowledge in so far as it does know the one thing which we can and must know in the sphere of this mystery, namely, that all Being is life, and that in loving self-devotion to other life we realize our spiritual union with infinite Being. [Indian, pp. 263 f.]

The Unanswered Question

Ethical mysticism humbly leaves unanswered the question in what manner the World-Spirit exists within the poor human spirit and in it attains to consciousness of itself. It holds only to the fact that the poor human spirit, by leaving behind its existence for itself alone, in the devotion of service to other life, experiences union with the World-Spirit and thereby becomes enriched and finds peace. [Indian, p. 264]

Primitive Mysticism

Mysticism may be either primitive or developed. Primitive mysticism has not yet risen to a conception of the universal, and is still confined to naïve views of earthly and super-earthly, temporal and eternal. The entry into the super-earthly and eternal takes place by means of a "mystery," a magical act. By means of this the participant enters into communion with a divine Being in such a way that he shares the latter's supernatural mode of existence. This view of a union with the divinity, brought about by efficacious ceremonies, is found even in quite primitive religions. The most fundamental significance of the sacrificial feast is, no doubt, that by this meal the partaker becomes in some way one with the divinity.   [Mysticism, p. 1]

The Higher Mysticism

When the conception of the universal is reached and a man reflects upon his relation to the totality of being and to Being in itself, the resultant mysticism becomes widened, deepened, and purified. The entrance into the super-earthly and eternal then takes place through an act of thinking. In this act the conscious personality raises itself above that illusion of the senses which makes him regard himself as in bondage in the present life to the earthly and temporal. It attains the power to distinguish between appearance and reality and is able to conceive the material as a mode of manifestation of the spiritual. It has sight of the eternal in the transient. Recognizing the unity of all things in God, in Being as such, it passes beyond the unquiet flux of becoming and disintegration into the peace of timeless being, and is conscious of itself as being in God, and in every moment eternal.   [Mysticism, pp. 1 f.]

Intellectual Mysticism

Intellectual mysticism is a common possession of humanity. Whenever thought makes the ultimate effort to conceive the relation of the personality to the universal, this mysticism comes into existence. It is found among the Brahmans and in Buddha, in Platonism, in Stoicism, in Spinoza, Schopenhauer, and Hegel.   [Mysticism, p. 2]

The Mysticism of Paul

The mysticism of Paul . . . occupies a unique position between primitive and intellectual mysticism. The religious conceptions of the Apostle stand high above those of primitive mysticism. This being so, it might have been expected that his mysticism would have to do with the unity of man with God as the ultimate ground of being. But this is not the case. Paul never speaks of being one with God or being in God.   He does indeed assert the divine sonship of believers. But, strangely enough, he does not conceive of sonship to God as an immediate mystical relation to God, but as mediated and effected by means of the mystical union with Christ.   [Mysticism, p. 3]

I Am in Christ

In Paul there is no God-mysticism; only a Christ-mysticism by means of which man comes into relation to God. The fundamental thought of Pauline mysticism runs thus: I am in Christ; in Him I know myself as a being who is raised above this sensuous, sinful, and transient world and already belongs to the transcendent; in Him I am assured of resurrection; in Him I am a child of God.   [Mysticism, p. 3]

The Spirit of Christ

The most obvious and natural thing, from our point of view, would have been that Paul should have developed on mystical lines that conception of sonship to God which Christ proclaimed and which was current in early Christianity. He, however, leaves that as he found it, and works out in addition to it the mystical conception of being-in-Christ, as though sonship to God needed for its foundation the being-in-Christ. Paul is the only Christian thinker who knows only Christ-mysticism, unaccompanied by God-mysticism. In the Johannine theology both appear alongside one another and intermingled with each other. The Johannine Logos-Christ speaks both of a being-in-him and a being-in-God, and represents the being-in-God as mediated by the being-in-Christ. From that point onward Christ-mysticism and God-mysticism interpenetrate.

What makes it more remarkable that the direct mystical relations of the believer to God should find no place in Paul's manner of thought, is that in his statements about the believer's possession of the Spirit he does not make any clear distinction between the Spirit of God and the Spirit of Christ. Passages in which he describes those who are in Christ as possessing the Spirit of Christ alternate with those in which he reminds them that they have the Spirit of God.

Rom. viii:9. "You are not in the flesh but in the spirit, if so be that the spirit of God dwells in you; but he who has not the Spirit of Christ is none of His."

Gal. iv:6. "But because you are sons, God has sent forth the Spirit of His Son into our hearts, who there cries Abba, Father."

Although he so unhesitatingly equates the possession of the Spirit of Christ with the possession of the Spirit of God,

Paul nevertheless never makes the being-in-Christ into a being-in-God.   [Mysticism, pp. 4 f.]

The Lighthouse of Paul's Mysticism

That Paul is prevented by his eschatological world-view from equating Christ-mysticism with God-mysticism has a deep significance. For all intellectual apprehension God-mysticism remains always something imperfect, and incapable of being perfected. Paul, by confining himself to seeing sonship to God realized in the union with Christ, without trying to make this sonship to God intelligible as a being-in-God, is a guiding light to lead Christianity back from all divagations into the course which it ought to follow. Like a lighthouse that throws its beam upon the ocean of the eternal, the Pauline mysticism stands firm, based upon the firm foundation of the historical manifestation of Jesus Christ.   [Mysticism, p. 379]

The Inner Essence of Paul's Mysticism

As radium by its very nature is in a constant state of emanation, so Pauline mysticism is constantly being transmuted from the natural to the spiritual and ethical. The spiritual and ethical significance shine through the naturalistic conception in a marvelous way. This shows that the naturalistic-eschatological constitutes only the outward character of his mysticism, whereas its inner-essence is determined by the close connection of the concept of redemption with the belief in the Kingdom of God, which retains its significance even when the concept of the Kingdom of God is transformed from the natural into the spiritual. That is why Paul's teaching about the dying and rising with Christ, which are to be experienced in the circumstances of our lives and in all our thinking and willing, are just as true for our world-view of today as they were for his.   [Mysticism, pp. 385 f.]

Surrender to Christ

Christianity is a Christ-mysticism, that is to say, a "belonging together" with Christ as our Lord, grasped in thought and realized in experience. By simply designating Jesus "our Lord" Paul raises Him above all the temporally conditioned conceptions in which the mystery of His personality might be grasped, and sets Him forth as the spiritual Being who transcends all human definitions, to whom we have to surrender ourselves in order to experience in Him the true law of our existence and our being.   [Mysticism, p. 378]

Mysticism and Everyday Piety

As a rule, the man who has once penetrated to the recognition and experience of the eternal amid the transient thenceforward scorns to have anything to do with the inadequate conception of ordinary thought and everyday piety. He is a mystic and nothing but a mystic. As possessed of a mode of apprehension coming from within and directed towards that which is within, he is exalted above all knowledge coming from without. If he tolerates naïve statements about the temporal and eternal as traditional pictures, he nevertheless constantly endeavors to illuminate this exoteric material with the penetrating light of mysticism and to show it up clearly in its inadequate relativity. But Paul's mysticism behaves quite differently. It shows no hesitation in allowing non-mystical views of redemption to take their place alongside of it as having equal right to expression.   [Mysticism, p. 24]

Union with Jesus Christ

All attempts to rob Christianity of the character of Christ-mysticism are nothing more or less than a useless resistance to that spirit of knowledge and truth, which finds expression in the teaching of the first and greatest of all Christian thinkers. Just as philosophy, after all its aberrations, has always to return to the primary truth that every genuinely profound and living world-view is of a mystical character, in the sense that it consists of some kind of conscious and willing surrender to the mysterious and infinite will-to-live, from which we are; so thought of an essentially Christian character cannot do other than conceive this surrender to God, as Paul conceived it long ago, as coming to pass in union with the being of Jesus Christ.   [Mysticism, p. 378]

God-Mysticism

God-mysticism, in the sense of a direct becoming-one with the infinite creative will of God, is impossible of realization. All attempts to extract living religion from pure monistic God-mysticism are foredoomed to failure, whether they are undertaken by the Stoics, by Spinoza, by Indian or by Chinese thought. They know the direction, but they do not find the way. From the becoming-one with the infinite essence of the being of the universal will-to-be there can result nothing but a passive determination of man's being, an absorption into God, a sinking into the ocean of the Infinite. Pure God-mysticism remains a dead thing. The becoming-one of the finite will with the Infinite acquires a content only when it is experienced both as quiescence in it and at the same time as a "being-taken-possession-of" by the will of love, which in us comes to consciousness of itself and strives in us to become act. Mysticism only takes the road to life when it passes through the antithesis of God's will of love with His infinite enigmatic creative will, and transcends it. Since human thinking cannot comprehend the eternal in its true nature, it is bound to arrive at dualism and be forced to overcome it, in order to adjust itself to the eternal. It must, no doubt, face all the enigmas of existence which present themselves to thought and harass it, but in the last resort it must leave the incomprehensible uncomprehended, and take the path of seeking to be certified of God as the will of love, and finding in it both inner peace and springs of action.   [Mysticism, pp. 378 f.]

Bach's Mysticism

In the last resort Bach's real religion was not orthodox Lutheranism, but mysticism. In his innermost essence he belongs to the history of German mysticism. This robust man, who seems to be in the thick of life with his family and his work, and whose mouth seems to express something like comfortable joy in life, was inwardly dead to the world. His whole thought was transfigured by a wonderful, serene longing for death. Again and again, whenever the text affords the least pretext for it, he gives voice to this longing in his music; and nowhere is his speech so moving as in the cantatas in which he discourses on the release from the body of this death. The Epiphany and certain bass cantatas are the revelation of his most intimate religious feelings. Sometimes it is a sorrowful and weary longing that the music expresses; at others, a glad serene desire, finding voice in one of those lulling cradlesongs that only he could write; then again a passionate, ecstatic longing, that calls death to it jubilantly, and goes forth in rapture to meet it. . . . We feel that we are in the presence of a musician who is not merely bent on rendering into tone the thoughts of his text, but has seized upon the words and made them his own, breathing into them something of himself that was yearning for expression.

This is Bach's religion as it appears in the cantatas. It transfigured his life. The existence that, considered from the outside, seems all conflict and struggle and bitterness, was in truth tranquil and serene.   [Bach, I, pp. 169 f.]

The Danger of Mysticism

The great danger for all mysticism is that of becoming supra-ethical, that is to say, of making the spirituality associated with the being-in-eternity an end in itself. This valuation of the spiritual in and for itself is found among the Brahmans, the Buddhists, and in Hegel. And the mysticism of Hellenistic personal religion is, it might almost be said, without ethical interests. Its efforts are directed only towards attaining for the individual man, through initiation, the assurance of immortality. It does not urge the man, born again to new life, to live as a new person an ethical life in the world. How difficult it is for the intellectual mysticism of the being-in-God to reach an ethic is seen in Spinoza. Even in Christian mysticism, whether medieval or modern, it is often the semblance of ethics rather than ethics itself which is preserved. There is always the danger that the mystic will experience the eternal as absolute impassivity, and will consequently cease to regard the ethical existence as the highest manifestation of spirituality.

In Paul's teaching, however, ethics comes to its full rights. He is never tempted to give to the thought, that those who are in Christ are already supernatural beings, the special complexion that they are now exalted above what is held in the natural world to be good or evil.   [Mysticism, pp. 297 f.]

The Desire to Be with God

When you preach, you must lead men out of the desire to
know everything to the knowledge of the one thing that
is needful, to the desire to be in God, and thus no more to
conform to the world but to rise above all mysteries as
those who are redeemed from the world. "If only I have
Thee, I care nothing for heaven and earth." * "All things
work together for good to them that love God." Point men
to these words as to the peaks of Ararat, where they may
take refuge when the flood of the inexplicable overwhelms
all around. [Christianity, pp. 81 f.]

Mysticism and Ethics

Ethics must make up its mind to base itself in mysticism. But
mysticism, on its side, must never suppose that it exists for
its own sake. It is not the blossom itself, but only the green
calyx which is its support. The blossom is ethics. Mysticism
that exists for its own sake is the salt which has lost its
savor. [Ethics, p. 247]

* Ps. lxxiii, 25 (Luther).

LIVING ETHICS

What Is Ethics?

Ethics is the activity of man directed to secure the inner perfection of his own personality.   [Decay, p. 94]

The Ethical Problem

The ethical problem is the problem of finding a foundation in thought for the fundamental principle of morality. What is the common element of good in the manifold kinds of good which we encounter in our experience? Does such a general notion of the good really exist?

If so, then what is its essential nature, and to what extent is it real and necessary for me? What power does it possess over my opinions and actions? What is the position into which it brings me with regard to the world?

Thought, therefore, must direct its attention to this fundamental moral principle. The mere setting up of lists of virtues and vices is like vamping on the keyboard and calling the ensuing noise music.   [Ethics, p. 25]

Reason and Goodness

Whatever is reasonable is good. . . . To be truly rational is to become ethical.   [Reverence, p. 231]

Good and Evil

Just as in my own will-to-live there is a yearning for more life, and for that mysterious exaltation of the will-to-live which is called pleasure, and terror in face of annihilation and that injury to the will-to-live which is called pain; so the same obtains in all the will-to-live around me, equally whether it can express itself to my comprehension or whether it remains unvoiced.

Ethics thus consists in this, that I experience the necessity of practising the same reverence for life toward all will-to-live, as toward my own. Therein I have already the needed fundamental principle of morality. It is *good* to maintain and cherish life; it is *evil* to destroy and to check life. [Ethics, p. 254]

The Relationship of Love

Let me give you a definition of ethics: It is good to maintain life and further life; it is bad to damage and destroy life. However much it struggles against it, ethics arrives at the religion of Jesus. It must recognize that it can discover no other relationship to other beings as full of sense as the relationship of love. Ethics is the maintaining of life at the highest point of development—my own life and other life—by devoting myself to it in help and love, and both these things are connected.   [Religion, p. 1521]

Resignation

Ethics is in fact reverence for the will-to-live both within and without my own personality. The immediate product of reverence for the will-to-live which I find in myself is the profound life-affirmation of resignation. I comprehend my will-to-live not only as something which lives itself out in fortunate moments of success, but also as something which is conscious of itself and its own experiences. If I do not allow this experiencing of myself to be dissipated by heedless lack of reflection, but, on the contrary, deliberately pause in it as one who feels its real value, I am rewarded by a disclosure of the secret of spiritual independence. I become a partaker in an unguessed-at freedom amid the destinies of life. At moments when I should otherwise have thought myself to be overwhelmed and crushed, I feel myself uplifted in a state of inexpressible joy, astounding to myself, in which I am conscious of freedom from the world and experience a clarifying of my whole view of life. Resignation is the vestibule through which we pass in entering the palace of ethics. Only he who experiences inner freedom from external events in profound surrender to his own will-to-live is capable of the profound and permanent surrender of himself for the sake of other life. [Ethics, pp. 258 f.]

The Progress of Ethics

There is a development under way by which the circle of ethics always grows wider, and ethics becomes more profound. This development has been in progress from primitive times to the present. It is often halted, hindered by the absence of thought among men—I dare to say through that absence of thought which characterizes thought! But yet the development goes on to its end. The circle described by ethics is always widening. Primitive man has duties only toward his nearest relations. All other living beings are to him only things; he mistreats them and kills them, without compunction. Then the circle widens to the tribe, to the people, and grows ever wider until at last man realizes his ethical association with the whole of humanity. This represents an enormous act of thinking. [Religion, pp. 1520 f.]

Ethics and Humanity

Consider Plato and Aristotle. Their ethics is narrow-hearted. They were occupied only with their fellow citizens. Slaves and foreigners did not concern them. Then with stoicism the circle begins to widen. That was the greatest manifestation of Greek thought. (Forgive me this heresy!) Then in Seneca, Epictetus, Marcus Aurelius, the idea suddenly crops up that ethics is concerned with all humanity. Thought arrives at that intuitive knowledge which you find already in the prophets of Israel and which is explained by Jesus. [Religion, p. 1521]

Purposeless Activity

We Westerners dream of a theory of the universe which corresponds to our impulse to action and at the same time clarifies it. We have not been able to formulate such a theory definitely. At present we are in the state of possessing merely an impulse without any definite orientation. The spirit of the age drives us into action without allowing us to attain any clear view of the objective world and of life. It claims our toil inexorably in the service of this or that end, this or that achievement. It keeps us in a sort of intoxication of activity so that we may never have time to reflect and to ask ourselves what this restless sacrifice of ourselves to ends and achievements really has to do with the meaning of the world and of our lives. And so we wander hither and thither in the gathering dusk formed by lack of any definite theory of the universe like homeless, drunken mercenaries, and enlist indifferently in the service of the common and the great without distinguishing between them. And the more hopeless becomes the condition of the world in which this adventurous impulse to action and progress ranges to and fro, the more bewildered becomes our whole conception of things and the more purposeless and irrational the doings of those who have enlisted under the banner of such an impulse.   [Decay, pp. 97 f.]

Beyond Utility

Jesus does not build up His ethic with a view to solving the problem of how to organize a perfectly ethical society, but He preaches the ethic of men who together strive to attain to a perfect yielding of themselves to the will of God. Because He thus turns away from the utilitarian, He attains to the absolute ethic. An ethic which is formulated on a principle of utility is always relative.

An illustration: Jesus tells us that we must always forgive, that we must never fight for our rights nor resist evil; He does not consider whether observance of these commandments makes legally ordered conditions possible in human society, but He leads us beyond all considerations of utility into the inward constraint to do the will of God.   [Christianity, p. 18]

Absolute Ethics

Every ethic has something of the absolute about it, just as soon as it ceases to be mere social law. It demands of one what is actually beyond his strength. Take the question of man's duty to his neighbor. The ethic cannot be fully carried out, without involving the possibility of complete sacrifice of self. Yet, philosophy has never bothered to take due notice of the distinction. It has simply tried to ignore absolute ethics, because such ethics cannot be fitted into tabulated rules and regulations. Indeed, the history of world

teachings on the subject may be summarized in the motto:
"Avoid absolute ethics, and thus keep within the realm of
the possible." [Reverence, p. 232.]

Incomplete Ethics

Materialism proclaims war against metaphysics. It wants
only the positive—what one can really know—and by that
it declares its intention of living. The ethics of materialism
consists in saying: You must live for the good of the community. Has this form of ethics really the significance of a
religion? Can a man understand the purpose of his life
when he says: I live for the good of the community?
No! The ethics of materialism is incomplete. It hangs in
the air. [Religion, p. 1519]

Unethical Religion

Karl Barth—whom I, personally, value greatly—came to
the point when he had to concern himself with the world,
which in theory he did not want to do. He had to defend
the freedom of religion against the state. And he did it with
courage. But it shows that his theory is false! It is something terrible to say that religion is not ethical. Karl Barth
is a truly religious personality, and in his sermons there is
much profound religion. But the terrible thing is that he
dares to preach that religion is turned aside from the world
and in so doing expresses what the spirit of the age is feeling. [Religion, p. 1484]

Justice and Love

As modern men we imagine the state of the perfect human
society to be one of harmony between legal organization
and the practice of love. Jesus does not attempt to har-

monize justice and love but says to man: If you want to be
in the spirit of God, you may not think or act otherwise
than in love.   [Christianity, pp. 18 f.]

Passive and Active Ethics

In the Epistle to the Romans Paul develops his mysticism
and his ethics side by side. And in this exposition the unity
of active and passive ethics is admirably shown. For the
only profound ethic is one which is able, on the basis of
one and the same conception, to give an ethical interpretation to all that a man experiences and suffers as well as to
all that he does. The great weakness of the utilitarian
ethic is at all times that it can relate itself only to man's
action and not to that which he undergoes, although for
his full development both must be taken into account. It
is only insofar as a man is purified and liberated from
the world by that which he experiences and endures, that he
becomes capable of truly ethical action. In the ethic of the
dying and rising again with Christ, passive and active ethics
are interwoven as in no other. The being "not as the world"
in action is the expression of the being made free from the
world, through suffering and dying with Christ. This constitutes the greatness and originality of Paul's ethics. And
therefore these chapters of the Epistle to the Romans are
among the most fundamental and impressive passages which
have ever been written about ethics.   [Mysticism, p. 302]

Living Ethics

Since, in virtue of his spirituality, Paul moves within the
narrow bounds of eschatology as a free man, he does not
suffer it to rob him of his direct humanity, which only
becomes the more profound. With tremendous certainty
and precision he goes in all things straight to the spiritually

essential. In the most natural way the mystical dying with Christ and rising with Him is transmitted into a living ethic. The problem of the relation between redemption and ethics finds in his teaching a complete solution. Ethic is for him the necessary outward expression of the translation from the earthly world to the super-earthly, which has already taken place in the being-in-Christ. And, further, that the man who has undergone this translation has placed himself under the direction of the Spirit of Christ, and so has become Man in the highest sense of the word.   [Mysticism, pp. 332 f.]

The Authority of the Ethical

By preserving this ethical spirituality amid the enthusiastic expectation of the glory of Christ, and laying down in such forceful words the ethical character of the belief in Christ, Paul shows himself the true disciple of Jesus. He has therein accomplished something essential to the preservation of the spirit of Jesus' message and work—something which is overlooked by those who are content simply to repeat His ethical sayings. Paul, alone of all the believers of this early period, recognized the faith in Jesus Christ essentially, and with all that it implies, must place itself under the absolute authority of the ethical, and must draw its warmth from the flame of love.   [Mysticism, p. 310]

The Spiritual Humanizing of Mankind

The religions which decisively deny the world and life (Brahminism and Buddhism) show no interest in civilization. The Judaism of the prophetic period, the almost contemporary religion of Zarathustra, and the religious thought of the Chinese include in their ethical world- and life-affirmation strong impulses to civilization. They want to improve social conditions, and they call men to purposeful action in the service of common aims which ought to be realized, whereas the pessimistic religions let men continue to pass their time in solitary meditation.

The Jewish prophets Amos and Isaiah (760–700 B.C.), Zarathustra (7th century B.C.), and Kung-fu-tse (560–480 B.C.) mark the great turning point in the spiritual history of mankind. Between the eighth and sixth centuries B.C. thinking men belonging to three nations, living in widely separated countries and having no relations whatever with one another, rise one and all to the perception that the ethical consists not in submission to traditional national customs, but in the active devotion of individuals to their fellow men or to aims which should produce an improvement of social conditions. In this great revolution begins the spiritual humanizing of mankind and, with that, the civilization which is capable of the highest development. [Life, p. 215]

Deeds Instead of Words

I wanted to be a doctor that I might be able to work without having to talk. For years I had been giving myself out in words, and it was with joy that I had followed the calling of theological teacher and of preacher. But this new form of activity I could not represent to myself as talking about the religion of love, but only as an actual putting it into practice. Medical knowledge made it possible for me to carry out my intention in the best and most complete way, wherever the path of service might lead me. In view of the plan for Equatorial Africa, the acquisition of such knowledge was especially indicated because in the district [the Gabun, one of the four colonies of French Equatorial Africa, bordering on the Atlantic] to which I thought of going, a doctor was, according to the missionaries' reports, the most needed of all needed things. They

were always complaining in their magazine that the natives
who visited them in physical suffering could not be given
the help they desired. To become one day the doctor whom
these poor creatures needed, it was worth-while, so I
judged, to become a medical student. Whenever I was inclined to feel that the years I should have to sacrifice were
too long, I reminded myself that Hamilcar and Hannibal
had prepared for their march on Rome by their slow and
tedious conquest of Spain.   [Life, pp. 114 f.]

Dives and Lazarus

I gave up my position of professor in the University of
Strassburg, my literary work, and my organ playing, in
order to go as a doctor to Equatorial Africa. How did that
come about?

I had read about the physical miseries of the natives in
the virgin forests; I had heard about them from missionaries,
and the more I thought about it the stranger it seemed to
me that we Europeans trouble ourselves so little about the
great humanitarian task which offers itself to us in far-off
lands. The parable of Dives and Lazarus seemed to me to
have been spoken directly of us! We are Dives, for, through
the advances of medical science, we now know a great deal
about disease and pain, and have innumerable means of
fighting them: yet we take as a matter of course the incalculable advantages which this new wealth gives us! Out
there in the colonies, however, sits wretched Lazarus, the
colored folk, who suffers from illness and pain just as much
as we do, nay, much more, and has absolutely no means of
fighting them. And just as Dives sinned against the poor
man at his gate because for want of thought he never put
himself in his place and let his heart and conscience tell
him what he ought to do, so do we sin against the poor
man at our gate.   [Edge, pp. 1 f.]

The Decision to Serve

The decision was made when I was one and twenty. In that year, while still a student, I resolved to devote my life till I was thirty to the office of preacher, to science, and to music. If by that time I should have done what I hoped in science and music, I would take a path of immediate service as man to my fellow men. What this path should be I counted on learning from circumstances during the interval.

The idea of devoting myself to the work of medical help in the colonies was not the first form that the resolution took. This one emerged after plans for giving other kinds of help had occupied my mind, and had been given up for the most varied reasons. Finally a chain of circumstances pointed out to me the road which led to the sufferers from leprosy and sleeping sickness in Africa. [Childhood, pp. 82 f.]

Individual and Social Ethics

The fact that it is impossible to develop the ethic of ethical personality into a serviceable ethic of society is closely connected with the subjective enthusiastic nature of ethics. It seems so self-evident that correct social ethics develops naturally from correct individual ethics, and that the one passes over into the other as a city does into its suburbs. But actually they cannot be so built on to one another that the streets of the one may run on into the other. . . .

In the last resort the antagonism between the two is due to the different values which they attach to humanitarianism. Humanitarianism consists in this principle, that a *man* is never to be sacrificed for an *end*. The ethic of ethical personality desires to preserve humanitarianism; that which is molded on the needs of society is unable so to preserve it.

When the individual has the alternative before him of either sacrificing in some way the happiness or existence of another man for the sake of his own interests, or of receiving injury himself, he is in a position to listen to the demand of ethics and to choose the latter course. But society, thinking supra-personally, and following supra-personal ends, cannot attribute such importance to the happiness and existence of an individual. Its ethic is in principle non-humanitarian.   [Ethics, pp. 233 f.]

Charity at Home and Abroad

Care for distress at home and care for distress elsewhere do but help each other if, working together, they wake men in sufficient numbers from their thoughtlessness, and call into life a new spirit of humanity.   [Edge, pp. 174 f.]

THE WILL–TO–LIVE

All Life Is Valuable

The deeper we look into nature, the more we recognize that it is full of life, and the more profoundly we know that all life is a secret and that we are united with all life that is in nature. Man can no longer live his life for himself alone. We realize that all life is valuable and that we are united to all this life. From this knowledge comes our spiritual relationship to the universe.   [Religion, p. 1520]

The Will-to-Live

The most immediate fact of man's consciousness is the assertion: "I am life which wills to live, in the midst of life which wills to live," and it is as will-to-live in the midst of will-to-live that man conceives himself during every moment that he spends in meditating on himself and the world around him.

As in my will-to-live there is ardent desire for further life and for the mysterious exaltation of the will-to-live which we call pleasure, while there is fear of destruction and of that mysterious depreciation of the will-to-live which we call pain: so too are these in the will-to-live around me, whether it can express itself to me, or remains dumb.

Man has now to decide what his relation to his will-to-live shall be. He can deny it. But if he bids his will-to-live change into will-not-to-live, as is done in Indian and indeed in all pessimistic thought, he involves himself in self-contradiction. He raises to the position of his world- and life-view something unnatural, something which is in itself untrue, and which cannot be carried to completion. Indian thought, and Schopenhauer's also, is full of inconsistencies because it cannot help making concessions time after time to the will-to-live which persists in spite of all world and life denial, though it will not admit that the concessions are really such. Negation of the will-to-live is self-consistent only if it is really willing actually to put an end to physical existence.

If man affirms his will-to-live, he acts naturally and honestly. He confirms an act which has already been accomplished in his instinctive thought by repeating it in his conscious thought. The beginning of thought, a beginning which continually repeats itself, is that man does not simply accept his existence as something given, but experiences it as something unfathomably mysterious. Life-affirmation is the spiritual act in which he ceases to live unreflectively and begins to devote himself to his life with reverence, in order to raise it to its true value. To affirm life is to deepen, to make more inward, and to exalt the will-to-live.

At the same time the man who has become a thinking being feels a compulsion to give to every will-to-live the same reverence for life that he gives to his own. He experiences that other life in his own. He accepts as being good: to preserve life, to promote life, to raise to its highest value life which is capable of development; and as being evil: to destroy life, to injure life, to repress life which is capable of development. This is the absolute, fundamental principle of the moral, and it is a necessity of thought. [Life, pp. 186 ff.]

Interest in Life

There is in each of us the will-to-live, which is based on the mystery of what we call "taking an interest." We cannot live alone. Though man is an egoist, he is never completely so. He *must* always have some interest in life about him. If for no other reason, he must do so in order to make his own life more perfect. Thus it happens that we want to devote ourselves; we want to take our part in perfecting our ideal of progress; we want to give meaning to the life in the world. This is the basis of our striving for harmony with the spiritual element.   [Reverence, pp. 225 f.]

The Impulse to Perfection

The essential nature of the will-to-live is found in this, that it is determined to live itself out. It bears in itself the impulse to realize itself to the highest possible degree of perfection.

In delicate blossoms, in the manifold wondrous forms of the jellyfish, in a blade of grass, in the crystal; everywhere it strives to reach that perfection which is implicit in its own nature. Imaginative power, determined by ideals, is at work in all that is. The impulse toward perfection is innate in us—beings, as we are, endowed with freedom and capable of reflective purposive action—in such a way that we naturally aspire to raise ourselves and every portion of existence affected by our influence to the highest material and spiritual degree of value.

We do not know how this aspiration came to be in us and how it has developed itself in us. It is an intrinsic part of our being. We must follow it if we will not be untrue to the secret will-to-live which is rooted in us.   [Ethics, p. 222]

The Insignificance of Man

When we consider the immensity of the universe, we must confess that man is insignificant. The world began, as it were, yesterday. It may end tomorrow. Life has existed in the universe but a brief second. And certainly man's life can hardly be considered the goal of the universe. Its margin of existence is always precarious. Study of the geologic periods shows that. So does the battle against disease. When one has seen whole populations annihilated by sleeping sickness, as I have, one ceases to imagine that human life is nature's goal. In fact, the Creative Force does not concern itself about preserving life. It simultaneously creates and destroys. Therefore, the will-to-live is not to be understood within the circle of Creative Force. Philosophy and religion have repeatedly sought the solution by this road; they have projected our will to perfection into nature at large, expecting to see its counterpart there. But in all honesty we must confess that to cling to such a belief is to delude ourselves.   [Reverence, p. 226]

What Knowledge Tells Me

I ask knowledge what it can tell me of life. Knowledge replies that what it can tell me is little, yet immense. Whence this universe came, or whither it is bound, or how it happens to be at all, knowledge cannot tell me. Only this: that the will-to-live is everywhere present, even as in me. I do not need science to tell me this; but it cannot tell me anything more essential. Profound and marvelous as chemistry is, for example, it is like all science in the fact that it can lead me only to the mystery of life, which is essentially in me, however near or far away it may be observed.   [Reverence, p. 230]

Is Man the End of Nature?

The effort for harmony never succeeds. Events cannot be harmonized with our activities. Working purposefully toward certain ends, we assume that the Creative Force in the world is doing likewise. Yet, when we try to define its goal, we cannot do so. It tends toward developing a type of existence, but there is no coordinated, definite end to be observed, even though we think there should be. We like to imagine that Man is nature's goal; but facts do not support that belief.   [Reverence, p. 226]

The Horrible Drama of the World

The world offers us the horrible drama of will-to-live divided against itself. One existence holds its own at the cost of another: one destroys another. Only in the thinking man has the will-to-live become conscious of other will-to-live, and desirous of solidarity with it. This solidarity, however, he cannot completely bring about, because man is subject to the puzzling and horrible law of being obliged to live at the cost of other life, and to incur again and again the guilt of destroying and injuring life. But as an ethical being he strives to escape whenever possible from this necessity, and as one who has become enlightened and merciful to put a stop to this disunion (Selbstentzweiung) of the will-to-live so far as the influence of his own existence reaches. He thirsts to be permitted to preserve his humanity, and to be able to bring to other existences release from their sufferings.   [Life, pp. 188 f.]

Know Thyself

The will-to-live which aspires to knowledge of the objective world is sure to make shipwreck, the will-to-live which aspires to knowledge of itself is a bold and skilful sailor. . . .

My knowledge of the world is a knowledge from the outside and must always remain incomplete. The knowledge derived from my will-to-live is, on the contrary, direct, and goes back to the secret springs of life as life exists in itself.

The highest knowledge is thus to know that I must be true to the will-to-live. This it is which plots the course for me that I must follow through the night without a chart. To live out one's life along its true course, to exalt it, to ennoble it, is natural. Every diminution of the will-to-live is an act of insincerity towards oneself or a definite symptom of ill-health.   [Ethics, p. 221]

Triumph over Circumstances

The will-to-live is not a flame which burns only when it has the fuel of events which it desires; it even gives a purer, clearer light when it has to depend on itself for nourishment. It shows itself as an actively working will even when surrounding events involve it in certain suffering. In profound reverence for life it makes the existence, which, according to our ordinary notions, is in no way any longer worthy of life, precious, in that in such beings also it develops and experiences its freedom from the world. Quietness and peace pass from such a man to others and they in turn are affected by the secret truth that we must all maintain our freedom in action and in suffering in order to live sincerely.

True resignation is not a becoming weary of the world, rather it is the quiet triumph over the circumstances of life which the will-to-live enjoys in its bitterest need.   [Ethics, pp. 223 f.]

Spiritual Exaltation

One realizes that he is but a speck of dust, a plaything of events outside his reach. Nevertheless, he may at the same time discover that he has a certain liberty, as long as he lives. Sometime or another all of us must have found that happy events have not been able to make us happy, nor unhappy events to make us unhappy. There is within each of us a modulation, an inner exaltation, which lifts us above the buffetings with which events assail us. Likewise, it lifts us above dependence upon the gifts of events for our joy. Hence, our dependence upon events is not absolute; it is qualified by our spiritual freedom. Therefore, when we speak of resignation it is not sadness to which we refer, but the triumph of our will-to-live over whatever happens to us. And to become ourselves, to be spiritually alive, we must have passed beyond this point of resignation. [Reverence, p. 229]

Sincerity

Resignation is the very basis of ethics. Starting from this position, the will-to-live comes first to veracity as the primary ground of virtue. If I am faithful to my will-to-live, I cannot disguise that fact, even though such disguise or evasion might seem to my advantage. Reverence for my will-to-live leads me to the necessity of being sincere with myself. And out of this fidelity to my own nature grows all my faithfulness. Thus, sincerity is the first ethical quality which appears. However lacking one may be in other respects, sincerity is the one thing which he must possess. Nor is this point of view to be found only among people of complex social life. Primitive cultures show the fact to be equally true there. Resignation to the will-to-live leads directly to this first virtue: sincerity.   [Reverence, p. 230]

The Mystery of Life

The essential thing to realize about ethics is that it is the very manifestation of our will-to-live. All of our thoughts are given in that will-to-live, and we but give them expression and form in words. To analyze reason fully would be to analyze the will-to-live. The philosophy that abandons the old Rationalism must begin by meditation on itself. Thus, if we ask, "What is the immediate fact of my consciousness? What do I self-consciously know of myself, making abstractions of all else, from childhood to old age? To what do I always return?" we find the simple fact of consciousness is this, *I will to live*. Through every stage of life, this is the one thing I know about myself. I do not say, "I am life"; for life continues to be a mystery too great to understand. I only know that I cling to it. I fear its cessation—death. I dread its diminution—pain. I seek its enlargement—joy.   [Reverence, pp. 227 f.]

I Cling to Life

When my will-to-live begins to think, it sees life as a mystery in which I remain by thought. I cling to life because of my reverence for life. For, when it begins to think, the will-to-live realizes that it is free. It is free to leave life. It is free to choose whether or not to live. This fact is of particular significance for us in this modern age, when there are abundant possibilities for abandoning life, painlessly and without agony.   [Reverence, p. 228]

Life Is a Trust

The question which haunts men and women today is whether life is worth living. Perhaps each of us has had the experience of talking with a friend one day, finding that person bright, happy, apparently in the full joy of life; and then the next day we find that he has taken his own life! Stoicism has brought us to this point, by driving out the fear of death; for, by inference it suggests that we are free to choose whether to live or not. But if we entertain such a possibility, we do so by ignoring the melody of the will-to-live, which compels us to face the mystery, the value, the high trust committed to us in life. We may not understand it, but we begin to appreciate its great value. Therefore, when we find those who relinquish life, while we may not condemn them, we do pity them for having ceased to be in possession of themselves. Ultimately, the issue is not whether we do or do not fear death. The real issue is that of reverence for life.   [Reverence, pp. 228 f.]

The Boundless Ocean

Most men are scantily nourished on a modicum of happiness and a number of empty thoughts which life lays on their plates. They are kept in the road of life through stern necessity by elemental duties which they cannot avoid.

Again and again their will-to-live becomes, as it were, intoxicated: spring sunshine, opening flowers, moving clouds, waving fields of grain—all affect it. The manifold will-to-live, which is known to us in the splendid phenomena in which it clothes itself, grasps at their personal wills. They would fain join their shouts to the mighty symphony which is proceeding all around them. The world seems beauteous . . . but the intoxication passes. Dreadful discords only allow them to hear a confused noise, as before, where they had thought to catch the strains of glorious music. The beauty of nature is obscured by the suffering which they discover in every direction. And now they see again that they are driven about like shipwrecked persons on the waste of ocean, only that the boat is at one moment lifted high on the crest of the waves and a moment later sinks deep into the trough; and that now sunshine and now darkening clouds lie on the surface of the water.

And now they would fain persuade themselves that land lies on the horizon toward which they are driven. Their will-to-live befools their intellect so that it makes efforts to see the world as it would like to see it. It forces this intellect to show them a map which lends support to their hope of land. Once again they essay to reach the shore, until finally their arms sink exhausted for the last time and their eyes rove desperately from wave to wave. . . .

Thus it is with the will-to-live when it is unreflective.

But is there no way out of this dilemma? Must we either drift aimlessly through lack of reflection or sink in pessimism as the result of reflection? No. We must indeed attempt the limitless ocean, but we may set our sails and steer a determined course.   [Ethics, pp. 220 f.]

The Light That Shines in Darkness

I can do no other than hold on to the fact that the will-to-live appears in me as will-to-live which aims at becoming one with other will-to-live. This fact is the light which shines for me in the darkness. My ignorance regarding the real nature of the objective world no longer troubles me. I am set free from the world. I have been cast by my reverence for life into a state of unrest foreign to the world. By this, too, I am placed in a state of beatitude which the world cannot give. If in the happiness induced by our independence of the world I and another afford each other mutual help in understanding and in forgiveness, when otherwise will would harass other will, then the will-to-live is no longer at variance with itself. If I rescue an insect from a pool of water, then life has given itself for life, and again the self-contradiction of the will-to-live has been removed.

Whenever my life has given itself out in any way for other life, my eternal will-to-live experiences union with the eternal, since all life is one. I possess a cordial which secures me from dying of thirst in the desert of life. [Ethics, p. 257]

The Unfinished Cathedral

I recognize it as the destiny of my existence to be obedient to the higher revelation of the will-to-live which I find in myself. I choose as my activity the removal of the self-contradiction of the will-to-live, as far as the influence of my own existence extends. Knowing as I do the one thing needful, I am content to offer no opinion about the enigma of the objective world and my own being.

Thought becomes religious when it thinks itself out to the end. The ethic of reverence for life is the ethic of Jesus brought to philosophical expression, extended into cosmical form, and conceived as intellectually necessary.

The surmising and longing of all deeply religious personalities is comprehended and contained in the ethic of reverence for life. This, however, does not build up a world-view as a completed system, but resigns itself to leave the cathedral perforce incomplete. It is only able to finish the choir. Yet in this, true piety celebrates a living and continuous divine service. . . . [Ethics, pp. 257 f.]

REVERENCE FOR LIFE

Reverence for Life

Slowly we crept upstream, [on one of the long African errands of mercy], laboriously feeling—it was the dry season—for the channels between the sandbanks. Lost in thought I sat on the deck of the barge, struggling to find the elementary and universal conception of the ethical which I had not discovered in any philosophy. Sheet after sheet I covered with disconnected sentences, merely to keep myself concentrated on the problem. Late on the third day, at the very moment when, at sunset, we were making our way through a herd of hippopotamuses, there flashed upon my mind, unforeseen and unsought, the phrase, "Reverence for Life." The iron door had yielded: the path in the thicket had become visible. Now I had found my way to the idea in which world- and life-affirmation and ethics are contained side by side! Now I knew that the world-view of ethical world- and life-affirmation, together with its ideals of civilization, is founded in thought. [Life, pp. 185 f.]

I Live for Other Life

Ethics is nothing else than reverence for life. Reverence for life affords me my fundamental principle of morality, namely, that good consists in maintaining, assisting and enhancing life, and that to destroy, to harm or to hinder life is evil. Affirmation of the world, that is to say, affirmation of the will-to-live which appears in phenomenal form all around me, is only possible for me in that I give myself out for other life. Without understanding the meaning of the world I act from an inner necessity of my being so as to create values and to live ethically, in the world and exerting influence on it. For in world- and life-affirmation and in ethics I fulfil the will of the universal will-to-live which reveals itself in me. I live my life in God, in the mysterious ethical divine personality which I cannot discover in the world, but only experience in myself as a mysterious impulse.   [Ethics, p. xvi]

The Highest Rationality

Today there is an absence of thinking which is characterized by a contempt for life. We waged war for questions which, through reason, might have been solved. No one won. The war killed millions of men, brought suffering to millions of men, and brought suffering and death to millions of innocent animals. Why? Because we did not possess the highest rationality of reverence for life. And because we do not yet possess this, every people is afraid of every other, and each causes fear to the others. We are mentally afflicted one for another because we are lacking in rationality. There is no other remedy than reverence for life, and at that we must arrive.   [Religion, p. 1521]

The Driving Force of the Ethical

Thought must strive to find a formula for the essential nature of the ethical. In so doing it is led to characterize ethics as self-devotion for the sake of life, motivated by reverence for life. Although the phrase "reverence for life" may perhaps sound a trifle unreal, yet that which it denotes is something which never lets go its hold of the man in whose thought it has once found a place. Sympathy, love, and, in general, all enthusiastic feeling of real value are summed up in it. It works with restless vitality on the mental nature in which it has found a footing and flings this into the restless activity of a responsibility which never ceases and stops nowhere. Reverence for life drives a man on as the whirling, thrashing screw forces a ship through the water.   [Ethics, p. 256]

Life Has Value

It is in reverence for life that knowledge passes over into experience. . . . My life bears its meaning in itself. And this meaning is to be found in living out the highest and most worthy idea which my will-to-live can furnish . . . the idea of reverence for life. Henceforward I attribute real value to my own life and to all the will-to-live which surrounds me; I cling to an activist way of life and I create real values.   [Ethics, pp. xv f.]

Pure Religious Feeling

To have reverence in the face of life is to be in the grip of the eternal, unoriginated, forward-pushing will, which is the foundation of all being. It raises us above all intellectual knowledge of external objects, and grafts us on to the tree which is assured against drought because it is planted by the rivers of water. All vital religious feeling flows from reverence for life and for the necessity and for the need for ideals which is implicit in life. In reverence for life religious feeling lies before us in its most elemental and most profound form, in which it is no longer involved in explanations of the objective world, nor has anything to do with such, but is pure religious feeling founded altogether in

implicit necessity and therefore devoid of care about results.   [Ethics, p. 223]

Hindering or Helping

What shall be my attitude toward other life? It can only
be of a piece with my attitude towards my own life. If I
am a thinking being, I must regard other life than my own
with equal reverence. For I shall know that it longs for
fulness and development as deeply as I do myself. Therefore, I see that evil is what annihilates, hampers, or hinders
life. And this holds good whether I regard it physically or
spiritually. Goodness, by the same token, is the saving or
helping of life, the enabling of whatever life I can influence
to attain its highest development.   [Reverence, p. 230]

Raising Life to Its Highest Level

As a matter of fact, everything which in the usual ethical
valuation of inter-human relations is looked upon as good
can be traced back to the material and spiritual maintenance
or enhancement of human life and to the effort to raise it
to its highest level of value. And contrariwise everything
in human relations which is considered as evil, is in the final
analysis found to be material or spiritual destruction or
checking of human life and slackening of the effort to raise
it to its highest value. Individual concepts of good and evil
which are widely divergent and apparently unconnected
fit into one another like pieces which belong together, the
moment they are comprehended and their essential nature
is grasped in this general notion.   [Ethics, p. 254]

Shadows

Two perceptions cast their shadows over my existence.
One consists in my realization that the world is inexplicably

mysterious and full of suffering; the other in the fact that I
have been born into a period of spiritual decadence in mankind. I have become familiar with and ready to deal with
each through the thinking which has led me to the ethical
world- and life-affirmation of reverence for life. In that
principle my life has found a firm footing and a clear path
to follow.   [Life, p. 254]

Taking the World as It Is

The world-view of reverence for life follows from taking
the world as it is. And the world means the horrible in the
glorious, the meaningless in the full of meaning, the sorrowful in the joyful. However it is looked at it remains to
many a riddle.

But that does not mean that we need stand before the
problem of life at our wits' end because we have to renounce all hope of comprehending the course of world-
events as having a meaning. Reverence for life brings us
into a spiritual relation with the world which is independent
of all knowledge of the universe. Through the dark valley
of resignation it leads us by an inward necessity up to the
shining heights of ethical world- and life-affirmation.

We are no longer obliged to derive our life-view from
knowledge of the world. In the disposition to reverence
for life we possess a life-view founded on itself, in which
there stands, firm and ready for us, the ethical world-view
we are in search of. It renews itself in us every time we look
thoughtfully at ourselves and the life around us.

It is not through knowledge, but through experience of
the world that we are brought into relation with it. All
thinking which penetrates to the depths, ends in ethical
mysticism. What is rational is continued into what is nonrational. The ethical mysticism of reverence for life is
rationalism, thought to a conclusion.   [Life, p. 235]

Natural and Spiritual Life

The mistake made by all previous systems of ethics has been the failure to recognize that life as such is the mysterious value with which they have to deal. All spiritual life meets us within natural life. Reverence for life, therefore, is applied to natural life and spiritual life alike. In the parable of Jesus, the shepherd saves not merely the soul of the lost sheep but the whole animal. The stronger the reverence for natural life, the stronger grows also that for spiritual life.   [Life, p. 270]

"There Shall Be No More Pain"

How can I describe my feelings when a poor fellow is brought me in this condition [strangulated hernia]? I am the only person within hundreds of miles who can help him. Because I am here and am supplied by my friends with the necessary means, he can be saved, like those who came before him in the same condition and those who will come after him, while otherwise he would have fallen a victim to the torture. This does not mean merely that I can save his life. We must all die. But that I can save him from days of torture, that is what I feel as my great and ever new privilege. Pain is a more terrible lord of mankind than even death himself.   [Edge, p. 92]

"All Ye Are Brethren"

When the poor, moaning creature comes [with strangulated hernia], I lay my hand on his forehead and say to him: "Don't be afraid! In an hour's time you shall be put to sleep, and when you wake you won't feel any more pain." Very soon he is given an injection of omipon; the doctor's wife is called to the hospital, and, with Joseph's help, makes everything ready for the operation. When that is to begin she administers the anaesthetic, and Joseph, in a long pair of rubber gloves, acts as assistant.

The operation is finished, and in the hardly lighted dormitory I watch for the sick man's awaking. Scarcely has he recovered consciousness when he stares about him and ejaculates again and again: "I've no more pain! I've no more pain!" . . . His hand feels for mine and will not let it go. Then I begin to tell him and the others who are in the room that it is the Lord Jesus who has told the doctor and his wife to come to the Ogowe, and that white people in Europe give them the money to live here and cure the sick Negroes. Then I have to answer questions as to who these white people are, where they live, and how they know that the natives suffer so much from sickness. The African sun is shining through the coffee bushes into the dark shed, but we black and white sit side by side and feel that we know by experience the meaning of the words: "And all ye are brethren" (Matt. xxiii:8). Would that my generous friends in Europe could come out here and live through one such hour! [Edge, pp. 92 f.]

Identity with Life

The idea of reverence for life offers itself as the realistic answer to the realistic question of how man and the world are related to each other. Of the world man knows only that everything which exists is, like himself, a manifestation of the will-to-live. With this world he stands in a relation of passivity and of activity. On the one hand he is subordinate to the course of events which is given in this totality of life; on the other hand he is capable of affecting the life which comes within his reach by hampering or promoting it, by destroying or maintaining it.

The one possible way of giving meaning to his existence is that of raising his natural relation to the world to a spiritual one. As a being in a passive relation to the world he

comes into a spiritual relation to it by resignation. True resignation consists in this: that man, feeling his subordination
to the course of world happenings, wins his way to inward
freedom from the fortunes which shape the outward side
of his existence. Inward freedom means that he finds
strength to deal with everything that is hard in his lot, in
such a way that it all helps to make him a deeper and more
inward person, to purify him, and to keep him calm and
peaceful. Resignation, therefore, is the spiritual and ethical
affirmation of one's own existence. Only he who has gone
through the stage of resignation is capable of world-
affirmation.

As a being in an active relation to the world he comes into
a spiritual relation with it by not living for himself alone,
but feeling himself one with all life that comes within his
reach. He will feel all that life's experiences as his own, he
will give it all the help that he possibly can, and will feel
all the saving and promotion of life that he has been able
to effect as the deepest happiness that can ever fall to his
lot.

Let a man once begin to think about the mystery of his
life and the links which connect him with the life that fills
the world, and he cannot but bring to bear upon his own life
and all other life that comes within his reach the principle
of reverence for life, and manifest this principle by ethical
world- and life-affirmation expressed in action. Existence
will thereby become harder for him in every respect than it
would be if he lived for himself, but at the same time it
will be richer, more beautiful, and happier. It will become,
instead of mere living, a real experience of life. [Life,
pp. 267 f.]

Reverence and Resignation

The first spiritual act in man's experience is reverence for
life. The consequence of it is that he comes to realize his
dependence upon events quite beyond his control. There-

fore he becomes resigned. And this is the second spiritual act: resignation.   [Reverence, p. 229]

Adventurers in Self-Sacrifice

Reverence for life does not allow me to appropriate my own happiness. At moments when I should like to enjoy myself without a care, it brings before me thoughts of the misery I have seen and surmised. It refuses to allow me to banish my uneasiness. Just as the wave has no existence of its own, but is part of the continual movement of the ocean, thus I also am destined never to experience my life as self-contained, but always as part of the experience which is going on around me. An uncomfortable doctrine prompts me in whispered words. You are happy, it says. Therefore you are called to give up much. Whatever you have received more than others in health, in talents, in ability, in success, in a pleasant childhood, in harmonious conditions of home life, all this you must not take to yourself as a matter of course. You must pay a price for it. You must render in return an unusually great sacrifice of your life for other life. The voice of the true ethic is dangerous for the happy when they have the courage to listen to it. For them there is no quenching of the irrational fire which glows in it. It challenges them in an attempt to lead them away from the natural road, and to see whether it can make them the adventurers of self-sacrifice, of whom the world has too few.   [Ethics, pp. 267 f.]

Losing One's Life

The ethic of reverence for life constrains all, in whatever walk of life they may find themselves, to busy themselves intimately with all the human and vital processes which are being played out around them, and to give themselves as men to the man who needs human help and sympathy. It does not allow the scholar to live for his science alone, even if he is very useful to the community in so doing. It does not permit the artist to exist only for his art, even if he gives inspiration to many by its means. It refuses to let the business man imagine that he fulfils all legitimate demands in the course of his business activities. It demands from all that they should sacrifice a portion of their own lives for others. In what way and in what measure this is his duty, this everyone must decide on the basis of the thoughts which arise in himself, and the circumstances which attend the course of his own life. The self-sacrifice of one may not be particularly in evidence. He carries it out simply by continuing his normal life. Another is called to some striking self-surrender which obliges him to set on one side all regard for his own progress. Let no one measure himself by his conclusions respecting someone else. The destiny of men has to fulfil itself in a thousand ways, so that goodness may be actualized. What every individual has to contribute remains his own secret. But we must all mutually share in the knowledge that our existence only attains its true value when we have experienced in ourselves the truth of the declaration: "He who loses his life shall find it."   [Ethics, pp. 269 f.]

THE SACREDNESS OF ALL THAT LIVES

All Life Is Sacred

To the man who is truly ethical all life is sacred, including that which from the human point of view seems lower in the scale. He makes distinctions only as each case comes before him, and under the pressure of necessity, as, for example, when it falls to him to decide which of two lives he must sacrifice in order to preserve the other. But all through this series of decisions he is conscious of acting on subjective grounds and arbitrarily, and knows that he bears the responsibility for the life which is sacrificed.   [Life, p. 271]

Ethics and the Animal Creation

Slowly in our European thought comes the notion that ethics has not only to do with mankind but with the animal creation as well. This begins with St. Francis of Assisi. The explanation which applies only to man must be given up. Thus we shall arrive at saying that ethics is reverence for *all* life.   [Religion, p. 1521]

Widening the Circle of Ethics

If thought once begins to occupy itself with the mysterious fact of ethics, it cannot succeed in defining the limits of solidarity with other life. It must widen the circle from the narrowest limits of the family first to include the

clan, then the tribe, then the nation and finally all mankind. But even when it has established the relationship
between man and every other man it cannot stop. By reason of the quite universal idea, which is as elastic as one
pleases, of participation in a common nature, it is compelled to declare the unity of mankind with all created
beings.   [Indian, pp. 261 f.]

The Principle Is Universal

Ordinary ethics seeks to find limits within the sphere of
human life and relationships. But the absolute ethics of the
will-to-live must reverence every form of life, seeking so
far as possible to refrain from destroying any life, regard-
less of its particular type. It says of no instance of life,
"This has no value." It cannot make any such exceptions,
for it is built upon reverence for life as such. It knows that
the mystery of life is always too profound for us, and that
its value is beyond our capacity to estimate. We happen
to believe that man's life is more important than any other
form of which we know. But we cannot prove any such
comparison of value from what we know of the world's
development. True, in practice we are forced to choose. At
times we have to decide arbitrarily which forms of life, and
even which particular individuals, we shall save, and which
we shall destroy. But the principle of reverence for life is
none the less universal.   [Reverence, p. 233]

Universal Ethics

The great fault of all ethics hitherto has been that they
believed themselves to have to deal only with the relations
of man to man. In reality, however, the question is what
is his attitude to the world and all life that comes within
his reach. A man is ethical only when life, as such, is sacred

to him, that of plants and animals as that of his fellow men, and when he devotes himself helpfully to all life that is in need of help. Only the universal ethic of the feeling of responsibility in an ever-widening sphere for all that lives—only that ethic can be founded in thought. The ethic of the relation of man to man is not something apart by itself: it is only a particular relation which results from the universal one.

The ethic of reverence for life, therefore, comprehends within itself everything that can be described as love, devotion, and sympathy whether in suffering, joy, or effort. [Life, p. 188]

Birth and Nature of Ethics

We have dared to say that ethics is born of physical life, out of the linking of life with life. It is therefore the result of our recognizing the solidarity of life which nature gives us. And as it grows more profound, it teaches us sympathy with *all* life. Yet, the extremes touch, for this material-born ethic becomes engraved upon our hearts, and culminates in spiritual union and harmony with the creative Will which is in and through all. [Reverence, p. 239]

The Solidarity of Life

The important thing is that we are part of life. We are born of other lives; we possess the capacities to bring still other lives into existence. In the same way, if we look into a microscope we see cell producing cell. So nature compels us to recognize the fact of mutual dependence, each life necessarily helping the other lives which are linked to it. In the very fibers of our being, we bear within ourselves the fact of the solidarity of life. Our recognition of it expands with thought. Seeing its presence in ourselves, we realize how closely we are linked with others of our kind. We might like to stop here, but we cannot. Life demands that we see through to the solidarity of all life which we can in any degree recognize as having some similarity to the life that is in us.   [Reverence, p. 237]

Ethics Consist in Responsibility

Ethics consist in responsibility towards all that lives—responsibility which has become so wide as to be limitless.

Action directed towards the world is only possible for man in so far as he strives for the maintenance and furtherance at its highest level of all life that comes within his range. In this becoming-one with all life he realizes the active becoming-one with the Primal Source of Being to which this life belongs.   [Indian, p. 262]

True Ethics Are World-Wide

True ethics are world-wide. All that is ethical goes back to a single principle of morality, namely, the maintenance of life at its highest level, and the furtherance of life. The maintenance of one's own life at the highest level by becoming more and more perfect in spirit, and the maintenance at the highest level of other life by sympathetic, helpful self-devotion to it—this is ethics. What we call love is in its essence reverence for life. All material and spiritual values are values only in so far as they serve the maintenance of life at its highest level and the furtherance of life.

Ethics are boundless in their domain and limitless in their demands. They are concerned with all living things that come within our sphere.   [Indian, p. 260]

The Fundamental Principle of Morality

A man is really ethical only when he obeys the constraint laid on him to help all life which he is able to succor, and when he goes out of his way to avoid injuring anything living. He does not ask how far this or that life deserves sympathy as valuable in itself, nor how far it is capable of feeling. To him life as such is sacred. He shatters no ice crystal that sparkles in the sun, tears no leaf from its tree, breaks off no flower, and is careful not to crush any insect as he walks. If he works by lamplight on a summer evening, he prefers to keep the window shut and to breathe stifling air, rather than to see insect after insect fall on his table with singed and sinking wings.

If he goes out into the street after a rainstorm and sees a worm which has strayed there, he reflects that it will certainly dry up in the sunshine, if it does not quickly regain the damp soil into which it can creep, and so he helps it back from the deadly paving stones into the lush grass. Should he pass by an insect which has fallen into a pool, he spares the time to reach it a leaf or stalk on which it may clamber and save itself.   [Ethics, pp. 254 f.]

Truth Is Always Ridiculed

It is the fate of every truth to be an object of ridicule when it is first acclaimed. It was once considered foolish to suppose that colored men were really human beings and ought to be treated as such. What was once foolishness has now become a recognized truth. Today it is considered as exaggeration to proclaim constant respect for every form of life as being the serious demand of a rational ethic. But the time is coming when people will be amazed that the human race was so long before it recognized that thoughtless injury to life is incompatible with real ethics. Ethics is in its un-

qualified form extended responsibility with regard to
everything that has life.   [Ethics, p. 255]

A Prayer for All Living Creatures

It was quite incomprehensible to me—this was before I
began going to school—why in my evening prayers I should
pray for human beings only. So when my mother had
prayed with me and had kissed me good night, I used to
add silently a prayer that I had composed myself for all
living creatures. It ran thus: "O, heavenly Father, protect
and bless all things that have breath; guard them from all
evil, and let them sleep in peace."   [Childhood, p. 40]

"Thou Shalt Not Kill"

A deep impression was made on me by something which
happened during my seventh or eighth year. Henry Bräsch
and I had with strips of india rubber made ourselves cata-
pults, with which we could shoot small stones. It was
spring and the end of Lent, when one morning Henry said
to me, "Come along, let's go on to the Rebberg and shoot
some birds." This was to me a terrible proposal, but I did
not venture to refuse for fear he should laugh at me. We
got close to a tree which was still without any leaves, and
on which the birds were singing beautifully to greet the
morning, without showing the least fear of us. Then stoop-
ing like a red Indian hunter, my companion put a bullet in
the leather of his catapult and took aim. In obedience to
his nod of command, I did the same, though with terrible
twinges of conscience, vowing to myself that I would shoot
directly he did. At that very moment the church bells began
to ring, mingling their music with the songs of the birds
and the sunshine. It was the warning bell, which began half
an hour before the regular peal ringing, and for me it was

a voice from heaven. I shooed the birds away, so that they flew where they were safe from my companion's catapult, and then I fled home. And ever since then, when the Passiontide bells ring out to the leafless trees and the sunshine, I reflect with a rush of grateful emotion how on that day their music drove deep into my heart the commandment: "Thou shalt not kill."   [Childhood, pp. 40 f.]

Respect for Life

There slowly grew up in me an unshakeable conviction that we have no right to inflict suffering and death on another living creature unless there is some unavoidable necessity for it, and that we ought all of us to feel what a horrible thing it is to cause suffering and death out of mere thoughtlessness. And this conviction has influenced me only more and more strongly with time. I have grown more and more certain that at the bottom of our heart we all think this, and that we fail to acknowledge it and to carry our belief into practice chiefly because we are afraid of being laughed at by other people as sentimentalists, though partly also because we allow our best feelings to get blunted. But I vowed that I would never let my feelings get blunted, and that I would never be afraid of the reproach of sentimentalism.

I never go to a menagerie because I cannot endure the sight of the misery of the captive animals. The exhibiting of trained animals I abhor. What an amount of suffering and cruel punishment the poor creatures have to endure in order to give a few moments' pleasure to men devoid of all thought and feeling for them!   [Childhood, pp. 44 f.]

Sympathy with Animals

Man comes again and again into the position of being able to preserve his own life and life generally only at the cost of other life. If he has been touched by the ethic of reverence for life, he injures and destroys life only under a necessity which he cannot avoid, and never from thoughtlessness. So far as he is a free man he uses every opportunity of tasting the blessedness of being able to assist life and avert from it suffering and destruction.

Devoted as I was from boyhood to the cause of the protection of animal life, it is a special joy to me that the universal ethic of reverence for life shows the sympathy with animals which is so often represented as sentimentality, to be a duty which no thinking man can escape. Hitherto ethics have faced the problem of man and beast either uncomprehending or helpless. Even when sympathy with the animal creation was felt to be right, it could not be brought within the scope of ethics, because ethics were really focused only on the behavior of man to man.   [Life, p. 272]

Wanton Pastimes

Whenever I injure life of any kind I must be quite clear as to whether this is necessary or not. I ought never to pass the limits of the unavoidable, even in apparently insignificant cases. The countryman who has mowed down a thousand blossoms in his meadow as fodder for his cows should take care that on the way home he does not, in wanton pastime, switch off the head of a single flower growing on the edge of the road, for in so doing he injures life without being forced to do so by necessity.   [Ethics, p. 264]

The Humane Treatment of Animals

Those who test operations or drugs on animals, or who inoculate them with diseases so that they may be able to help human beings by means of the results thus obtained,

ought never to rest satisfied with the general idea that their
dreadful doings are performed in pursuit of a worthy aim.
It is their duty to ponder in every separate case whether it
is really and truly necessary thus to sacrifice an animal for
humanity. They ought to be filled with anxious care to
alleviate as much as possible the pain which they cause.
How many outrages are committed in this way in scientific
institutions where narcotics are often omitted to save time
and trouble! How many also when animals are made to
suffer agonizing tortures, only in order to demonstrate to
students scientific truths which are perfectly well known.
The very fact that the animal, as a victim of research, has
in his pain rendered such services to suffering men, has
itself created a new and unique relation of solidarity between him and ourselves. The result is that a fresh obligation is laid on each of us to do as much good as we possibly can to all creatures in all sorts of circumstances.
When I help an insect out of his troubles all that I do is
to attempt to remove some of the guilt contracted through
these crimes against animals.   [Ethics, p. 264]

Animal Suffering

Wherever any animal is forced into the service of man,
the sufferings which it has to bear on that account are the
concern of every one of us. No one ought to permit, insofar
as he can prevent it, pain or suffering for which he will
not take the responsibility. No one ought to rest at ease
in the thought that in so doing he would mix himself up
in affairs which are not his business. Let no one shirk the
burden of his responsibility. When there is so much mal-
treatment of animals, when the cries of thirsting creatures
go up unnoticed from the railway trucks, when there is
so much roughness in our slaughter houses, when in our
kitchens so many animals suffer horrible deaths from un-

skilful hands, when animals endure unheard-of agonies from heartless men, or are delivered to the dreadful play of children, then we are all guilty and must bear the blame.   [Ethics, pp. 264 f.]

Beasts That Perish

For some days a blue haze has been hanging over the forest. At night the low-hanging smoke-clouds are replaced by myriad darts of flame, stabbing the dark horizon. For it is the dry season, when the thick woods must be cleared to make way for new plantations. Yet, despite the dryness, the heavy timber burns slowly and incompletely: when the first rains come toward the end of September, the fallen trees are only partially consumed. As a result, it is quite common to see corn and banana saplings sprouting up through a morass of charred branches, logs and stumps.

At this time of the year, with the red reflections against the evening sky, I am seized by compassion for the poor beasts that perish in these fires. In ancient China the burning of forests was regarded as a crime, because it meant painful death to so many creatures. Here it is necessity for the natives. The forest giants cannot be cut up and removed.   [Letter, p. 70]

The Boundlessness of Ethics

Indian thought, starting from world- and life-negation, presses forward to a stage of knowledge which is quite outside the purview of European thinking. It reaches the point of taking into account the fact that our ethical behavior must not only concern our human neighbor but all living things. The problem of the boundlessness of the field of ethics and the boundlessness of the claims which ethics make upon us—a problem from which even today European thought is trying to escape—has existed for Indian thought for more than two thousand years, although Indian thought too has not yet felt its whole weight nor recognized the whole range which it covers.   [Indian, p. 10]

Ahimsa

In accordance with the Ahimsa commandment, the Jains give up bloody sacrifices, the use of meat, hunting and wild beast fights. They also make it their duty to be careful not to trample unawares on creeping things and insects as they walk. The Jain monks go so far as to tie a cloth in front of their mouths in order that as they breathe they may not swallow the tiny creatures of the air. Jainism also sees itself forced to abandon field work because it is impossible to dig up the earth without damaging minute living things. That is why the Jains are mainly engaged in trade.

The laying down of the commandment not to kill and not to damage is one of the greatest events in the spiritual history of mankind. Starting from its principle, founded on world and life denial, of abstention from action, ancient Indian thought—and this in a period when in other respects ethics have not progressed very far—reaches the tremendous discovery that ethics know no bounds! So far as we know this is for the first time clearly expressed by Jainism.   [Indian, pp. 82 f.]

The Law of Necessity

However seriously man undertakes to abstain from killing and damaging, he cannot entirely avoid it. He is under the law of necessity, which compels him to kill and to damage both with and without his knowledge. In many ways it may happen that by slavish adherence to the commandment not to kill compassion is less served than by breaking it. When the suffering of a living creature cannot be alleviated, it is more ethical to end its life by killing it mercifully than it is to stand aloof. It is more cruel to let domestic animals which one can no longer feed, die a painful death by starvation than to give them a quick and painless end by violence. Again and again we see ourselves placed under the necessity of saving one living creature by destroying or damaging another.

The principle of not-killing and not-harming must not aim at being independent, but must be the servant of, and subordinate itself to, compassion. It must therefore enter into practical discussion with reality. True reverence for morality is shown by readiness to face the difficulties contained in it.

If Indian thought were occupied with the whole of ethics, and not merely with the ethics of non-activity, it could not avoid, as it does, nor endeavor to escape, the practical confronting of reality.

But once again, it is just because it simply lays down non-killing and non-harming as a dogma, that it succeeds in preserving safely through the centuries the great ethical thought which is connected with it.   [Indian, pp. 83 f.]

The Ethics of the Flock

A flock of wild geese had settled to rest on a pond. One of the flock had been captured by a gardener, who had clipped its wings before releasing it. When the geese started to resume their flight, this one tried frantically, but vainly, to lift itself into the air. The others, observing his struggles, flew about in obvious efforts to encourage him; but it was no use. Thereupon, the entire flock settled back on the pond and waited, even though the urge to go on was strong within them. For several days they waited until the damaged feathers had grown sufficiently to permit the goose to fly. Meanwhile, the unethical gardener, having been converted

by the ethical geese, gladly watched them as they finally
rose together, and all resumed their long flight.   [Rever-
ence, p. 238]

Life Is Linked Together

I have the virtue of caring for all stray monkeys that come
to our gate. (If you have had any experience with large
numbers of monkeys, you know why I say it is a virtue
thus to take care of all comers until they are old enough or
strong enough to be turned loose, several together, in the
forest—a great occasion for them—and for me!) Sometimes
there will come to our monkey colony a wee baby monkey
whose mother has been killed, leaving this orphaned infant.
I must find one of the older monkeys to adopt and care for
the baby. I never have any difficulty about it, except to
decide which candidate shall be given the responsibility.
Many a time it happens that the seemingly worst-tempered
monkeys are most insistent upon having this sudden burden
of foster parenthood given to them.   [Reverence, p. 238]

Mutual Dependence

A friend in Hanover owned a small café. He would daily
throw out crumbs for the sparrows in the neighborhood.
He noticed that one sparrow was injured, so that it had difficulty getting about. But he was interested to discover that
the other sparrows, apparently by mutual agreement, would
leave the crumbs which lay nearest to their crippled com-
rade, so that he could get his share, undisturbed.   [Rever-
ence, pp. 238 f.]

A Complete Ethic

Only a complete ethic has mystical significance. An ethical
system which is only concerned with the attitude of man

to his fellow man and to society cannot really be in harmony with a world-view. It has no relationship with the universe. To found an ethical world-view on ethics which are only concerned with our fellow man and human society is a logical impossibility. It is the fault of too narrow a conception of ethics that thought has so far been unable to present an ethical world-view in a way that carries conviction.   [Indian, pp. 259 f.]

RETROSPECT AND PROSPECT

Misery in Paradise

I saw a man lying on the ground with his head almost buried in the sand and ants running all over him. It was a victim of sleeping sickness whom his companions had left there, probably some days before, because they could not take him any further. He was past all help, though he still breathed. While I was busied with him I could see through the door of the hut the bright blue waters of the bay in their frame of green woods, a scene of almost magic beauty, looking still more enchanting in the flood of golden light poured over it by the setting sun. To be shown in a single glance such a paradise and such helpless, hopeless misery, was overwhelming . . . but it was a symbol of the condition of Africa. [Edge, pp. 168 f.]

The Lord Whose Name Is Pain

"The natives who live in the bosom of nature are never so ill as we are, and do not feel pain so much." That is what my friends used to say to me, to try to keep me at home, but I have come to see that such statements are not true. Out here there prevail most of the diseases which we know in Europe, and several of them—those hideous ones, I mean, which we brought here—produce, if possible, more misery than they do amongst us. And the child of nature feels them as we do, for to be human means to be subject to the power of that terrible lord whose name is Pain.

Physical misery is great everywhere out here. Are we justified in shutting our eyes and ignoring it because our European newspapers tell us nothing about it? We civilized people have been spoiled. If any one of us is ill the doctor comes at once. If an operation is necessary, the door of some hospital or other opens to us immediately. But let every one reflect on the meaning of the fact that out here millions and millions live without help or hope of it. Every day thousands and thousands endure the most terrible sufferings, though medical science could avert them. Every day there prevails in many and many a far-off hut a despair which we could banish. Will each of my readers think what the last ten years of his family history would have been if they had been passed without medical or surgical help of any sort? It is time that we should wake from slumber and face our responsibilities!   [Edge, pp. 170 f.]

The Joy of Work

However limited one's means are, how much one can do with them! Just to see the joy of those who are plagued with sores, when these have been cleanly bandaged up and they no longer have to drag their poor, bleeding feet through the mud, makes it worth while to work here. How I should like all my helpers to be able to see on Mondays and Thursdays—the days set apart for the bandaging of sores—the freshly bandaged patients walking or being carried down the hill, or that they could have watched the eloquent gestures with which an old woman with heart complaint described how, thanks to digitalis, she could once more breathe and sleep, because the medicine had made "the worm" crawl right away down to her feet!

As I look back over the work of two months and a half, I can only say that a doctor is needed, terribly needed, here; that for a huge distance round the natives avail themselves of his help, and that with comparatively small means he can accomplish a quite disproportionate amount of good. The need is terrible. "Here, among us, everybody is ill," said a young man to me a few days ago. "Our country devours its own children," was the remark of an old chief. [Edge, pp. 37 f.]

Appeal to Sympathy

Believing it, as I do, to be my life's task to fight on behalf of the sick under far-off stars, I appeal to the sympathy which Jesus and religion generally call for, but at the same time I call to my help also our most fundamental ideas and reasonings. We ought to see the work that needs doing for the colored folk in their misery, not as a mere "good work," but as a duty that must not be shirked.

Ever since the world's far-off lands were discovered, what has been the conduct of the white peoples to the colored ones? What is the meaning of the simple fact that this and that people has died out, that others are dying out, and that the condition of others is getting worse and worse as a result of their discovery by men who professed to be followers of Jesus? Who can describe the injustice and the cruelties that in the course of centuries they have suffered at the hands of Europeans? Who can measure the misery produced among them by the fiery drinks and the hideous diseases that we have taken to them? If a record could be compiled of all that has happened between the white and the colored races, it would make a book containing numbers of pages, referring to recent as well as to early times, which the reader would have to turn over unread, because their contents would be too horrible.

We and our civilization are burdened, really, with a great debt. We are not free to confer benefits on these men, or not, as we please; it is our duty. Anything we give them is not benevolence but atonement. For everyone who scattered injury, someone ought to go out to take help, and when we have done all that is in our power, we shall not have atoned for the thousandth part of our guilt.   [Edge, pp. 171 f.]

A Brother to All Who Suffer

The necessity for taking medical help to the natives in our colonies is frequently argued on the ground that it is worthwhile to preserve the human material without which the colonies would become valueless. But the matter is in reality something much more important than a question of economics. It is unthinkable that we civilized peoples should keep for ourselves alone the wealth of means for fighting sickness, pain, and death which science has given us. If there is any ethical thinking at all among us, how can we refuse to let these new discoveries benefit those who, in distant lands, are subject to even greater physical distress than we are? In addition to the medical men who are sent out by the governments, and who are never more than enough to accomplish a fraction of what needs doing, others must go out too, commissioned by human society as such. Whoever among us has through personal experience learned what pain and anxiety really are must help to ensure that those who out there are in bodily need obtain the help which came to him. He belongs no more to himself alone; he has become the brother of all who suffer. On the "Brotherhood of those who bear the mark of pain" lies the duty of medical work, work for humanity's sake, in the colonies. Commissioned by their representatives, medical men must accomplish among the suffering in far-off lands, what is crying out for accomplishment in the name of true civilization.

In reliance upon the elementary truth which is embodied

in the idea of the "Brotherhood of those who bear the mark of pain," I ventured to found the Forest Hospital at Lambaréné. [Life, p. 227]

The Fellowship of Those Who Bear the Mark of Pain

The Fellowship of those who bear the Mark of Pain. Who are the members of this fellowship? Those who have learned by experience what physical pain and bodily anguish mean, belong together all the world over; they are united by a secret bond. One and all they know the horrors of suffering to which man can be exposed, and one and all they know the longing to be free from pain. He who has been delivered from pain must not think he is now free again, and at liberty to take life up just as it was before, entirely forgetful of the past. He is now a "man whose eyes are open" with regard to pain and anguish, and he must help to overcome those two enemies (so far as human power can control them) and to bring to others the deliverance which he has himself enjoyed. The man who, with a doctor's help, has been pulled through a severe illness, must aid in providing a helper such as he had himself, for those who otherwise could not have one. He who has been saved by an operation from death or torturing pain, must do his part to make it possible for the kindly anaesthetic and the helpful knife to begin their work, where death and torturing pain still rule unhindered. The mother who owes it to medical aid that her child still belongs to her, and not to the cold earth, must help, so that the poor mother who has never seen a doctor may be spared what she has been spared. Where a man's death agony might have been terrible, but could fortunately be made tolerable by a doctor's skill, those who stood around his deathbed must help, that others, too, may enjoy that same consolation when they lose their dear ones.

Such is the Fellowship of those who bear the Mark of Pain.   [Edge, pp. 173 f.]

Practical Idealism

The idealism that I preach is no nebulous thing; it has stood the test of practical achievement. I am confident that a group of men who appeal without too much fanfare to the generosity of any country for the creation of a medical station in the midst of the most underprivileged colonial peoples will be listened to and will succeed in their plans, especially if they are resolved, contrary to present tendencies, to begin modestly.   [Secours, p. 404]

Burden and Blessing

In my own life, anxiety, trouble, and sorrow have been allotted to me at times in such abundant measure that had my nerves not been so strong, I must have broken down under the weight. Heavy is the burden of fatigue and responsibility which has lain upon me without a break for years. I have not much of my life for myself, not even the hours I should like to devote to my wife and child.

But I have had blessings too: that I am allowed to work in the service of mercy; that my work has been successful; that I receive from other people affection and kindness in abundance; that I have loyal helpers, who identify themselves with my activity; that I enjoy a health which allows me to undertake most exhausting work; that I have a well-balanced temperament which varies little, and an energy which exerts itself with calmness and deliberation; and, finally, that I can recognize as such whatever happiness falls to my lot, accepting it also as a thing for which some thank offering is due from me.   [Life, pp. 281 f.]

Glorious Activity

Again and again we unite with gratitude to the God who has directed us to such a glorious sphere of activity, gratitude to the kind people who make it possible for us through the gifts they send for the work.   [Busy Days, p. 357]

Continuing Courage

I have not lost courage. The misery I have seen gives me strength, and faith in my fellow men supports my confidence in the future. I do hope that I shall find a sufficient number of people who, because they themselves have been saved from physical suffering, will respond to requests on behalf of those who are in similar need. . . . I do hope that among the doctors of the world there will soon be several besides myself who will be sent out, here or there in the world, by "the Fellowship of those who bear the Mark of Pain."   [Edge, p. 176]

Grace for Work

Our real strength for the work we find every day anew in the realization of the grace which comes to us in that we are allowed to be active in the service of the mercy of Jesus among the poorest of the poor. It is this consciousness which unites us. In this we feel ourselves lifted above the not always small difficulties which work among primitives who cannot be accustomed to any discipline brings with it. [Busy Days, p. 357]

A Free Man

I feel it deeply that I can work as a free man at a time when an oppressive lack of freedom is the lot of so many;

as also that though my immediate work is material, yet I have at the same time opportunities of occupying myself in the sphere of the spiritual and intellectual.

That the circumstances of my life provide in such varied ways favorable conditions for my work, I accept as something of which I would fain prove myself worthy.   [Life, p. 282]

We Wander in Darkness

We wander in darkness now, but one with another we all have the conviction that we are advancing to the light; that again a time will come when religion and ethical thinking will unite. This we believe, and hope and work for, maintaining the belief that if we make ethical ideals active in our own lives, then the time will come when peoples will do the same. Let us look out toward the light and comfort ourselves in reflecting on what thinking is preparing for us. [Religion, p. 1521]

Retrospect and Prospect

My hair is beginning to turn. My body is beginning to show traces of the exertions I have demanded of it, and of the passage of the years.

I look back with thankfulness to the time when, without needing to husband my strength, I could get through an uninterrupted course of bodily and mental work. With calmness and humility I look forward to the future, so that I may not be unprepared for renunciation if it be required of me. Whether we be workers or sufferers, it is assuredly our duty to conserve our powers, as being men who have won their way through to the peace which passeth all understanding.   [Life, pp. 282 f.]

BIOGRAPHICAL DATA

BIOGRAPHICAL DATA

January 14, 1875. Born at Kaysersberg, Haute Alsace. During this year his father became pastor at Gunsbach, in the Munster Valley, Haute Alsace.

1880–1884. In the village school.

Autumn 1884 to autumn 1885. Realschule at Munster.

Autumn 1885 to August 1893. Gymnasium at Mulhouse, Haute Alsace.

June 18, 1893. Passed his matriculation examination for the university at the Mulhouse Gymnasium.

October, 1893. First sojourn in Paris. Studied the organ under Widor.

November 1893 to spring 1898. Student at the University of Strassburg in theology, philosophy, and musical theory, living in the Theological Seminary of St. Thomas (Collegium Wilhelmitanum). While at the university wrote his first book, a small brochure in French upon the life and activity of Eugène Munch, his former organ teacher at Mulhouse, who died of typhoid fever at the beginning of his career, a book intended for the friends and pupils of this artist. The book was printed at Mulhouse in 1898.

April 1, 1894 to April 1, 1895. Military service in infantry regiment 143.

Autumn 1897. Wrote thesis required of all candidates for the first examination in theology upon the topic prescribed by the faculty: "The Idea of the Last Supper in Daniel Schleiermacher, Compared with the

Ideas of Luther, Zwingli and Calvin." In studying
Schleiermacher's idea of the Last Supper he was
struck by the fact that Schleiermacher insisted that
Jesus did not ask the disciples to repeat this meal,
and that the disciples had done so of their own
initiative.

May 6, 1898. Passed his first theological examination before
the faculty. The examination consisted of four
written papers on the New Testament, the Old
Testament, Church History and Dogmatics; an
oral examination in five parts, New Testament, Old
Testament, Church History, Dogmatics and Practical Theology; and a sermon preached in a church
with two of the examiners present. As a result of
this examination he received the Goll Scholarship,
the recipient of which was pledged to take his
licentiate in theology at Strassburg within six years
or return the money received.

Summer 1898. Continued to study philosophy at the University of Strassburg under Ziegler and Windel-
band. At the end of the summer he proposed to
Professor Ziegler as the theme of his doctoral thesis
a study of Kant's philosophy of religion in relation
to the different stages of what seemed to him its
constant evolution. At this time he was not living
at the Theological Seminary.

Autumn 1898 to spring 1899. Student at the Sorbonne in
Paris, living at 20 Rue de la Sorbonne. He neglected
the courses at the college, devoting himself to his
organ studies under Widor, and to his thesis on
Kant. He paid almost no attention to the books
about Kant, confining his attention to the minute
study of the text and the language peculiarities, in
order to discover the different stages in the development of the thought of Kant which was in a
state of constant flux.

March 12, 1899. Returned to Gunsbach and revised his manuscript.

April to July, 1899.   At Berlin for the study of philosophy
    and organ.
End of July, 1899.   Returned to Strassburg for his examination
    in philosophy with Windelband and Ziegler.
Autumn of 1899.   Returned to his old room in the Collegium
    Wilhelmitanum (St. Thomas Foundation) as a
    paying guest.
December 1, 1899.   Appointed Lehr-Vicar at St. Nicholas in
    Strassburg, in compliance with the rules requiring
    a student to serve in a church for a period between
    his first and second theological examination. There
    were two aged pastors at the church, Gerold who
    was the leader of the liberal party, and Knittel in
    whom orthodoxy and pietism mingled. Schweitzer
    began to work on a thesis upon the historical origin
    of the Last Supper, to submit in fulfilment of the
    requirements for the degree of licentiate in The-
    ology which one had to have to become a Privat-
    Dozent. This study led him to new conceptions
    about Jesus' messianic consciousness and his idea
    of sacrifice. At the same time Schweitzer worked
    on another book, *Das Messianitäts- und Leidens-
    geheimnis Jesu.* (The Secret of the Messiahship and
    Passion of Jesus.)
End of December, 1899.   *The Religious Philosophy of Kant
    from the "Critique of Pure Reason" to "Religion
    within the Bounds of Mere Reason,"* published by
    J. C. B. Mohr, at Tübingen, to whom Professor
    Holtsmann had recommended the book. Schweitzer
    received from the editor about 600 marks and the
    copies which he had to furnish to the faculty.
July 15, 1900.   Passed second theological examination before
    a commission of learned pastors among whom sat
    a member of the faculty. The subjects were the
    same as in the first examination except that more
    emphasis was placed on practical theology. Busy
    with his studies of the Last Supper and the messi-
    anic consciousness of Jesus, he had not taken the

time to review his previous studies in the various fields of theology and barely passed the examination.

July 21, 1900. Obtained the degree of licentiate in Theology with his study of the Last Supper. To obtain this degree he also had to pass a very difficult colloquium before a commission of the faculty. Schweitzer passed "magna cum laude."

September 23, 1900. Ordained at St. Nicholas as a regular curate.

May 1, 1901 to September 30, 1901. Received provisional appointment as Principal of the Theological Seminary (Collegium Wilhelmitanum) upon the death of Erichson until Gustav Anrich could assume the office.

1901. *Das Abendmahlproblem auf Grund der wissenschaftlichen Forschung des 19. Jahrhunderts und der historischen Berichte*, published by J. C. Mohr at Tübingen. The American edition was published by Dodd, Mead and Company in New York, under the title *The Mystery of the Kingdom of God*, and the English edition by A. and C. Black in 1925 in London.

1902. Appointed Privat-Dozent, thanks to the influence of Professor Holtzmann, and gave his inaugural lectures before the faculty upon the structure and tendencies of the Fourth Gospel. There followed in the summer of this year his first regular course on the Pastoral Epistles.

October 1, 1903. Received permanent appointment as Principal of the Theological Seminary, when Anrich was appointed Extraordinarius in Church History in succession to Ernst Lucius, who had suddenly died. Moved from the city to his official quarters on the Embankment of St. Thomas, using earlier student room for his study. Received stipend of 2400 marks.

January 14, 1905. Thirtieth birthday. Decided to devote the rest of his life to the natives of equatorial Africa as a doctor of medicine.

1905. *J. S. Bach, le musicien-poète* published by Costallat in Paris, and in 1908 by Breitkopf & Härtel in Leipzig. The German edition was not a translation of the French book, but an entirely new work. The first chapter had been written in Bayreuth in 1905. Published also in English under the title *J. S. Bach*.

October 13, 1905. Made known his decision to serve as a missionary doctor, and entered into discussion with the Paris Missionary Society.

Spring 1906. Resigned from the directorship of the Theological Seminary. Went to live in the mansard story of the house occupied by Dr. Curtius, the president of the Superior Consistory, in the same block of buildings with the Theological Seminary. There were three small rooms and a kitchen.

1906 to 1913. Studied as a medical student at the University of Strassburg.

1906. Published *Von Reimarus zu Wrede. Eine Geschichte der Leben-Jesu-Forschung* (J. C. B. Mohr, Tübingen.) Reimarus had been the first to emphasize the eschatological in Jesus and Wrede, who died in 1907, had tried to eliminate all eschatology and all messianic ideas from the thought world of Jesus. The English edition, under the title *The Quest of the Historical Jesus*, was published in London by A. & C. Black in 1910. This year there also appeared the treatise, *Deutsche und französische Orgelbaukunst und Orgelkunst* (German and French Organ-Building and Organ-Playing,) published by Breitkopf & Härtel, in Leipzig.

1906 to 1912. In the very restricted leisure moments left by his medical studies, his services as curate at St. Nicholas, his concert tours, and a very heavy correspondence he began his study of the Pauline ideas. He was trying to find out how Paul, beginning with primitive, eschatological Christianity, arrived at a mysticism of dying and being born again "in Jesus Christ," and how this eschatological mysticism prepared the way for the hellenization of

Christianity in the mysticism of "being in the
Logos." He hoped to be able to finish the book
before his departure for Africa, but succeeded
only in completing the introduction, a history of
the various interpretations of the writings of St.
Paul. The completion of his work was delayed by
three other tasks. Towards the end of this period
of medical study he prepared in collaboration with
Widor an edition of Bach's organ works. He was,
secondly, engaged in enlarging and completing the
second edition of his *Geschichte der Leben-Jesu-
Forschung*. To do this he had to go through a great
many new books, and particularly to study the
whole question of the historical existence of Jesus,
which had been brought to the fore by Drews.
Thirdly, he was engaged in preparing his thesis
for the degree of doctor of medicine, a study of
the books which dealt with the question of Jesus'
mentality from a psychiatrical point of view. This
book necessitated a profound study of psychiatrical
questions, and completed his history of the written
lives of Jesus.

1911. His *Geschichte der Paulinischen Forschung von der
Reformation bis auf die Gegenwart* was published
by J. C. C. Mohr at Tübingen. The English edition
under the title of *Paul and His Interpreters* was
published by A. & C. Black in London in 1912.
This book bore the dedication "Der medizinischen
Fakultät der Universität Strassburg in tiefer Dank-
barkeit für die gewährte Gastfreundschaft."

Autumn 1911. Played the organ for Widor's Second Symphony for Organ and Orchestra at the Festival of
French Music at Munich.

Autumn to December 1911. Passed his examination in medicine at Strassburg, during a period of terrible ex-
haustion.

Spring 1912. Resigned his posts as a teacher in the university
and as a preacher at St. Nicholas. His last lectures

were on the evaluation of religion from the point of view of historical criticism and the natural sciences.

June 18, 1912. Married Helene Bresslau, daughter of the Strassburg historian. Afterwards retired to his father's house in Gunsbach to work on the second edition of his *Geschichte der Leben-Jesu-Forschung*, assisted by his wife.

February 1913. Having completed his year of interneship, and having finished his thesis, he received the degree of doctor of medicine.

March 26, 1913. Embarked at Bordeaux for Africa, where he established a hospital on the grounds of the Lambaréné station of the Paris Missionary Society. The place was called Andende.

1913. The second edition of his *Geschichte der Leben-Jesu-Forschung* was published by J. C. C. Mohr at Tübingen. In the same year J. C. C. Mohr published in Tübingen *Die Psychiatrische Beurteilung Jesu*, (The Psychiatrical Study of Jesus.) The proofs of the former book were corrected on the train from Paris to Bordeaux, where he was to embark for Africa. The proofs of the latter were corrected by a friend in Strassburg while Schweitzer was at sea. Six volumes in the edition of Bach's works were finished before his departure. The last three volumes of choral compositions were completed in Africa during the first few months after his arrival there, but for various reasons these volumes have not yet been published.

August 5 to end of November 1914. Interned with his wife at Lambaréné as an enemy alien. Began his work on *The Philosophy of Civilization*, about which he had been thinking since the summer of 1899, and which an editor in England had requested about 1910. This work was continued even after November when he was allowed more liberty to continue his hospital work.

September 1915.   While on a two hundred kilometre journey
up the Ogowe River to N'Gomo, suddenly the
words "Reverence for Life" came to him as the
elementary and universal conception of ethics for
which he had been seeking. Upon this principle
his whole philosophy of civilization was subse-
quently based.

September 1917.   Transferred with his wife to France as a
civil interne. At Garaison in the Pyrenees continued to work on his philosophy.

Spring 1918.   Transferred to St. Rémy de Provence. Served
as a doctor during the daytime and worked on his
philosophy during the evenings.

End of July 1918.   Returned to Alsace in an exchange of prisoners.

1919 to 1921.   Accepted a post as preacher at St. Nicholas, and
also a post as physician in the City Hospital of
Strassburg. Occupied the empty parsonage on the
Nicholas Embankment through the courtesy of the
Chapter of St. Thomas. Submitted to operation,
from which he did not fully recover for two years.

January 14, 1919.   Daughter born on his birthday.

About Christmas 1919.   Received invitation to give course of
lectures at Upsala in Sweden.

After Easter 1920.   Delivered lectures on the Olaus-Petri
Foundation at the University of Upsala, using as
his subject the problem of world- and life-affirmation and ethics in philosophy and world-religions,
working up the material afresh, as he had left his
manuscripts in Africa. Gave a series of organ concerts and lectures in Sweden to pay off the debts
which he had incurred for the hospital.

Middle July 1920.   Returned to Strassburg to write in a few
weeks a book on his experiences in Africa, which
the editor Lindblad at Upsala had requested.

1920.   Honorary doctorate from theological faculty in Zürich.
The Swedish edition of *Zwischen Wasser und
Urwald* was published by Lindblad at Upsala. This

book was published in German in 1921 by Paul
Haupt at Berne, and in 1925 also by C. H. Beck in
Munich. Published in English under the title *On
the Edge of the Primeval Forest.*

Spring 1921.   Played the organ at the Orféo Català in Barce-
lona for the first production of the St. Matthew
Passion in Spain.

April 1921.   Gave up both positions at Strassburg depending
thenceforth for his support on his pen and his
organ. Returned to Gunsbach, where he was appointed vicar to his father, in order to work quietly
on his *Philosophy of Civilization.* Retained a room
in Strassburg on the rue de l'Ail (Knoblauchgasse).

Autumn 1921.   In Switzerland.

November 1921.   In Sweden.

January and February 1922.   Course of lectures in England
at Oxford at Mansfield College on Dale Foundation, and at the Selly-Oak Colleges at Birmingham
on "Christianity and the World-Religions," and at
Cambridge on "The Meaning of Eschatology," and
at the Society for the Science of Religion in London on "The Pauline Problem." Also gave a series
of organ concerts in England.

Spring 1922.   Three more weeks of lectures and concerts in
Sweden, followed by lectures and concerts in
Switzerland.

Summer 1922.   Working undisturbed on *The Philosophy of
Civilization.*

Autumn 1922.   More lectures and concerts in Switzerland, a
series of lectures in Copenhagen on the invitation of
the theological faculty, followed by lectures and
concerts in various Danish cities.

January 1923.   Spoke in Prague on "The Philosophy of
Civilization."

Spring 1923.   *The Philosophy of Civilization* published by
C. H. Beck in Munich and Paul Haupt in Berne in
1923 in two volumes, I. *The Decay and Restoration of Civilization,* and II. *Civilization and Ethics.*

Also in the same year Allen and Unwin published in London *Christianity and the World-Religions*. The German edition appeared in 1924 with Paul Haupt in Berne.

February 1924. Wrote *Memoirs of Childhood and Youth*. The English edition was published by Allen and Unwin in London the same year.

February 14, 1924. Left Strassburg for Africa, leaving his wife behind in Europe because of her poor health. Carried with him preliminary drafts of his book on *The Mysticism of Paul* on which he had been working during all the years of his first sojourn in Africa and during his sojourn in Europe from 1917 to 1924.

April 19, 1924 to July 21, 1927. Second sojourn in Africa. Compelled to reconstruct the hospital, which had fallen into ruin, and later to transfer it to a new and roomier site at Adolinanongo, where the new buildings were constructed of hardwood and corrugated iron. During this period of rebuilding he was compelled to abandon all literary work. In the morning he worked as a doctor, in the afternoon as a laborer. The number of patients constantly increased and he was obliged to send to Europe for two more doctors and two more nurses. Just as he was about to resume work on *The Mysticism of St. Paul* a severe famine and an epidemic of dysentery set in, and again his writing had to be abandoned. He was able, however, to keep up his regular practice on his piano with organ pedals. Reports of his work in Africa were sent to Europe in the form of letters to friends and supporters and published in three small volumes, under the title *Mitteilungen aus Lambaréné*, by C. H. Beck in Munich and Paul Haupt in Berne. The first covered the period from spring to autumn 1924, and appeared in 1925; the second the period from autumn 1924 to autumn 1925, and appeared in 1926; and the third the period from autumn 1925 to summer 1927 and appeared in 1928.

July 1927 to December 1929. In Europe. Lectures and concert tours in Sweden, Denmark, Holland, Germany, Switzerland, England, and Czechoslovakia. During this period devoted all his spare time to his book on *The Mysticism of St. Paul.* A large part of this book was written in Königsfeld in the Black Forest, where he had established a summer home. The book was finished on the boat which took him back to Africa.

August 28, 1928. Received Goethe Prize from the City of Frankfort, delivering an address there on his indebtedness to Goethe. This was the second time that this prize had been awarded, Stephan George having been the first to receive it. With the money he received he built a home in Gunsbach where he planned also to house the personnel of his hospital while on vacation in Europe. Schweitzer's address on Goethe was published by Henry Holt in New York in 1929, following the text published in the *Hibbert Journal* in July of the same year.

December 26, 1929 to January 7, 1932. Third sojourn in Africa. During this sojourn he wrote his autobiography. In 1929 he had written for the editor Felix Meiner in Leipzig a brief autobiographical sketch for the seventh volume of his *Philosophie der Gegenwart in Selbstdarstellungen* (Present Day Philosophy in Self-Portraits.) This particular chapter was republished by the editor as a small book, but as Schweitzer considered that readers might consider this a real autobiography and draw false conclusions from it, he decided to enlarge it to include a review of his life and his literary works. The book appeared in German under the title *Aus meinem Leben und Denken,* published by Felix Meiner in Leipzig in 1931, and the following year it was published in England under the title *Out of My Life and Thought*. Upon the completion of the autobiography, Schweitzer continued his work on the third volume of his *Philosophy of Civilization*. This work in turn was interrupted by an invitation received in October 1931, from the burgermeister of Frankfort to deliver a memorial address on the anniversary of the death of Goethe. The acceptance of this invitation necessitated an earlier return to Europe than he had contemplated. The first draft of the address was prepared at Lambaréné towards the close of 1931 and the address was completed on the steamer that took him to Europe in January 1932.

1931.   *More from the Primeval Forest* was published in England by A. & C. Black. This was a translation of the German book *Das Urwaldspital zu Lambaréné*, which had been published by Beck at Munich in 1931. This latter book in turn brought together into a single volume the three little books, *Mitteilungen aus Lambaréné*, which had been published in 1925, 1926, and 1928. The American edition, published by Henry Holt and Company in New York, bore the title, *The Forest Hospital at Lambaréné*.

February 1932 to April 1933.   In Europe. Lectures and concerts in Holland, England, Sweden, Germany and Switzerland. Worked on the third volume of *The Philosophy and Civilization*, completing the plan for the whole book and sketching out the different chapters.

March 22, 1932.   Memorial address in Frankfort on 100th anniversary of death of Goethe. The address was published in the same year by C. H. Beck in Munich.

April 21, 1933 to January 11, 1934.   Fourth sojourn in Africa. All of his leisure was employed upon the third volume of his philosophy, and in preparation of the Gifford Lectures which were to be given in 1934 and 1935.

February 1934 to February 1935.   In Europe. The spring and summer were spent upon the third volume and upon the preparation of the Gifford Lectures.

Autumn 1934.   Hibbert Lectures at Manchester College, Oxford, under the subject "Religion in Modern Civilization." These lectures were later repeated at London University College. They have not yet been published, but a fairly adequate summary of them was printed in *The Christian Century* in November 1934.

November 1934.   Gifford Lectures at Edinburgh, in which he endeavored to trace the progress of human thought from the great thinkers of India, China, Greece, and Persia. The chapter upon the evolution of Indian thought grew to such an extent that he decided to publish it as a separate book. It was issued under the German title of *Die Weltanschauung der indischen Denker* by Beck at Munich in 1934; under the French title *Les Grands Penseurs de l'Inde* by Payot at Paris in 1936; and under the English title *Indian Thought and Its Development* by Hodder and Stoughton at London in 1936. The same year it was published by Henry Holt and Company in New York.

February 26, 1935 to August 22, 1935. Fifth sojourn in Africa. This stay was terminated by his obligation to return to Europe for the second series of Gifford Lectures, which were largely written in Africa.

September 1935 to February 1937.   In Europe.

November 1935.   Second course of Gifford Lectures. Lectures and concerts in England.

1936.   Working on his philosophy, translating into French his book *Les Grands Penseurs de l'Inde*, and in October making records of organ music for Co-

lumbia Records in London upon the organ of St.
Aurelia's at Strassburg.

February 18, 1937 to January 10, 1939. Sixth sojourn in
Africa. He carried with him the manuscript for his
philosophy, believing that now at last he would be
able to finish it, but the increasing responsibilities
of the hospital left him little leisure. For some time
he thought that the volume of material would
make it necessary to publish two volumes instead
of one. He could not bring himself to this decision,
however, and finally set to work to compress his
thought into the compass of a single book. In
order to simplify the problem he then planned to
publish separately the chapters on the Chinese
thinkers in whom he had become deeply interested.

1938. Wrote *From My African Notebook*, a little volume of
anecdotes upon the ideas and the lives of the
natives. Meiner of Leipzig published it under the
title of *Afrikanische Geschichten* in 1938; Payot in
Paris issued the French edition in 1941; Allen and
Unwin in London issued the English edition in
1938.

January 10, 1939. Left for Europe with the hope of completing his third volume.

February 1939. Arrived in Europe, only to decide that war
could not be avoided, and might break out at any
moment. Decided, therefore, to return immediately to Africa.

February 12, 1939. Embarked again for Africa.

March 3, 1939 to date. Seventh sojourn in Africa. During
the first two years of the war he was able to work
continuously on his book, but afterwards the lack
of white personnel at the hospital made it necessary for him to devote himself almost exclusively
to the care of the sick and to other hospital duties.
Towards the end of 1945 he wrote an account of
the war years at Lambaréné, which was pub-

lished in 1946, in Switzerland, Alsace, England and
America. The close of the war brought little relief,
and it was not until 1947 that a rather more adequate personnel became available. Dr. Schweitzer
now looks forward to a sojourn in Europe in
order to give final form to the third volume of
his *Philosophy of Civilization,* which will be called
Reverence for Life.

INDICES

INDEX OF SUBJECTS

INDEX OF TITLES